Labor People

Labor People

The Stories of Six True Believers

Chris Bowen

MONASH
UNIVERSITY
PUBLISHING

Labor People: The Stories of Six True Believers
© Copyright 2021 Chris Bowen
All rights reserved. Apart from any uses permitted by Australia's Copyright Act 1968, no part of this book may be reproduced by any process without prior written permission from the copyright owners. Enquiries should be directed to the publisher.

Monash University Publishing
Matheson Library Annexe
40 Exhibition Walk
Monash University
Clayton, Victoria 3800, Australia
https://publishing.monash.edu/

Monash University Publishing brings to the world publications which advance the best traditions of humane and enlightened thought.

ISBN: 9781922464729 (paperback)
ISBN: 9781922464736 (pdf)
ISBN: 9781922464743 (epub)

Design: Les Thomas

Typesetting: Jo Mullins

A catalogue record for this book is available from the National Library of Australia.

CONTENTS

Acknowledgments... vii

Introduction... ix

1   Gregor McGregor: The First Number Two 1

2   Lilian Locke: The Labor Suffragist 24

3   Frank Tudor: A Leader for the Darkest Days 51

4   John Dedman: A Man Curtin and Chifley Could Rely On.... 88

5   Gertrude Melville: A Tough Pioneer 140

6   Ken Wriedt: A Quiet Achiever........................... 185

Notes 232

Index 236

About the Author 246

For Labor's True Believers.
The branch members and supporters who are there at every election,
without fail.

This book was mainly written in my home,
which is on the land of the Cabrogal People of the Darug Nation.
I pay my respects to their elders, and the elders of
First Nations peoples across our country.

ACKNOWLEDGMENTS

My first thanks must go to Louise Adler. A book on "forgotten figures of Labor history" would not immediately appeal to every publisher, but her commitment to books that contribute to bringing Australian history and public policy to life remains as strong as ever. She has now arranged the publication of four of my books across three publishing houses. Australian publishing is all the richer for her ongoing, unstinting efforts.

Thanks also to the team at Monash University Publishing, led by Greg Bain. Monash recognises the ongoing importance of universities being strongly involved in publishing, but also recognises that not all academic works have to be written by academics! As some other universities have unfortunately pared back their publishing efforts, Monash plays an ongoing vital role.

Thanks also to the others in the small but highly productive Monash University Publishing team: Joanne Mullins, Sarah Cannon, Les Thomas and Sam van der Plank.

This book is edited by John Mahony, who was professional, patient and appropriately exacting at each turn; thank you. Thank you also to Mei Yen Chua for providing such a comprehensive index.

John Faulkner and Rodney Cavalier both read every word in early manuscript and both, as expected, provided invaluable advice of fact and interpretation. It goes without saying any errors are mine and mine alone.

James Mack assisted me in obtaining access to the original records of the NSW Supreme Court from the 1920s when I had very little idea how to do so. The helpful staff at the Supreme Court Registry should also be thanked.

Ken Wriedt's daughters Sonja and Paula were generous with their time and feedback, which I also appreciate.

The staff in the Reading Room of the Mitchell Library within the State Library of NSW were of enormous assistance in helping me locate esoteric, long unread files and resources. The staff in the Parliamentary Library were their usual, ever helpful selves.

To Thomas McCrudden, thanks as always.

And to Bec, Grace and Max, who don't quite understand why I have spent hours on the laptop typing away about long-dead Labor figures but who have supported me in doing so anyway, all my love.

INTRODUCTION

The history of the Australian Labor Party is dominated by the big names. The big, sweeping personalities dominated the party and the politics of their times: Watson, Fisher, Hughes, Scullin, Curtin, Chifley, Evatt, Calwell, Whitlam, Hawke, Keating, Rudd, Gillard.

Labor has a rich written history. There are thousands of books already written. They tend to focus on the big names or the big dramatic moments: the election wins, the reforms, the splits, the challenges.

But the history of the Labor Party is a lot more complex and a lot richer than even this.

Tens of thousands of people have been members of the Labor Party since it was founded in 1891. Thousands have served in the various Australian parliaments. As good and grand as our leaders have (mainly) been, the Labor Party is about much more than just its leaders and big names. The late great Labor speech-writer and historian Graham Freudenberg called the Labor Party "A collective memory in action". It is the memories of all members that drive it forward.

The prime ministers have relied on hundreds of people each to help them guide the party to a position of power and reform. Not all politics is glamorous. Most of it isn't. There is hard work to be done and thousands of people have done it.

I've written *Labor People* to bring the stories of just some of these people to life. The six people I've chosen for pen portraits all made big contributions to the Labor Party. They have been, to some degree, forgotten. Most of them haven't had full-length biographies written about them.[1]

LABOR PEOPLE

But what stories they are! The Scottish garden-labourer who went blind and went on to be Labor's first federal deputy leader. The earnest campaigner for women's rights who went on to be one of the inspirations for an important character in Australian literature. The unassuming hatter whom the party turned to when the prime minister of the day got up and left the Caucus room, splitting the party asunder. The Scottish soldier who became a key lieutenant for both Curtin and Chifley in their massive undertakings of invigorating the war effort and building the peace. The first woman to be elected to the oldest parliamentary chamber in Australia who stayed loyal to Labor during several big splits and was a campaigner against police corruption and brutality when it was far from fashionable. A reforming minister for Whitlam, who is mainly remembered for a conversation that didn't happen.

Gregor McGregor, Lilian Locke, Frank Tudor, John Dedman, Gertrude Melville and Ken Wriedt are no longer household names. Indeed some of them were low profile even when they were active. But their stories are an important part of the Labor story. They, and the people they represented and worked with, were important parts of the collective memory in action that is the history of the Labor Party.

Chris Bowen
Smithfield
January 2021

Chapter 1

GREGOR MCGREGOR

The First Number Two

Who was the first federal deputy leader of the Australian Labor Party?

This is a trivia question that stumps some of the best informed aficionados of Labor history.

Add in a question about his disability and only a couple of people across the country can answer correctly.

But Gregor McGregor was far from a trivial figure in Labor history. He deserves a more prominent place. Labor's first federal deputy leader was a powerful force in Australian politics for a decade and a half. He voted on perhaps the most important piece of progressive legislation that any Australian jurisdiction has given the world – South Australia's legislation to provide women with the vote – and rose to be the second most senior member of the first national Labor government anywhere in the world. He was the deputy in each of Australia's first three Labor governments. Any history of the pioneering Watson and Fisher governments is incomplete without a consideration of his role.

A strong personality, his speeches were legendary for their force and mastery of details; a phenomenon made more remarkable by the fact that McGregor could not use speech notes – by the time he reached the peak of his political powers, he was completely blind.

His blindness was the result of a workforce accident earlier in his life (possibly compounded by cataracts) which gradually and eventually removed his eyesight. His blindness meant the only way he could make speeches was from memory and without notes, which made him one of the most powerful parliamentary speakers of his era.

McGregor was the archetypal perfect deputy – completely loyal to Watson and Fisher, the latter of whom he became personally very close to. His well-developed sense of humour exhibited in his public performances was a useful foil to the dry personae of his two leaders, for whom he was often the "warm up act" on the stump, at a time when the stump speech was the pre-eminent form of political campaigning.

He was never seriously considered for the party leadership – mainly because he was in the Senate. The practice of having the party's leader in the Senate serve as the deputy leader of the broader party outlived McGregor, but not for very long. It was his personality as much as his position that determined his role as second among equals.

Gregor McGregor has long since ceased to be a household name. But he was a deeply respected and indeed loved figure in the 14 years he bestrode the national political stage. It is impossible to find a bad word written about him in the memoirs and histories of the time. On the contrary, he was lauded for his abilities. Future federal Labor MP and historian Norman Makin went as far as to write: "Possibly no man in the history of the Commonwealth Parliament attained such [high] standards as parliamentarian as did this seasoned veteran of Labor".[1]

His political opponents also recognised his abilities, although in one instance it was under a pseudonym. Australia's second Prime Minister, Alfred Deakin, had a sideline as correspondent for the London *Morning Post*. Writing regular columns on Australian politics as "Our Special Correspondent", Deakin didn't mind giving his political opponents an anonymous adverse character assessment. But he was happy to tell his British readers about McGregor's qualities in January 1902. It's an assessment worth quoting at some length:

> Senator McGregor, who leads the Labor members of the Senate, is one of the most picturesque and striking figures in the Federal Parliament. A sturdy Scotsman, powerfully built, with rugged features and large, grizzled head, he has but one weakness, that of his voice, which is thin in quality, though penetrating and clear. A working man until middle age, he has a large store of experience to draw on, besides being exceptionally thoughtful and well read. He is a trenchant speaker, bold, incisive and humorous, ready and caustic in retort. An almost total loss of his sight from which he suffers seems only to have accentuated the retentiveness of his memory, his reflective powers, the resolute vigour of his character. The high place he won and held in South Australian politics has been more than justified by his career in the Commonwealth, where his clear-headedness, courtesy, and caution have placed and kept him in the front rank. He is recognised as head of the Labor Party as a whole, and acts as its unquestioned leader in the Senate.[2]

He was a man of strong views: a devout Presbyterian and teetotaller who objected to the recital of the Lord's Prayer in parliament as a "parade of religion" defying the separation of church and state; a strong protectionist at a time when free trade versus tariffs was the key economic question of the era; about as close to being a Republican as it was possible for a mainstream politician to be at the time, objecting to the glorification of the role of governor-general and calling for the High Court of Australia to be the ultimate Australian court of appeal as opposed to the Privy Council in London; and opposed to the Boer War and dismissive of excessive jingoism. He played as big a role as any of his colleagues in setting the tone and agenda of the new force of federal Labor. He deserves an honoured place in Labor history.

Early Life

The small, picturesque town of Kilmun in the Argyll region of Western Scotland is where Gregor McGregor was born to his parents Malcolm and Jane in 1848. A seaside village, the town had developed into a type of resort for Glasgow merchants and seamen. It is unclear whether Malcolm and Jane knowingly named their son after the (in)famous soldier and conman Gregor MacGregor, who had died three years previously. Although hard to imagine given his exploits,[3] he had his defenders so it is possible. Malcolm was a gardener and moved the family to Ireland when he landed a job as Chief Gardener to Sir Gerald Aylmer, who was a member of Irish Baronetcy with a substantial estate in County Tyrone.

Young McGregor returned to Scotland and worked both as an agricultural labourer and in the Glasgow shipyards.

He migrated to Australia in 1877, and procured a job as an agricultural labourer for Sir Richard Baker, with whom he would later serve in both the Legislative Council of South Australia and the Senate. A conservative free-trader, Baker was a keen proponent of Federation and, unusually for any politician of the era, let alone one of the right, an advocate for an Australian Republic. We don't know if McGregor and Baker ever discussed politics before McGregor ran for office, but it is unlikely the master and gardener ever imagined they would serve together in a national parliament some decades later.

It was while working for Baker that McGregor suffered a workplace accident which would have a huge influence over his life and career.

While felling a tree, a branch fell into his face. His eyesight was damaged and would, over time, disappear. His injury may have been worsened in later years by cataracts which were, at that time, impossible to treat. But for whatever reason he was completely blind by the time he entered the federal cabinet. This would have a profound but not negative impact on his ability to make speeches.

In April 1880, McGregor married Julia Jane Stegall, but she died in December of the same year. Her death certificate records her age at death as 28 and her cause as death as a "cold after confinement", indicating that McGregor would have been doubly mortified, with the loss of his wife and baby. The fact that such bereavements were much more likely in his time does not make it any more likely he was consolable, although there is no record of his feelings. He remarried, to Sarah Brock, in 1882. Sarah had been born in Kilcardine, a town about 150 kilometres away from his birthplace in Scotland. This was her second marriage, her husband having died in 1877. Sarah had two children, Fred and Charles, to her first husband. Fred would die in 1883 aged eight, one year after she and McGregor married. Charles lived on, and took the McGregor name as his own even though he was not a blood relative. Sarah and Gregor would have no children together, and Sarah would outlive him.

Following his gardening accident, McGregor gave up agricultural labouring and moved to Victoria to work as a stonemason between 1885 and 1891. It was in the construction industry that McGregor became involved in the union movement. He became active in the United Builders Labourers Society.

It was following his return to South Australia that his involvement in unions and Labor politics went to new levels.

Entering Politics

In 1892, he was elected to the United Trades and Labor Council of South Australia and in 1893 became President of the United Labor Party of South Australia, that is, of the South Australian Labor Party.

In 1894, he became one of the first people anywhere in the world to be elected to a parliament under a Labor banner, and it was to one of the more conservative chambers in the British Empire: the Legislative Council of South Australia.

The Labour League had proven remarkably successful in the Legislative Council, with three members elected in 1891, another in 1893 and McGregor and another colleague coming into the chamber in the 1894 colonial election. This was despite the Council having a property qualification franchise. Only male citizens who owned property to a value of 50 pounds freehold or 20 pounds leasehold qualified to vote in Council elections. Luckily for McGregor and his Labor colleagues, the property qualification only applied to the vote, not to service. So the Labor candidates only had to appeal to property owners to vote for them, not be owners themselves.

It was hard enough for a Labor candidate to be running in an election with a property franchise, but McGregor didn't choose an easy electorate to put his name forward in. The "Southern District" constituency covered the Adelaide Hills, the Fleurieu Peninsula and the south-east of South Australia. As it was heavily agricultural, McGregor was no doubt helped by his background as an agricultural labourer. But he was helped more by his work ethic. By the end of the campaign he had visited every mainland hamlet that was part of the electorate.

There were five candidates vying for the two available places as Member for Southern District. McGregor was up against the extremely popular and high-profile Sir Edwin Smith who was a former Mayor of Adelaide and long-serving Member of the House of Assembly. Smith ran for the seat after a petition of 1260 electors beseeched him to do so (who wouldn't want that sort of start to a campaign?). Other candidates included Friedrich Krichauff, a serving member and leader of the German community; Lewis Cohen, another serving MP who was seeking to switch seats (and would later go on to become Adelaide's first Jewish Lord Mayor); and Samuel Tomlinson, a very conservative Alderman on Adelaide Council. McGregor's hard work paid off, with a strong second-place vote of 2458 to Smith's 3750, seeing him narrowly beat Tomlinson on 2117.

One of the reasons for Labor's comparative success in South Australia was Labor's reputation for moderation and sensible pragmatism. As Scarfe puts it: "Socialism in South Australia was basically practical, claiming to provide a more efficient plan for society than private enterprise."[4] However, this of course did not stop conservatives railing against the "radical" agenda of McGregor and his colleagues.

The most controversial debate McGregor was involved in was the extension of the vote to women just after the 1894 election. Since the early 1880s, progressive liberals had repeatedly moved in parliament to extend the franchise and had consistently failed. But 1894 was the year. Following the election, the Kingston Liberal government moved to legislate for votes for women. Sensing defeat, conservatives proposed what they thought was a "poison pill" amendment, moving that women not only be able to vote but they also be entitled to serve in parliament – a concept they thought so preposterous that it would guarantee the defeat of the bill. But both houses were actually happy enough to allow the reform and the bill passed. This was remarkable: while other Australian colonies and then states granted the right to vote to women over the course of the next 15 years, South Australia was the only state that allowed women to actually run for parliament until Queensland made the reform in 1915 and other states followed. (Ironically, although South Australia was the first jurisdiction to allow women MPs, it was the last Australian state to actually have a female MP, with no woman elected until 1959. It is also the only Australian state at the time of writing to not have had a female premier.)

McGregor's contributions in the debate were fairly brief and workmanlike as opposed to high oratory about democratic principles, but he spoke for and voted for the bill, making him part of an important moment in Australian democratic history, as South Australia became a world leader in female suffrage.

McGregor spoke in favour of a reduction in taxation on tea, coffee and kerosene, with land tax to make up the revenue foregone, saying of the arguments of some of his opponents that they had "no more logic than the music in Patrick Weldon's street organ", in reference to a prominent Adelaide busker with a limb deformity and a broken organ he refused to replace.[5] He argued for an extension of the upper-house franchise to a broader class of property owners (which failed to get the required two-thirds majority for constitutional change). These speeches were given without notes, because while his sight did not completely disappear until 1906, it was severely limited. He could quote biblical passages at length in support of his arguments and would pick up colleagues on errors in quotations. It was later said of McGregor's contributions in the Senate, "Here, as in the Legislative Council, he became renowned for his cheeky and ready wit and his frequent use of biblical imagery."[6]

The final years of the nineteenth century were, however, not dominated by domestic colonial issues, but by a continent-wide debate about whether and how the colonies should federate into one country.

McGregor was originally sceptical about federation, but, as the debate ensued, became a supporter. He was a Labor candidate for the 1896 Federation Convention. No Labor candidates were successful.

Despite the lack of Labor representation, the convention elected in 1896 successfully advanced the work of federation, refining the draft constitution through three meetings in Adelaide, Sydney and Melbourne. It is unknown how much interest McGregor paid to its deliberations, but one key development would have very significant ramifications for the future Commonwealth and McGregor's place in it: the method of election of the Senate. The 1891 draft of the constitution had had senators appointed by state parliaments. The second convention settled on direct election of senators and set the size of the Senate at half that of the House of Representatives. The people of South Australia voted for federation at both their opportunities: the referenda of 1898 and 1899 (with a 67% yes vote in 1898 and a 79% yes vote the second time). The 1899 referendum received the necessary approval in each colony (except Western Australia which waited until 1900 to vote) and federation hurtled towards reality.

Because of his popularity and experience, McGregor was an obvious candidate to lead Labor's Senate ticket in the 1901 election. Despite his campaigning skills, he only just made it: elected to the sixth and last position with 52.2% of the vote (compared to 74.8% for the popular Sir Josiah Symon and 70% of the vote for his former boss Sir Richard Baker). He saw off the candidate who came seventh by just 644 votes. (The 1901 election was the only election in Australian history in which states used different voting systems. In the South Australian Senate election, voters were asked to strike a line through candidates they didn't want to see elected. The six with the fewest lines through their name were elected. The new parliament would enact the Commonwealth Electoral Act which harmonised voting methods across the states.) This result was similar to Victoria's, where Labor also won the last spot in the Senate. It was inferior to Queensland and Western Australia (three and two Labor senators respectively) but better than New South Wales which failed to elect a Labor senator, and Tasmania in which Labor neglected to even field a candidate for the Senate. This would be the last time that McGregor would struggle in an election, given he topped the South Australian Senate poll in both 1903 and 1910.

McGregor was known and well regarded by his colleagues. George Pearce, elected a Labor senator from Western Australia on the same day as McGregor, called the South Australian Senate delegation (which consisted of Sir Josiah Symon, former Premiers Thomas Playford and Sir John Downer, Sir Richard Baker and David Charleston as well as McGregor) "the most outstanding team sent in at the first election".

The first Labor Caucus of 16 members and nine senators met in the basement of the Victorian Parliament House (which served as home to the Federal Parliament until 1927) on 8 May 1901. The first head of a Labor government anywhere in the world, Andrew Dawson, chaired the meeting in deference to his status as the former Premier of Queensland. A ballot was held for the party's spokesman in both the House and the Senate. It was clear the House spokesman would be the party's leader although how much authority that position held and what other structures the party would embrace was very much a work in progress. While John Christian Watson of New South Wales prevailed over Queenslander Andrew Fisher in a ballot for House leader, McGregor was elected as the party's spokesman in the Senate unopposed. Dawson (a Queensland Senator) was a potential rival but his ill health and alcoholism effectively ruled him out.

That first Caucus meeting also established a committee, with a representative from each state, to devise a permanent Caucus structure. That committee reported to the Caucus 12 days later and recommended that the Caucus be chaired by the leader in the House of Representatives and that the deputy chair be the leader in the Senate. The Caucus Executive would consist of the two leaders, two whips and three other MPs elected by the Caucus. Thus McGregor became Labor's first deputy leader.

As Crisp notes of the deputy leadership:

> In later years there was sometimes elected a Deputy Leader of the Party in the House and sometimes not. In 1905 Fisher was elected to that position when Watson notified the Caucus of his desire, on health grounds, to resign the leadership of the party but was persuaded to carry-on… but the Leader in the Senate still for many years ranked as second in charge, as Deputy Leader of the FPLP as a whole, presiding over the Caucus in the absence of the Leader.

That first meeting of the Caucus also resolved that given the party was the "the third force" in the parliament, holding the balance of power in the House between the Free Traders with 31 seats and the Protectionists with 28 seats as well as the balance of power in the Senate (Free Trade 17, Protectionist 11, Labor 8), Labor would not contest the speakership or presidency of the Senate but rather "conserve its full strength intact for manoeuvre and deployment on the floors of the two chambers".

While Labor was numerically far from being able to form a government, it did use its numbers to considerable effect, and in relation to McGregor it was noted that "He came to dominate the Senate through tactical shrewdness." He was disarmingly explicit about Labor's tactics of demanding policy concessions from the two big parties in return for its support on the floor of parliament when he declared in 1901 that Labor was "for sale, and we will get the auctioneer when he comes, and take care that he is the right man".

He also indicated in early sittings of the Senate that "the more progressive the legislation, the more… he liked it" and also argued for the extension of the vote to women in the new nation just as South Australia had done, arguing in his first speech that "it is the feeling of every member of the Party that I belong, no matter from what State he may come, that adult suffrage must ultimately be adopted as the franchise for federated Australia". He went on in this first speech to argue for comprehensive social security in the new nation: "It is a standing disgrace to a civilized country that we should have old men and old women at the corners of our streets in the State capitals selling newspapers and matches – men and women who are the monuments of misery."

His next contribution in the Senate was one that he was clearly worried about. Somewhat unusually for a party leader, he warned that "For what I am about to say, I take the whole responsibility; I wish to disassociate the Party to which I belong in reference to the views which I am about to express." In a time of high religiosity, McGregor was arguing that parliament should not open with prayer, noting that the Constitution stated the parliament could not impose a national religion, nor any religious observances. While he had a literal reading of the Constitution on his side, it was a courageous argument to run. This devout Presbyterian lost the argument that the parliament should not adopt a religious ceremony. At the time of writing, 118 years later, parliament still opens with the Lord's Prayer.

The 1903 election, which saw McGregor move from last place to first in the list of successful senators from South Australia, also saw the

Labor Party increase its representation the House of Representatives from 15 to 22. This was the first federal election in which women received the vote. Labor was also gaining increasing respect as a rational and sensible force. Parliament was now very evenly split, with Alfred Deakin's Protectionists on 26 seats, George Reid's Free Traders on 24 seats and Watson's Labor Party not far behind on 22 seats. This would be the parliament that Deakin would not unreasonably describe as the parliament "of the three elevens" in reference to three fairly evenly matched cricket teams.

The post-election Caucus agreed to continue to support the Deakin Protectionist government, but, given the small majority of the government, all concerned knew that its life expectancy was not particularly good.

The flashpoint for the Deakin government's fall came from an area in which passions were always likely to run particularly strongly in the Labor Party: industrial relations. The conservative government in Victoria led by Thomas Bent engaged in a robust anti-union response to a railway strike, leading Labor to insist on the inclusion of state public servants in the Federal Conciliation and Arbitration Bill.

This had been an ongoing sore point between the Protectionists and Labor. When Prime Minister Barton had moved the Conciliation and Arbitration Bill, Labor moved an amendment to cover state public servants. While this was defeated, an amendment to include railway workers was passed. Barton's response was to simply drop the bill.

Labor had campaigned strongly on all workers being covered by federal arbitration in the 1903 election and was always going to stick to its guns on this issue.

Deakin was being fatalistic when he reintroduced the Conciliation and Arbitration Bill after the election and announced he would resign the government's commission if an amendment to include state public servants was carried. He knew his government's hold on power was tenuous and was deliberately bringing matters to a head.

Labor moved an amendment in the House to insist on public servants inclusion, which was carried with the support of the Free Trade Party (voting tactically in the hope of bringing down the government, rather than out of any deep-seated views that the Commonwealth should be providing succour for the industrial rights of public servants).

His government having lost an important vote on the floor, Deakin set an Australian precedent by resigning his government's commission.

He also advised the governor-general to send for Watson as Prime Minister.

Accordingly, Watson advised his Caucus colleagues on 23 April 1904 that he had accepted the governor-general's commission. Thus the first national Labor government in the world was born.

The Caucus was torn about whether to seek to govern alone or whether to seek an alliance with the Protectionists, or at least with their more radical and progressive element. There was also a debate how the ministry should be selected.

It was McGregor who, at the Caucus meeting moved the key and successful motion that Watson be given a "free hand" to determine these matters. Having had his power to determine the ministry confirmed, Watson appointed his deputy as Vice-President of the Executive Council. McMullin argues, "Detailed departmental administration was impossible for McGregor. The position of Vice-President of the Executive Council was tailor made for him."[7] While McGregor's blindness was possibly a factor in the decision to give him a wide ranging brief as opposed to a single department to administer, it is unfair to him to dismiss his abilities so brusquely. While the position of Vice-President of the Executive Council is a minor office today, the cabinet hierarchy was viewed differently then and the seniority of the role of being putative deputy to the governor-general cannot be readily dismissed.

Just as McGregor memorised statistics and arguments for his speeches, he listened carefully to the oath of office being recited by his colleagues and recited it word for word without notes or assistance.

The question about whether Labor should seek to govern alone or in a coalition dragged on. Without a majority in either house, no member was under any illusions about what the government could achieve. In May, the Caucus authorised Watson to seek a coalition with Deakin (24 votes to 8, with McGregor and all other ministers supporting the proposition). However, the Protectionists themselves were divided about whether and whom to go into coalition with. Deakin advised Watson that a coalition was not presently possible. Hence, more by accident than design, the tradition of Labor governing alone or not at all was established.

The numbers in the parliament meant that the first Labor government's achievements were never going to be legion. Perhaps its greatest achievement was establishing the precedent that Labor could govern and, despite the frantic anti-Labor shrieking in elements of the media that predicted disaster with members of the working class in control of government levers, nothing went spectacularly wrong for the country during their tenure. As Faulkner and Macintyre put it, "In fact… the Cabinet's competent administration was significant and worthwhile in itself, gradually accustoming Australians to the notion of a Labor Government."[8]

But Watson was realistically fatalistic about the chances of an evenly divided parliament to achieve anything: "I despair of seeing any good come out of this Parliament," he told Attorney-General Henry Bourne Higgins.⁹

By August, the same piece of legislation that saw Watson and his colleagues form government also saw the government fall. The government lost a vote on an amendment to the Conciliation and Arbitration Bill to provide for preferential employment for members of a union. Having previously discussed the situation with Caucus, Watson resigned the government's commission. Reid, as leader of the Free Traders, became the third prime minister of the term (forming a coalition with the conservative end of the Protectionist Party) and Labor returned to Opposition until 1908.

Royal Commissions

Much of the time in McGregor's early years in parliament was spent on Royal Commissions. The practice at the time was that serving politicians would be called upon to serve as Royal Commissioners to ensure political balance in the investigations that were undertaken. In fact, he served on as a commissioner on Australia's first ever Royal Commission.

The SS *Drayton Grange* was returning Australian soldiers from the Boer War, but the conditions were so bad and overcrowded that five of 2000 soldiers on board died on board and another 12 would die in the weeks after disembarkation. So much was the nation scandalised by this poor treatment of our Boer War veterans that there were demands for a full inquiry. But there was no legislative basis for an inquiry with the power to subpoena witnesses. Hence the Commonwealth Royal Commissions Act was quickly passed, and McGregor found himself the Labor representative on the Commission, chaired by the Protectionist Member for Gippsland Allan McLean. The Commission reported in

October 1902 and apportioned blame to various authorities in both South Africa and Australia. The findings were unanimous among commissioners.

In 1904, McGregor was appointed to Australia's seventh Royal Commission (there had been Royal Commissions into the location of the new national capital, the butter industry and navigation among other things after the *Drayton Grange* Commission). In 1904, a Royal Commission was appointed to work through the correct tariff rate for hundreds of items. It was a big task, with hearings in Sydney, Melbourne, Adelaide, Perth, Hobart, Kalgoorlie, Launceston and Maryborough. There would have been no easy consensus with the Commission consisting of three Labor members (McGregor, Senator William Higgs and the Member for Perth James Fowler), three Protectionist members and two Free Traders. The Commission took three years and reported in 1907, making recommendations for tariff levels on many goods and noting that "It is clear from the evidence… that as a whole, employment in secondary industries has greatly increased since the Commonwealth Tariff has been introduced."

Opposition and Return to Government under Fisher

While Labor won three more seats at the 1906 federal election, taking its total to 26, it was not as good a result as it could have been, with the party losing three seats in Queensland due to the first head of a Labor government anywhere in the world, former Premier Andrew Dawson, leaving the party to run as an independent, thus leading to the party's first significant split. While Deakin's Protectionists held only 21 seats and Reid's Free Traders held 27, it was unthinkable for Labor to lend its support to the conservative Reid. Following the frustrations of the first Labor government, there was little appetite to form another minority Labor government, hence the Deakin government continued with Labor's support.

Watson and McGregor were re-elected unopposed as leader and deputy following the 1906 election. Watson had tried to resign as leader in 1905 due to the stress of the job. To convince Watson to stay, the Caucus created the position of deputy leader in the House of Representatives and elected Andrew Fisher to the role. McGregor was still the more senior of the two and recognised as deputy leader of the party as a whole.

In 1907, Watson again resigned, this time insisting on his right to go. Fisher and Hughes ran for the leadership with the two candidates playing a game of billiards while their colleagues voted. Fisher prevailed, with McGregor continuing as deputy leader, with the position of deputy leader in the House of Representatives not being filled. Fisher would come to rely on McGregor even more than Watson had, and they became close friends.

In 1908, the Caucus became increasingly dissatisfied with Deakin's lack of progress on legislation and the government fell when Labor withdrew its support. Fisher was commissioned as Labor's second prime minister. The Caucus engaged in a robust debate about how ministers should be chosen, with Watson (who remained a Caucus member) moving that the leader be entitled to appoint the ministry. McGregor supported Watson's motion but the majority of the Caucus did not, and thus the ministry was selected by Caucus ballot with both Fisher and McGregor exempt from the ballot as they were to be regarded as ministers automatically as the party's leaders.

This too was to be a fairly short-lived government. It had long been apparent that the cleavages in parliament were not sustainable and some sort of permanent realignment of the parties was inevitable. It was likely that the Protectionists would not survive and would either go into a progressive alliance with Labor or an anti-Labor alliance with the Free Traders. George Reid worked shrewdly to bring the latter development about, renaming his Free Trade Party the Anti-Socialist Party and appealing to the Protectionists to work together on the things that united them. The Fisher government fell when the two parties combined to bring him down in 1909. This was a precursor, though, to Labor's greatest moment in the Commonwealth so far. It would also be when McGregor would play his biggest and most important role, as leader of the government in the Senate in the first majority government in the history of the Commonwealth: the Fisher Labor government elected in 1910.

Campaigning and Majority Government

The 1910 election campaign effectively started when Prime Minister Fisher returned to his home town of Gympie on 30 March 1909 to deliver a major policy speech on behalf of the Labor government. This was the most important speech by a Labor leader in the first decades of nationhood. The vision Fisher laid out was an expansive one, committing Labor to a land tax, funding for pensions, a railway across the country, increased military expenditure given heightened tensions, the development of Canberra, a takeover of the Northern Territory, protection for the sugar industry, a national paper currency and re-writing of the fiscal relationship between the Commonwealth and the states. Labor MP William Spence described it reasonably as "the boldest and most national Australian policy ever enunciated".

The speech was substantial but not well delivered. Fisher was halting in his style. This couldn't be said for his warm-up act, his deputy McGregor. He and Fisher had developed a partnership and friendship forged as McGregor accompanied him on political tours around the country, and McGregor's usual role was to introduce the leader and warm up the audience. He did this in front of the 2000 people at the Olympic Theatre in Gympie and his relaxed and natural style somewhat contrasted with Fisher's more reserved nature. He weaved plenty of humour into his address, but his main theme was to skewer the imperialist conservatives who were demanding the Fisher government help the British Government in the purchase of dreadnought battleships to keep up with the Germans. Fisher and Labor preferred to concentrate resources on the creation of an Australian Navy. He described such imperialist demands as "blatherskite".

The program that Fisher put forward met with the approval of the Australian people and the election of April 1910 saw Labor elected to government. The new government also commanded a majority in the Senate. Labor won 16 new seats in the House, on a swing of 13%, and won an extra seven senators, giving it a commanding majority of 36 to 18 in the Senate.

Thus one of the most reforming and productive eras in Labor's history began, with Fisher firmly in control in the House and McGregor guiding the government's program through the Senate. For the third time, McGregor was sworn in as Vice-President of the Executive Council, giving him a broad brief across the government and allowing him to concentrate on the Senate agenda.

One hundred and thirteen Acts entered the statute book during the three years of Labor government.

The conservatives by and large recognised Labor's mandate to a surprising degree, seeking to amend and quibble, not oppose outright. The exception to this was the proposal for national land tax, which was an affront to conservative interests. In introducing the legislation to the Senate, McGregor argued that if tariffs were to work they would reduce imports over time, meaning less money would be raised, requiring other sorts of revenue to fund government services. One of the government's objectives in introducing a land tax was to break up the large estates of the squattocracy in order to generate greater development in smaller land holdings. Little wonder that this was the one measure the conservatives chose to oppose most vociferously in parliament. Labor's superior numbers in both houses carried the day. It was a lasting reform: federal land tax stayed in place until it was abolished by the Menzies government in 1952.

The agenda of the Fisher government closely followed the program that Fisher had laid out in the Gympie address, with the exception that the government also enacted a government bank in the guise of the Commonwealth Bank. By the time the Fisher government faced the people in 1913, they had successfully passed through both houses the creation of the Royal Australian Navy and the Commonwealth Bank, taken over the administration of the Northern Territory with a view to economic development, started the Adelaide to Perth railway, introduced bank notes for the first time, carried the Maternity Allowance Act and started work on Canberra as the nation's capital.

With this record of achievement, Fisher, McGregor and their colleagues were probably hopeful of re-election. But it was to be narrowly denied them. The government put six referenda to the people on election day, with Attorney-General Billy Hughes determined to continue in efforts to expand Commonwealth power, despite the fact that people had already rejected a Labor bid to expand its power in 1911. The Fisher government asked for powers over trade and commerce, corporations, industrial matters, trusts and the nationalisation of monopolies. This political miscalculation enabled the conservatives to not only campaign against the referenda but also to run a scare campaign about the risks of a re-elected Labor government with expanded powers if the referenda were to be carried. In addition, the winds of discord were clearly blowing in Europe and the leader of the Opposition Joseph Cook campaigned on the basis that Labor's loyalty to Britain in these troubled times was questionable. It wouldn't be the last time conservatives would attempt to play this card. This scare campaign was effective enough, just.

The Fisher government received 48.47% of the national vote, narrowly pipped by the Commonwealth Liberal Party on 48.94% of the vote. Labor lost a net five seats, meaning Cook commanded a mere one seat majority.

The Senate was a different story, however. With only half the senators facing the people, and the Labor senators elected in the landslide of 1910 not facing election, Labor was able to actually increase its numbers in the upper house. While McGregor returned to being leader of the Opposition in the Senate, he led a team of 29 senators facing a rump of just seven government senators. McGregor and Labor could deny the Cook government any legislative success and the new government's legislative position was not sustainable.

Sawer notes that the Cook government "did not make any very serious attempt at finding and carrying out a policy which would be supported by the Opposition as well as itself… it was more concerned to provoke the conditions for a double dissolution than to conciliate a Senate majority".[10]

The Cook government's chosen double-dissolution trigger was legislation to end the preference for trade unionists in the federal public service, a measure that would never had received the support of the Labor Senate majority, and the election was set for 5 September 1914.

Labor was to be distracted in the campaign by the illness of its Senate leader McGregor, however, and would be denied his considerable campaign skills. Fisher visited Adelaide during the campaign and spoke at a rally at Adelaide Town Hall. Absent from the meeting was his usual partner on the platform. McGregor was suffering from heart troubles and did not actively campaign. He was nevertheless nominated as lead Labor candidate for the Senate in South Australia. It wasn't to be. He succumbed to heart disease on 13 August 1914, during the election campaign.

Gregor McGregor, Labor's first deputy leader, was buried in the West Terrace Cemetery, Adelaide. The tributes flowed freely. *The Bulletin* remembered him as "the Labor leader for whom the Senate had genuine affection". His successor as Labor's Senate leader, George Pearce, said, "very few men make so many friends". Billy Hughes said hearing of McGregor's death was like "a limb being ripped off our own body" and his leader and friend Andrew Fisher said, "Australia has lost a great citizen... a man of rare ability with a big heart and indomitable courage in fighting the battles of the people".

McGregor was survived by his wife Sarah who would live another six years and his stepson Charles. An area of 260 square kilometres on the Eyre Peninsula had been named the "Hundred of McGregor" (a medieval term that refers to an administrative region) in honour of his service in the South Australian Parliament, but apart from that he has passed from Australia's memory. It's time that was rectified.

Chapter 2

LILIAN LOCKE

The Labor Suffragist

Of all Australia's social and political achievements, being one of the first nations in the world to provide votes to women is surely among the most remarkable.

Australia doesn't revere the women who campaigned so effectively to bring about this outcome in an impressive timeframe. Perhaps it's because they were so effective and didn't have to resort to violence or long decades of campaigning that Australia doesn't celebrate its suffragists[1] like the United Kingdom honours the Pankhursts and the United States reveres Susan B. Anthony.

To the extent we do honour the campaigners for female suffrage in Australia, it tends to be those who eschewed formal party politics, like the admirable Vida Goldstein and Catherine Spence, who are better known.

The Australian Labor Party was an important force in bringing female suffrage about. Women who were active in the early Labor movement were key in pressuring the nascent party to adopt an enlightened position on issues of female rights. Names like Mary Lee and the three Golding sisters deserve recognition.

But no-one deserves more recognition than Lilian Locke. Her story has it all. She was a pioneer of Labor; the first female to be a paid official of the party;[2] the first female delegate to a Labor national conference.

She was an active suffragist who saw the battle for women's rights and the battle for the cause of Labor as one and the same. She was prepared to sacrifice friendships with other campaigners for female suffrage if they came into conflict with her loyalty to Labor. From the middle class, she devoted her life to the improvement of the working class. She really was a True Believer.

Lilian came from a remarkable family. Her sisters were talented in their own ways, and in fact the Locke family has been enshrined in Australian literary history, but few people are aware of the important connection with Labor and suffragist history.

Her nephew, Sumner Locke Elliott, became a celebrated Australian novelist and several of his novels were autobiographical, drawing heavily for inspiration on Lilian's life and the dysfunctional nature of the family in later years. His most famous novel, *Careful, He Might Hear You*, would win the Miles Franklin Award and be turned into an acclaimed movie. The love of Sumner Locke Elliott for his favourite aunt and guardian Lilian shines through in several of his novels, but especially his most famous one.

The thousands of Labor women and men who came after Lilian Locke owe her a debt for her pioneering role in carving a place for women in the Labor family. She was a Labor loyalist but not an unquestioning one: when frustrated she would castigate her own party for not being inclusive enough of women. For this, the generations that came after her owe her a debt. Yet she is not well remembered or honoured. She deserves much better.

Early Life and the Battle for Suffrage

Lilian Locke's upbringing could not have been more respectable. Her father and both grandfathers were Church of England clergy, and her father had a Bachelor of Arts degree from Cambridge University, a particularly rare achievement in the era.

Born in 1869 in Melbourne a year after the marriage of her parents, Reverend William Locke and Annie Seddon, Lilian was the first of 11 children. Eight of the children lived beyond infancy. The family of seven daughters and one son was heavily focused on female achievement. Among her sisters, one became an actress, one a World War One nurse, one an accomplished novelist and one a Christian Science pastor. As the eldest child, Lilian played the "unenviable role of surrogate mother during her own mother's never-ending pregnancies".[3]

Lilian's role as the surrogate parent for her siblings brought out an early maturity in her, and in some senses robbed her of a carefree childhood. She would always be the more serious of the siblings, focused firstly on her role assisting her mother bringing them up and then on the serious business of suffrage and the Labor Party. Eventually, the task of being the adoptive mother to her talented nephew would be the focus of her life.

Moving around Australia due to her father's appointments to different parishes was good training for Lilian. Her service to the Labor Party in her adult years caused her to move between Melbourne, Hobart, Charters Towers, Wollongong and Sydney.

Although not from a Labor background, a concern for the underprivileged ran strongly through her family. Her paternal grandfather, Reverend William Locke Senior, was a key member of the 'ragged school' movement in Victorian England, which opened schools for the poor children of London. Charles Dickens was another key member of the movement.

Although some histories of the suffrage movement have referred to her as a schoolteacher, this is almost certainly incorrect. A collection of her newspaper clippings now held at the State Library of New South Wales includes an article on her support for her husband's campaign for parliament in 1904 and refers to her as "a former public school teacher" but four question marks have been written next to the reference in her hand, indicating she was perplexed to be referred to as such.

In fact, Lilian ran, with her some of her sisters, a "town shopper and general agent" business, in which she and her sisters purchased goods in Melbourne ordered by rural women on a commission basis and despatched them to far-flung parts of the colony.

Despite showing a penchant for business, Lilian "was much influenced by her middle class parents' sympathetic attitude to the underprivileged; she took up the cause of the working class, particularly working class women".[4] Business wasn't going to keep her attention long; there were two passions which drew her and dominated her professional life: the Labor Party and the political advancement of women.

By and large these causes were complementary. The Labor Party was in favour of female enfranchisement and improving the conditions of female workers. Votes for women was achieved in each jurisdiction by a coalition of progressive liberals and Labor, working against reactionary conservatives. Many of Lilian's prominent suffragist sisters eschewed party politics and felt they had to keep the Labor Party distant, even if they generally believed in progressive causes. This caused tension in Lilian's professional and personal life. Despite the frustrations that she inevitably endured, and despite the doubt that she occasionally exhibited, her belief in the cause of Labor meant her path was clear: in case of conflict, she would back Labor.

Lilian took on three roles: she became the first woman appointed to an organising role for the nascent Labor Party, the first "Woman

Organiser" of the Political Labour Council of Victoria (forerunner of the Victorian branch of the ALP). She was the only female member of the Victorian Trades Hall Council and became Secretary of the United Council for Women's Suffrage, the main advocacy group for votes for women, in the last jurisdiction in the nation to provide them, Victoria. In carrying out these roles she also became a regular contributor to the socialist journal *The Tocsin*, one of the few women to do so.

Suffrage and Reform

It is commonly understood that South Australia was among the first jurisdictions in the world to give women the vote and Australia was the second country to do so. South Australia did so in 1894 and the Commonwealth in 1902. It is widely recognised that Australia was at the vanguard of the suffragist movement, compared to, for example, the United Kingdom which didn't deign to give women the vote until 1918 and the United States which waited until 1920. This self-congratulatory snapshot doesn't give due recognition to the women who campaigned so long to get the vote for Australian females. Their work was far from over in 1902.

Lilian saw the causes of the female enfranchisement and the Labor Party as entirely complementary. She knew that the Labor Party members had been instrumental in voting female suffrage into reality in 1893, following it being adopted as South Australian Labor official policy in 1892. It had been added to the Tasmanian party platform in 1896 and "one adult one vote" had very significantly been the first item on the federal Labor platform in 1900.

She also saw votes for women as being just the first step on a ladder of women's rights issues which included better industrial conditions for workers and more women in parliament.

The granting of the vote to women in South Australia in 1894 was a significant milestone, but the battle for female enfranchisement across the country was far from over. Within the victory in South Australia, though, lay the key to granting women the vote in the new Federation seven years later.

Western Australia followed the South Australian example and provided women the vote in 1899, but no other state had at the time of Federation. So it is unsurprising that, when former South Australian Premier Sir Frederick Holder proposed that full female suffrage be enshrined in the new Constitution at the 1897 Constitutional Convention, he was voted down by 23 votes to 12. He was not done yet, however. Soon after being defeated in this resolution, he told his fellow delegates that it would be unconscionable if South Australian women had the right to vote at the state level but were denied it at the Commonwealth level (or worse still, lost the rights they had won). Hence he moved that "no elector now possessing the right to vote shall be deprived of that right".

His fellow delegates, worried that South Australia would walk away from the federation project if the rights of their female voters were not so protected, voted in favour of the Holder resolution by a margin of three. Thus Holder ensured that the first election for the Commonwealth would involve female suffrage for South Australian voters (and West Australian voters given they passed such a law in 1899). While the first Commonwealth election denied the vote to women in other states, such an illogical franchise made no sense and Holder made universal female suffrage virtually inevitable in that deft move at the convention. (Holder would mainly be remembered in Australian political folklore for becoming the first Speaker of the new House of Representatives and, after eight years in office, clutching his chest during a fiery debate, yelling "Horrible, Horrible!" and dying on the floor of the chamber. In fact, he should be remembered as a father of female voting rights.)

It was in this context that Lilian joined the United Council for Women's Suffrage. Women could vote in two states and federally, but not in other state jurisdictions and certainly not in Victoria. The Council had been formed in 1894 and represented a broad church of views, including not only Trades Hall but the Woman's Christian Temperance Union and the Vigilance Society (a Catholic dominated pro-life group). It had been formed by Annette Bear Crawford but had been reinvigorated after Crawford's death by the woman who went on to become probably the best remembered of Australia's suffragists, Vida Goldstein.

Goldstein and Locke had a longstanding friendship and collaboration. Just how close they were is indicated by Lilian's decision to follow Vida into adherence to Christian Science, despite being the daughter and grand-daughter of Church of England ministers. The Church of England, together with most traditional churches, was hostile to the cause of suffrage, believing that the male is the head of the household. The Church of Christ (Scientist), however, was formed by a woman, Mary Baker Eddy, in the United States in 1879 and was pro-suffrage in outlook. Teaching that "to be spiritually minded is to be scientifically minded", Christian Scientists opened their first church in Melbourne in 1898. Despite her Jewish heritage, Vida Goldstein joined the church in 1902 and Lilian soon followed. So would Lilian's sister Agnes who took Christian Science so seriously that she moved to Boston to train as a pastor. It was to be a lifelong adherence, with Lilian being buried according to Christian Science rites in 1950.

Despite their agreement on religion, there was to be a considerable point of tension between them: a disagreement about which cause should receive priority: the cause of women or the cause of Labor.

Following the passage of national female suffrage in 1902, Goldstein decided the next step was for a woman to run for parliament. Although she didn't expect to be elected, she ran a serious campaign as an independent candidate for the Senate in Victoria. She was a political progressive, indeed radical (she would later run for parliament during World War One on a pacifist platform). But she was never a member of the Labor Party and doubted the party would seriously promote women for parliament until forced to.

This is when tension arose in Lilian's joint passions for the first time. She was the Secretary of the Council for Women's Suffrage. While Goldstein was running as an independent, the Council clearly supported her campaign. The Labor Party asked Lilian to resign as Secretary of the Council as it was a conflict with her duty to support the election of Labor candidates. In no doubt as to where her loyalties lay, she willingly immediately resigned as Secretary and made it clear she only recommended votes for official Labor candidates, however worthy independent candidates might be. "Locke believed that women's salvation lay with the Labor Party," as historian Betty Searle put it.[5]

This caused considerable tension between the two leading suffragists. Goldstein did not take Lilian's resignation lightly, and it was clear that there was personal tension between the two of them over her decision. Goldstein was reasonably diplomatic in her public statements, however, lamenting that "the broad basis of the Women's Political Association is not acceptable to Labor women, but I rejoice to see women organising on any lines".[6]

Goldstein's biographer Janette Bomford believes Goldstein and Locke remained on good terms personally despite their political fissure. The tension between the middle-class bourgeois advocates of suffrage and those like Lilian who believed in the broader progressive cause was underlined by Vida's sister Isobella who demonstrated her anti-working-class prejudices when she wrote privately, trying to show sympathy for Lilian's predicament, that "to rub shoulders with the uncultured must be very trying".[7]

Locke was still an ardent suffragist, although no longer a member of the key organisation. On 18 January 1904, for example, she argued in the *Portland Guardian* that "in the sphere of Federal politics we have been admitted to the full citizenship long enjoyed and prudently exercised in their several states, by the women of New Zealand and South Australia and, in more recent years, granted to the women of Western Australia, New South Wales and Tasmania… What have the women of Victoria done to deserve this?"

Lilian's departure from the Women's Suffrage Council coincided with her full-time employment as an organiser with the Victorian Labor Party and, simultaneously, the Victorian Trades Hall Council. She campaigned alongside the British socialist Tom Mann. Mann was influential in the party, and while encouraging of Lilian's work he was adamant that the organisation of females should be part of the broader party structure, with no deals or alliances struck with non-Labor women's groups. This view was clearly influential, and Lilian subscribed to it.

As remarkable as her early employment as female organiser was, the Labor Party's commitment to female organisation was not yet permanent or serious. The Women's Committee of the party, which Lilian was employed by for example, was established for the 1903 election and was disbanded in July 1904. She was re-employed (for three pounds a week) in 1905.[8] At the 1905 Victorian Labor Party conference, Lilian succeeded in having "civil equality of the sexes" put into the party platform, which was quite an achievement for the time.

She reported on her activities as the female organiser in *The Tocsin* and was clearly working hard: "Visits were paid to Prahran, St Kilda, Essendon, Fitzroy, Carlton, East Melbourne, Williamstown and North Melbourne districts with encouraging results," she reported. A "grand meeting" was held in Prahran with standing room only and "a really fine musical programme provided by Comrades Gibbons and Emmett. The subject of the evening was 'Women and the Socialist Movement'... Great enthusiasm was displayed." A smaller gathering was held a few days later. Lilian reported to *The Tocsin* readers that "A cottage meeting was held at Mrs Malchow's house... We had a Labour song and a short address on the 'Labour Party and the Home' and we finished with some excellent tea and cakes provided by the hostess. Several women present promised to attend the next local branch meeting and also to bring others." She knew the size of her task, reporting that "My next meeting was at Meredith where I spoke at a social evening. A number of women were present, and listened with great interest; but so far, politics has been a dead language to them, and it will take a great deal of continuous and patient work to rouse them to any active effort."[9] Representing the women of the Labor Party, Lilian led a delegation to the Victorian Premier William Irvine, urging that the humiliation of being denied the vote be removed "on behalf of the 120,000 women workers who had to earn their own bread".[10]

Although employed by Victorian Labor, she was in much demand as an impressive platform speaker in elections around the country. Newspaper reports of her speeches give us a flavour of her arguments and her persuasive abilities. The *Brisbane Worker* described her as a "brilliant organiser and propagandist". Not only did she give speeches, but she was influential in extending the reach of trade unionism into regional centres that she visited, especially the organisation of female workers.

It was her organising role that took her to Tasmania to campaign in the first elections in which women had the vote in that jurisdiction – the South Hobart by-election of 1903 and the 1904 state election. She was popular in Tasmania and moved there in 1904 to continue full-time campaigning and remained a popular speaker interstate. She was invited to speak at a rally in the mining town of Zeehan in August 1904 which the *Zeehan and Dundas Herald* on 11 August reported on extensively. She started her remarks by arguing in favour of the female franchise which had recently been granted, although her argument was fairly grounded in the norms of the time. She debunked the ridiculous arguments of those who opposed female suffrage that were common at the time (that women would become more masculine if given the vote or that chivalry would die).

She put the simple but powerful argument in favour of the female franchise: "If a woman has to pay taxes, obey laws, and work under certain conditions, she ought to be able to have a voice in the matter." She somewhat optimistically argued that suffrage would bring about equal pay (equal pay wasn't of course legislated until 1969 and is not yet a reality almost 120 years later). After making the case for female enfranchisement, she then went on to provide a solid defence of the Labor program: "Women should support the Labor Party, as the franchise for women had been secured through the exertions of the Labor Party." The *Herald* reported that "Another reason was because [Labor] was the great humanitarian movement of the world, and as women were humanitarian, her interests and sympathies must be with the Labor Party." Arbitration, improvements of working conditions through the *Factory Act*, and (shamefully but not prominently) the White Australia policy were other elements of the speech.

Although her arguments in favour of female suffrage and equality were radical for their time, a common theme to her speeches was to assure listeners both male and female that improved rights for females would not upset the existing order or domestic harmony. She told a rally outside the Geelong Wool Mills in 1904 that "There is no reason why the woman's sphere should be circumscribed. Her duty begins at home but it doesn't end there. No woman could be so much interested in a budget speech or an electoral bill to forget to put the chops on."[11]

A report from 22 January 1904 also gives us a good flavour of Lilian's technique. She would hold afternoon meetings in local halls advertised as a "Pleasant Sunday Afternoon". There she would advertise another meeting for the evening:

> There was a good attendance (chiefly of men) and Miss Locke, during the course of her address impressed upon them the importance of going home and rousing up their women for the evening meeting. Accordingly, at 8.30PM a large assembly of women, girls and a fair sprinkling of men gathered outside the hall, waiting for the conclusion of a Salvation Army Service. It came to an end in due time and as the Army congregation filed out, Miss Locke's audience filed in and a very enthusiastic meeting was held, although the hour was late.[12]

Lilian was a radical in many ways but also deeply grounded in her respectable middle-class roots in others. Not only did she argue that female suffrage would not upset the natural order of women being the provider in the home, but she was also a lifelong adherent to temperance.

In June 1905 she was invited to Broken Hill to organise female workers for a trade union. The meeting at Broken Hill Trades Hall overflowed, such was the attraction in hearing a powerful female platform speaker. A union was formed at her urging.

The *Adelaide Herald* reported in October 1905 that "Port Pirie has been favoured by a visit from Miss Locke, and long shall we remember the day. Her address was one of the most clear and fluent that any Port Pirie audience has had the pleasure of listening to." Lilian also addressed the laundry workers of Port Pirie, who resolved, after hearing from her about the virtues of trade unionism, to form The Federated Laundry Employees of Australia, South Australia branch.

She became the first ever female delegate to Labor's Interstate Conference (a forerunner to the current National Conference) when she was elected a Tasmanian delegate in 1905. This inevitably attracted some attention. The *Queensland Worker* noted:

> Tasmania sent the only woman delegate, Miss Locke, at the Interstate Conference. We can guess from her public speeches how that delegate voted on the momentous issues raised. She is for socialism before free trade or protection and no socialist objective is red hot enough for her to burn her fingers.

It was at this conference that she met George Mason Burns, who had been elected as the Labor Member for Queenstown in 1903. Exactly the same age as Lilian, they soon became more than friends, and returned to Melbourne to be married at Christ Church, South Yarra, in 1906. "An interesting ceremony took place at Christ Church, South Yarra," the *Adelaide Critic* reported on January 17:

> when Ms Lilian Locke, daughter of the Rev WE Locke, was united in the bounds of holy matrimony to Mr George Burns, Labor Member for Queenstown Tasmania… The wedding was of great interest to the Labor Party, Miss Lilian Locke being the lady lecturer of the Trades Hall Council. As the happy pair were

leaving the church a bouquet tied with the two Labor colours – red and black – was thrown into their carriage by a member of the Labor Party… A reception was afterwards held at Muir Street Hawthorn, the residence of the bride's father. Among those present was Miss Vida Goldstein. A social was also given at the Trades Hall in the afternoon to celebrate the event.

Although not reported, prominent Labor politician and fellow Tasmanian King O'Malley was also at the wedding.

In keeping with the norms of the time, some assumed incorrectly that marriage would mean Lilian would cease to be active in her own right. A supporter of her work from Broken Hill, for example, published a poem to mark her wedding:

> We have lost you Lilian dear,
> You who were our dear delight
> Our sweet champion, warm, sincere
> Bathing in the cause of Right
>
> You denounced monopoly
> And all other forms of greed,
> Now have changed – but we can sigh
> For our loved one past remede
>
> For, oh see what you have done –
> You whom we so dearly prized –
> Give away yourself to one,
> And are now monopolized.

George was re-elected as Member for Queenstown in the 1906 state election, but resigned from State Parliament that November to try his hand at federal politics as the Labor candidate for Denison. The seat was held for the Protectionist Party by former premier and one of the fathers of Federation, Sir Philip Fysh. Labor hadn't contested the 1903 election, so running in 1906 against a high-profile sitting member was a speculative exercise. It is not known how Lilian felt about her new husband risking his career like that. We can deduce that, given her passion for the Labor cause, she was in favour of him trying to wrest the seat. George did creditably, but not well enough, polling 38% of the vote to Fysh's commanding 59%.

Married for a year, the newlyweds were now without their main income. Neither was about to leave active involvement in the Labor Party. In fact, the Labor cause took them about as far from Queenstown as it was possible to travel while remaining in Australia, with George taking the post of Secretary of the Miners Association based in Charters Towers, Queensland. Lilian took up the role of Secretary of the North Queensland Women's Organising Committee of the Labor Party.

There was a welcoming rally of unionists and supporters when George and Lilian arrived in Charters Towers. While most wives of arriving officials would have quietly accepted welcome notes and the odd bouquet of flowers from the women of the town, Lilian spoke at the rally:

> Let women cultivate a little conceit – so that every woman, in the kitchen, in the nursery, in the parlour or in the workshop, may realise they are responsible for humanity; that upon them resolves the responsibility for purifying this world – and leaving it for our children better than we found it.

In 1907, Lilian had her first (publicly known at least) crisis of confidence in the strength of Labor's support for women. Whereas her previous contributions to *The Tocsin* had been detailed reports on the success of exercises to organise women voters, she grew agitated that Labor was not treating women with the respect they deserved as serious political figures.

> During the recent state and federal elections it was clear that women were not wanted on the platform but were needed out there canvassing or making tea. Nominations for the soft Labor seat of Batman included a woman for preselection but the men without exception threw up their hands in horror and cried "You wouldn't waste it on a woman surely?"

This was quite the turnaround in four years for the woman who had cut her ties with Victoria's leading suffragist movement because it undermined support for Labor's candidates. At the time, Lilian had said, "had Vida Goldstein attached herself to a Party she might now be in Federal Parliament". Now she was recognising that the Labor Party had a long way to go before it embraced women as equals in terms of potential parliamentary representation. Alas, both Goldstein and Locke were right: it would be another 36 years before either major party would put a woman in Federal Parliament (Labor and the conservatives at the same 1943 election). However, the road that Lilian took was ultimately the right one and the road that Vida Goldstein chose – standing aloof from political parties – was doomed to failure.

George and Lilian stayed for three years in Charters Towers before moving to New South Wales in 1910. They chose Wollongong for their new home and before long George was attempting to re-enter parliament via the federal seat of Illawarra, so it was probably for this reason that they relocated. George had been born in Mogo on the New South Wales south coast, so his links to the area provided a valuable launching pad to enter Federal Parliament. Soon after their relocation to the Illawarra, the 1910 election was called and George was endorsed as the Labor candidate. This was to be a good election for Labor, with Andrew Fisher forming the first majority government in the federation's short history. Burns did well, achieving a 12% swing against the sitting member and future New South Wales Premier, the popular George Fuller. He fell short of unseating him, however, with 48% of the vote. George was employed in the Government Printing Office and was an official of the Storemen's Union as he prepared for another run.

Despite Labor narrowly sliding out of office at the 1913 election, George pushed the Labor vote in Illawarra up slightly to pass 50%, and unseated Fuller with a vote of 50.2%. The 1914 election saw him slightly consolidate his hold with 54% of the vote (against Fuller again). The disastrous 1917 election saw George bundled out of parliament like so many of his colleagues, as he suffered an 8.5% swing, defeated by the expelled former President of the New South Wales Labor Party, Hector Lamond, who had followed Billy Hughes into the Nationalist Party. George had been an ardent and early opponent of conscription within the Labor Caucus. Relatives would later speculate that he was defeated because he supported prohibition[13] (he shared with Lilian a lifelong belief in temperance and prohibition), but given the widespread big swings against Labor, this seems unlikely to have played a big role in his defeat.

While George was an active parliamentarian, Lilian remained extremely active in the organisational sphere of the women's movement, becoming president of the New South Wales Association of Women Workers. As George fought for his political life while the Labor Party collapsed over the issue of conscription, Lilian wrote to the *Gosford Times and Wyong District Advocate* saying, "I must congratulate the electors of Robertson on the chance they will next Saturday have of voting for a woman candidate for the Federal Parliament. It is pleasing to find the old traditional ideas regarding 'woman's sphere' gradually dying out" (the 1917 election was the first in which a major party nominated female candidates, with Eva Seery the Labor candidate in Robertson and Henrietta Greville the Labor candidate in Wentworth). Seery, whom Lilian was supporting, suffered a 3% swing away from her, but this was significantly below the national average and she scored a creditable 43.8% of the vote in a very difficult election for Labor.

1917 was a tumultuous year for the Burns-Locke family. Not only did George lose his seat in one of the most hostile and bitter election campaigns in Australian history (see the Frank Tudor chapter for a fuller explanation of the rancorous campaign), in October a tragedy struck which changed the lives of Lilian and George forever.

While Lilian had been progressing the cause of Labor and women, her talented younger sister Helena Sumner Locke had been making her name as a novelist and playwright. She was also a pioneer for women, becoming the first woman dramatist to have a play produced in Australia by commercial theatrical management. She married Henry Logan Elliott in December 1916, a few weeks before he was posted to the Western Front. He was a journalist and accountant and by all accounts an alcoholic. He was reported to be a drinking partner of the great Henry Lawson, who had by these times fallen into alcoholism (both Helena and Henry went by their middle names: Sumner and Logan). He was in Australia long enough to get his young wife pregnant before leaving for the war.

On 17 October 1917, she gave birth to their son, whom she named Sumner. Tragically, she did not get an opportunity to have a bigger role in her son's life, as she died from eclampsia a day after giving birth. Her funeral was held in the Hurstville home that Lilian and George had relocated to following his electoral defeat a few months earlier.

The childless couple took custody of the newborn nephew. They were, in terms of location and stable home life, the best placed of the Locke family to provide a loving home for the baby. His father no doubt would have been able to achieve a discharge from the army for the purpose of caring for his newborn son, but showed no interest in doing so. Betty Searle noted that "This child became the centre of Lilian's life. She loved and cared for her nephew… Lilian's interest in labour politics never waned but much of her time from 1917 was spent caring for her nephew."[14]

By all accounts, Lilian ran a fairly austere, but happy household with young Sumner receiving much love and attention from her in particular, but also George. Sumner Locke Elliott's biographer Sharon Clarke wrote that Lilian "made him the centre of her entire life and kept the atmosphere in the house as happy as possible".[15]

George continued active involvement in politics; however, he was involved in a Labor schism when he joined the Independent Socialist Labor Party, which had been formed by supporters of the Industrial Workers of the World and One Big Union movement. He was one of only two parliamentary candidates for the party in the 1919 federal election and scored a mere 2075 votes in his final contest for Illawarra.

There is no evidence of Lilian's involvement in his campaign, although she presumably was supportive of her husband. She was now more focused on care for young Sumner than politics. When the Industrial Socialist Labor Party inevitably folded, some of its adherents drifted to other small socialist parties, but George wanted to return to the official Labor fold. His return to Labor was so complete that he was a Labor candidate for the (then) New South Wales state seat of St George in the 1925 state election.

Under the prevailing electoral system, St George was a multi-member district electing five members. Three Labor members were elected, including the future Premier Joseph Cahill and two conservatives (including Thomas Ley who was later charged with murder in the United Kingdom and acquitted on grounds of insanity). Burns received 7.5% of the vote: a creditable performance which might have been enough to see him enter his third parliament with a more favourable preference flow. It wasn't to be. The election, which saw his old adversary in the federal seat of Illawarra, Sir George Fuller, defeated as Premier by Jack Lang, and the first woman (Millicent Preston-Stanley) elected to the Legislative Assembly for the Nationalists, was George's last parliamentary foray.

From Politics to Family Law

Lilian and George's happy home-life with young Sumner was dealt a huge blow in 1921 when Lilian's sister Jessie returned from the United Kingdom "for the sole purpose of taking over the custody of the infant".[16] Despite their middle-class upbringing, the broader Locke family did not have considerable means. Lilian and George had devoted their professional lives to the Labor cause and had not amassed significant savings.

Following the death of their father William, Jessie moved to the United Kingdom where she was employed as a companion by a wealthy cousin, Aggie Barclay. This had given Jessie independent wealth and access to the upper strata of British society, leading to a view that she had superior social standing and could give Sumner access to a better start in life than could Lilian and George. There was also no doubt some snobbery involved in Jessie's disdain for Lilian's ability to raise their nephew. She referred to the neighbourhood and friends of Lilian and George as "common".

Jessie's location in London had enabled her to have strong influence over Logan Elliott's determination of the custody arrangements of his son. Jessie convinced him to sign a deed which named Lilian, herself and the child's godfather (and former lover of the child's mother Helena) Ernest Ewart as joint guardians. With Ewart also in London, and largely uninterested in his role as joint guardian, Jessie started sending instructions to Lilian as to how young Sumner should be raised, asserting that she had Ewart's support and therefore majority support among the guardians. This made Lilian's role as *in loco parentis* difficult and frustrating, but she did her best to shield young Sumner from the tension. This tension existed for three years, until Jessie returned to Australia. This return didn't improve the situation. An emotional tug of war ensued with an unsatisfactory arrangement for all concerned which involved shared custody between Jessie and Lilian. Jessie enrolled Sumner in exclusive junior schools in Sydney's eastern suburbs (first Miss Piles School for Infants, then Edgecliff Preparatory School and finally Cranbrook), which Sumner hated and rebelled against. When, in 1927 young Sumner simply refused to return to Jessie and demanded to stay with "Aunt Lily", Jessie began legal action (she was on strong ground as a joint custodian and had superior wealth to pay for legal representation).

There was a clear political element to the case. Jessie was no Labor voter. Her affidavit to the court stated, "I felt obliged to urge greater care in the choice of [Sumner's] associates. The respondent and her husband have by their actions and socialistic tendencies and doctrines caused the infant's mother before her death great anxiety… a fear I have always had was the influences arising there from might give the infant improper ideas." She went on to say, "I fully admit that it has been my aim to keep the infant's mind free of such doctrines and this has been one of the chief reasons for my keeping him as much as possible away from such influences." In response, Lilian admitted that Helena was not a Labor voter, but denied this had ever caused any tension between the sisters or would have caused the deceased mother any concern.

Lilian and George supplied several witnesses attesting they were good parents for young Sumner. As Sumner Locke Elliott's biographer Sharron Clarke describes the outcome: "Jessie, fearing that she had lost ground due to court evidence that supported Lily, suggested a compromise: that her nephew be placed in Cranbrook School as a boarder at her expense."[17] Perhaps to relieve young Sumner of the tug of war between his two aunts, the judge agreed to this solution. But it hardly seemed like a solution to young Sumner, who hated being away from Lilian and George and despised his time at the exclusive boarding school for the rest of his life. Jessie died in 1929 and Sumner returned to the mutually happy embrace of Lilian and George.

We know more about this sorry saga because Sumner went on to become an accomplished novelist. Australia's only Literature Nobel Laureate Patrick White would modestly come to describe him as "the finest living Australian novelist apart from myself".[18] He moved to the United States in 1948 where he became an accomplished playwright and screenwriter.

In 1963, he published his first novel, *Careful, He Hear Might Hear You*, which like many of his future novels was openly autobiographical. It is easy for a reader with knowledge of the Locke family to deduce who is who. His loving adoptive Aunt and Uncle are Lila and George Baines. George is a Trades Hall official who was previously a Labor candidate for parliament. While Lila is clearly Lilian, there is no indication in the novel of Lila having been a Labor and suffragist activist, although other family details like Aunt Agnes being a serious adherent of Christian Science and Sumner's grandfather being a Church of England Minister appear. By the time of the span covered by *Careful, He Might Hear You* Lilian was very much devoted to young Sumner's care. Her activism was increasingly a thing of the past, but there was no doubt about the political views of the household. Sumner told his biographer decades after he left Australia, "Ours was a Labor house. My Uncle George was a Labor politician and I was brought up to vote Labor and did so, always."[19]

Although not as well-known as his Miles Franklin Award winning *Careful, He Might Hear You*, it is his later novel, *Waiting for Childhood* (1987), which perhaps pays deeper tribute to his Aunt Lilian. Clearly inspired by Lilian and her sisters, it is the story of six sisters and their solitary brother. By this time, Sumner had learnt more about Lilian's active role in politics before he was born. In this novel, he more accurately paints Lilian as an activist in her own right, rather than as simply a supportive spouse to her politically active husband. He names his beloved aunt "Lillian Lord" on this occasion and George became George Barnes. He imagines the meeting of Lilian and George:

> Miss Lillian Lord
>
> She had almost been drowsing when she heard her name announced… she stood up and went to the lectern in a splatter of applause. "Let us begin" Lily began, as she always did, dramatically, taking them all in from one side of the hall to the other, and from one side of the hall to the other there was silence. But not the silence that she was used to, respectful, hushed, an amicable bridge between her and the audience over which she

would carry her message to them and to the world. Almost at once she recognised something sinister in this silence, there was hostility in it… The first time she had not held an audience in her palm… she knew she was speaking badly… Catcalls had begun to sound… At this point Mr Barnes stepped forward boldly and holding out his arms to the crowd called "Quiet, *quiet*, please now, ladies, give her a chance…" A hush came over the hall… But whatever power and authority she had started with had gone… she sat down to perfunctory applause…

Lilian did not live long enough to read about the characters based on her life or to see her beloved nephew become an acclaimed author.

George Burns passed away at the home that he and Lilian had moved to in Cremorne in Sydney in 1932.

The death of her partner of 26 years inspired Lilian to pick up her pen. She called her poem "Solitary". The grief and loneliness of a woman who once had a busy life shone through:

>All through the dreary mist of years
>I walk alone.
>The tired world is sick of tears
>And so through seeming endless years
>I walk alone.
>
>I hear the sound of hurrying feet,
>And joy, and laughter – (Life is Sweet) –
>But in the winter's rain and sleet
>I walk alone
>
>Once down the road of Memory,
>With laughing eyes you came to me,
>And where the headland meets the sea
>We walked alone

> But now I blindly grope my way,
> And know not if 'tis night or day
> The curlew cries across the bay
> I walk alone.

Lilian's days of very active political involvement were over, but she remained loyal to her party until the end.

There was to be more sadness in her later years. Her sister Blanche, an actress who struggled with alcohol, began to experience increasingly acute mental ill-health.

As Sumner's biographer recorded it:

> During these years Blanche turned on Lily, who was then her only means of shelter and support. Even in public she was unspeakably rude to the aged Lily, who was such a proper and polite woman herself. According to those of Sumner's friends who witnessed his aunt Blanche's outrages, she was consumed by jealousy of the relationship between Lily and her nephew. Sumner and his youngest aunt had many heated rows during this period.

The relationship between Lilian and Blanche remained an issue as Lilian approached the end of her life. Lilian had remained an adherent of Christian Science throughout her life, although not as fanatically as her sister Agnes. So did Blanche despite her party-girl lifestyle, career as an actor and dancer and her alcoholism. One of the tenets of Christian Science (ironically for a religion that celebrates science) is that medicine has no place in interfering with God's will. As Sharon Clarke described the sad situation:

> During Lily's last illness her adherence to the Christian Science doctrine of healing that "disease has no place within those properly attuned to the Divine Spirit" prevented any conventional medical

intervention on her behalf. Sumner Locke Elliott's friends remember that Blanche, as Lily's nurse-cum-warden during this time, urged her to maintain this stand against her "perceived" illness. Even when Lily herself began to ask for medical help, Blanche baulked and by the time a doctor was called Lily's condition was already too advanced… It seems ironic that Lily eventually died in such circumstances, when both Blanche and Agnes later died in hospitals with their pain and distress relieved as much as possible by medical science.[20]

Her nephew Sumner, who by now was working as a screenwriter in the United States, managed to get back to Australia a couple of days before the death of his beloved aunt. Lilian died on the first of July 1950 at the age of 81, and was buried according to the rites of Christian Science.

Some newspapers carried small obituaries which noted her passing. These didn't really capture the length and magnitude of her service to Labor. *The Age*, for example, reported: "Mrs. Lilian Burns, one of the early women leaders of the Labor movement, died, at her home at North Sydney yesterday, aged 81. Mrs. Burns was one of the organisers, and founders of the Women's Political Organisation, a group which campaigned for votes for women. Mrs. Burns travelled Australia as an organiser for the Labor party. Her late husband, Mr. George Burns, was a member of the House of Representatives." Much fuller obituaries outlining her contribution to suffrage, women's rights and the Labor Party would have been more appropriate.

Conclusion

Lilian Locke's life was a life well-lived. Her combined passions of an improved role for women in national politics and the cause of Labor would be shared by thousands of activists who would follow her, but in most cases would not know of her existence in order to honour her appropriately. Some (but not all) students of the suffrage movement know of Lilian's important work, and students of Sumner Locke Elliott understand her importance to his literature, but very rarely are the two strands of her life combined in any study.

It is ironic that characters based on Lilian are an important part of Australia's literary history but that the woman herself has been lost to history. The Labor Party, to which she was so loyal, sometimes disappointed her. She knew the way to improve the fealty of Labor to the cause of women was to stay in the party and fight for more. The achievement of votes for women and the improvement of working conditions for female employees, to which she devoted so many years of effort, stand as her ultimate testament.

Chapter 3

FRANK TUDOR

A Leader for the Darkest Days

I was standing in the boardroom of the Richmond Tigers Football Club, admiring the portraits of club presidents past, when I said to the senior Tigers official with me, "Oh look, you have a former leader of the Labor Party as one of your presidents." "Really?" he replied, "Which one?"

It's not just in his beloved home town of Richmond that Frank Tudor has been forgotten. One faded picture on the wall of the Labor Caucus room in Canberra serves as pretty much the only remaining tribute to his tenure as Labor leader. But he deserves his enormous contribution to Labor to be honoured in a much better fashion. Parliamentary contemporary and historian Norman Makin said of Tudor "No man of greater personal quality and honour ever held the position of Leadership to the Commonwealth Labor Party."[1] High praise indeed.

He was the first leader of an Australian political party to have been born in Australia, the first Labor leader not to assume the prime ministership, and was at the vanguard of the campaign to stop his Prime Minister, Billy Hughes, imposing conscription on an unwilling party and nation. Although he led the Labor Party at its darkest hour, Frank Tudor wasn't a natural leader. He was elected one largely by default after the incumbent walked out on the party and the movement imploded over the issue of conscription. He led the party to two election defeats and for the latter part of his leadership was stalked by a more charismatic and popular contender for the job. But Tudor held the Labor Party together when its very existence was under threat. The conscription issue succeeded in crippling Labor for a generation; but it failed to destroy the party, as it might easily have done. The Labor splits of the 1930s and 1950s were very difficult for Labor and its leaders, but on balance not as difficult as the task that faced Tudor when Prime Minister Hughes simply walked out on the party one day and began his own party. Hughes and his colleagues then hurled invective and accusations of disloyalty and lack of patriotism against Tudor and the other Labor loyalists which Tudor had to withstand and repel. For nursing Labor through that difficult canyon modern Labor owes Tudor a debt of gratitude.

Early Life

Francis Gwynne Tudor was born in Williamstown in Victoria in January 1866 to John Llewellyn Tudor and Ellen (nee Burt). John was ballastman (a worker who managed the ballast on ships). Frank was their second surviving son.

Soon after Frank's birth, the family moved to the inner-Melbourne suburb of Richmond, and his love of the suburb and its football team began. He attended Richmond Central School. After leaving school he tried his hand at saw milling and boot making. He soon realised that he was a better hat maker than boot maker and began an apprenticeship at the Denton Hat Mills in Abbotsford.[2]

His trade took him on an overseas adventure, travelling to the United Kingdom and the United States to further develop his skills. It was overseas that he also developed his involvement in, and love for, the trade union movement. He worked in Birmingham, Liverpool, Manchester and London but it was in Connecticut in the United States that he observed the operation of the "union label", a system in which hats made by union labour were labelled as such so that fellow unionists knew which products they could buy that would not undermine working conditions. He was clearly well-respected and influential in the English union because he not only rose to the Vice-Presidency of the London branch of the Felt Hatters Union, but also persuaded them to adopt the same system.

When he returned to Melbourne he returned to a job at the Denton Factory. Armed with not only passion but international experience, he rose to the Presidency of the Victorian Felt Hatters Union and took a seat on the Victorian Trades Hall Council.

It was trade unionism, rather than the great Federation debates that took his interest (he wasn't convinced the new Commonwealth Constitution was democratic enough to win his support)[3] and he rose to be President of the Victorian Trades Hall Council in 1900.

He was also active in his community, being a deacon of the Congregational Church. It is a common misconception that the early Labor Party was dominated by Catholics, when in fact many of the senior pioneers of the party were active participants in the Protestant churches.[4] Tudor was also President of the Victorian Life Saving Society (he had won a Bronze Medallion).

While in Britain he had met and fell in love with a Lancashire girl Alice Smale. They married in a Congregational chapel in Lancashire in January 1894 but planned a life together in his native Melbourne, arriving on the steamship *The Austral* on 24 April, which means they embarked for Australia soon after marriage. Alice was pregnant during the journey, giving birth to Alfred Gwynne Tudor in October.

But tragedy was to strike the young couple, with Alice dying as a result of childbirth. The tragedy facing the young widower would be compounded by the death of little Alfie just four months later. It was a simple death notice that appeared in *The Age* on 2 February 1895: "TUDOR: on 1st February at 24 York St Richmond, Alfred Gwynne, son of Frank and the late Alice Tudor, aged 4 months."

Tudor would never publicly speak or write about his bereavement on losing both a young wife and son. There is no record of him ever mentioning either of them in public. His grief was a private one.

It would be three years before he would re-marry, to Fannie Mead in 1897, and they went on to have six children together.

A combination of his trade union and community activity led him to be selected as the Labor candidate for Yarra in the new Commonwealth Parliament's first election in 1901. Based around working-class Richmond, Collingwood and Abbotsford, Yarra was a contest between Tudor for Labor and three different varieties of Protectionist candidate. At a time when the electoral system was first-past-the-post, Tudor prevailed with 33% of the vote compared to his main rival, the official Protectionist candidate, with 28%. It would be the first and last time the seat of Yarra would be close while Tudor was a candidate. Two years later in 1903, he would beat the Protectionist candidate 68% to 32%.

Into Parliament

Despite his active trade unionism, Tudor was regarded as a political moderate. His dedication to the Congregational Church led him to be a teetotaller, non-smoker and consistent observer of the Sabbath. As Janet McCalman put it, with "high principles tempered by genuine liberalism, Tudor was very much in the mould of respectable artisan radicalism".[5] He was regarded as the most moderate of the Victorian Labor MPs.

His organisational skills were clearly well-regarded by his colleagues and he was elected to one of only three positions at the first Labor Caucus meeting: the position of Whip, followed in 1904 by his appointment as Caucus Secretary. State representation factors might also have been at play here, given the leader (Watson) was a New South Welshman and the deputy (McGregor) was a South Australian.

At the 1908 Labor Federal Conference, Tudor successfully moved that Labor adopt the policy of citizen-initiated referenda and that a Commonwealth Bank be established. Many years later, Kim Beazley Senior would assert that "King O'Malley's pamphlet of 1923 falsified the conference record"[6] to claim credit for the idea of establishing a Commonwealth Bank, an idea that was actually Tudor's.

Tudor wasn't called upon to serve in the Watson ministry, but was on Fisher's list of preferred ministers that was put to the Caucus ballot for the Labor administration which took office in 1908. He was appointed Minister for Trade and Customs in the short-lived 1908–1909 government but didn't really get the chance to make a mark.

In the Caucus ballot for the 1910 ministry, he polled in the top three and was declared elected on the first ballot. Fisher appointed him to the same portfolio and he held it through the entire Fisher administration.

He held the same portfolio on Labor's return to office in 1914, and maintained it on the transition of the prime ministership from Watson to Hughes in 1915.

Tudor's time as Minister for Trade and Customs wasn't marked by any great reforms or stirring parliamentary speeches. In fact, his most descriptive defence of his policies while minister came after he had left the portfolio. When addressing parliament as leader of the Opposition in August 1917, he informed the House that the Member for Corangamite (the rather brilliantly named Chester Manifold) had told his constituents that "We can thank the conscription campaign for one thing – it got rid of Frank Tudor from the Customs Department." Then, as now, Corangamite was a seat heavily influenced by dairy farmers and there was policy tension between ensuring access to cheap milk for consumers and higher prices for producers. At this point, the main issue was about how much butter was allowed to be exported, with producers wanting a permissive export licence regime to keep prices high. Tudor was unapologetic, indeed proud, that he had restricted butter exports to ensure strong domestic supply and downward pressure on prices: "I regard as good testimonial to my administration the statement that these people were glad that I had left the Department. I am not sorry for what I did as Minister for Trade and Customs in connexion with the regulation of butter, meat and other commodities," he told the House. He was unashamedly on the side of consumers and lower prices. Makin added that "Frank Tudor was noted in public departments as being a very good administrator."[7]

It was 1916 that was the most tumultuous year of Tudor's political life and it was not his portfolio that was the cause of the tumult. Hughes was convinced that his government must introduce conscription to ensure an adequate supply of young men for the front. Tudor, as a member of his cabinet, was equally convinced this was an abomination of an idea.

Some have suggested that his opposition to conscription was driven solely by the virulent opposition of his branch members in Richmond. Conscription supporter Senator George Pearce claimed that Tudor had told him that, while conscription might be justified, "Richmond won't stand for it". While there can be little doubt that Tudor's supporters were strongly against conscription, this claim ignores his longstanding opposition to compulsory military service. He had voted against it being written into the Labor platform when former leader Chris Watson moved so at the Federal Conference in 1908. Tudor spoke against Watson's proposition and said, "There was too much gold lace, glorification and frills about military armaments now, and if shorn of these gorgeous trappings he did not think there would be much intense anxiety on the part of some people to be in the defence forces."[8] His opposition to conscription was genuine and he was prepared to pay a heavy political price to stand by his beliefs.

Hughes knew that he only had the support of Pearce and Postmaster-General William Webster in the cabinet, and so delayed taking the matter of conscription to the cabinet and Caucus for as long as possible. He also knew that even if he succeeded in getting the cabinet and the Caucus to support conscription, the government's numbers in the Senate were not strong enough to withstand Labor senators crossing the floor, which was likely given that many party State Executives were opposed to conscription and would protect the preselection of opponents of Hughes. Hence he decided to ask the government to support a plebiscite on conscription, giving the people the ultimate say. Even this proposal would tear his government apart.

"The atmosphere is electrical and a storm is appearing which is calculated to rend us in twain," wrote Treasurer William Higgs on the night before the Caucus meeting. The Caucus began meeting to discuss Hughes' demand that the Labor government adopt conscription as policy to be put to the people on Thursday 24 August 1916. It was to be the longest and arguably most tumultuous Labor Caucus meeting in history. Meetings of the Caucus and cabinet continued interchangeably over the Friday, Saturday, Sunday and Monday. At

2 a.m. on Monday 28 August, Hughes finally prevailed, securing a narrow Caucus majority of 23 to 21 for his plebiscite proposal.

On 14 September, Hughes introduced the Military Service Referendum Bill 1916. This was the day Tudor decided to resign from the cabinet as he could not support his government's position. This was an act of considerable bravery and principle on his behalf. While others would follow later, Tudor was not joined by any other colleagues in resigning on this point of principle at this point. He was the first, and for a good while the only anti-conscriptionist to resign his commission.

Higgs resigned as treasurer in October over Hughes' handling of the issue, and Albert Gardiner resigned as Vice-President of the Executive Council on the same day (Senator Edward Russell also resigned as an assistant minister but soon after joined Hughes in leaving the Labor Party, considerably diminishing his claim in history for having taken a point of principle). Frank Tudor was the first and one of only three Labor ministers who was prepared to give up the salary and trappings of office due to the fact he could not support conscription.

He was one of many Labor politicians campaigning for a No vote. With the support of the conservatives in parliament and a conservative press, the Yes vote was widely expected to prevail. It wasn't to be. It was a narrow vote with 48.39% supporting conscription and 51.6% opposing. But regardless of how narrow his defeat, Hughes' position as the head of a Labor administration was now untenable.

Following the plebiscite defeat, the Member for Brisbane, William Finlayson, moved a motion of no confidence in Hughes' position as Labor leader. The debate was predictably personal and brutal. While one of Hughes' fiercest critics, the Member for Cook James Catts, was in full flight, Hughes had enough. He simply rose from his chair, audibly said, "Enough of this" and walked out of the Caucus, and the Labor Party, for ever.

Close to a third of the Labor members followed him out. Those who were left carried the no-confidence motion unanimously.

The Caucus proceeded to elect a temporary leader, and went with the Speaker of the House, the Member for Kennedy Charles McDonald. Although Speaker, McDonald was not a bipartisan figure. His nickname was "Fighting Mac" because of his belligerent and aggressive campaigning style (being the Labor member for the outback Far North Queensland seat of Kennedy required a fighter).

The records are unfortunately unclear how things proceeded when it was time to elect a permanent leader of the Opposition. The Caucus minutes for the meeting of November are unhelpful, noting only that Tudor was elected. This implies he was unopposed for the position, but this was not the case.

While the *Sydney Morning Herald* and Melbourne *Australasian* newspapers noted that McDonald did not contest the leadership, a very different (and detailed) account appeared in the Melbourne *Age*. According to the paper, Tudor and McDonald were both candidates, with the Member for Capricornia, former treasurer William Higgs, and Member for Brisbane William Finlayson, also running. *The Age* reported that:

> most of the candidates dropped out on the first count… in the end the selection resolved itself into a close contest between the Speaker of the House of Representatives (Mr McDonald) and Mr Tudor (late Minister for Trade and Customs). The latter was finally chosen by the narrowest of margins.

The Catholic Press had an even more detailed and slightly different account, suggesting that McDonald and Tudor had actually tied for votes, with McDonald eventually agreeing to give way for Tudor who was formally then elected unopposed.

Given the detailed nature of these alternative accounts, there is little reason to disbelieve that there was a ballot and Tudor only narrowly prevailed against the three Queenslanders, with McDonald foremost among them.

The choice between McDonald and Tudor was stark. McDonald was a scrapper and fierce partisan. Tudor's reputation was for good administration and professional courtesy. He was not a noted orator and nor had he previously been touted for leader. However, he had the moral authority of having been willing to sacrifice his place in the Hughes ministry on the principle of opposing conscription. The Melbourne *Argus* was right to conclude that:

> The election of Mr Tudor to the leadership... seems to suggest that a policy of sustained obstruction is not contemplated. Had Mr McDonald, the present speaker, been selected, it is safe to assume that, from the moment that Parliament met, every form of the House would have been employed to harass the Ministry, and to emphasise the views of the Party. Neither by temperament nor by his mental qualities is Mr Tudor fitted for such a role. He will probably be content to act the part played by Mr Fisher when leader, and allow the rank and file to do all the obstruction, whilst he maintains courtesies between himself and the leaders of the other parties.

Despite the rancorous nature of the times and toxic robustness of the public debate (the 1917 and 1919 elections would be among the most rhetorically bitter in Australian history, see below), Tudor did maintain civil private relations with the man who had been his prime minister since 1915 and was now the prime minister whom he needed to usurp as part of his job description. Hughes reflected on this in parliament some time later when responding to a motion of no confidence in his government that had been moved by Tudor: "The honourable gentleman is a man whose disposition is by nature so kindly that it is with difficulty that he makes any remarks that are offensive, or even irritating, to his opponents."[9]

Regardless of whether the Caucus had made the right choice or not, the task of keeping the Labor Party alive and returning it to being a viable force after the Labor government had been defenestrated by Hughes' defection now fell to Frank Tudor. He was under no illusions as to the size of the task ahead of him, writing: "We are in for a very bad time, industrially as well as politically, and it is quite possible the movement will be set back at least ten years."

1917 Election

Billy Hughes was nothing if not an effectively cunning political operator. He did not walk out of the Caucus room on a whim. There can be little doubt that Hughes had predicted that he would lose the leadership of the party had he stayed and had a well-planned strategy to maintain power when he walked out. There can also be little doubt that he had communicated with the conservatives in parliament and knew a new government, with him at the head, was feasible.

His first move was to form a new party, the National Labor Party, with each of the 24 former Labor MPs who joined him in the Caucus walkout joining it. The new party did not have a majority on the floor of the House. Hughes and Joseph Cook, who led the Commonwealth Liberal Party, quickly settled an agreement that Cook's party would support Hughes' government on matters of confidence.

In practical terms, there was little to distinguish the National Labor Party and the Commonwealth Liberal Party, so their separate existence did not last long, with Hughes and Cook agreeing to merge the parties in February 1917, with Hughes continuing as party leader and Prime Minister.

Hughes moved fairly quickly to seek a mandate for the new government, calling an election for 5 May 1917.

In keeping with the practice of the time, Tudor launched Labor's campaign with a major speech in his electorate. His essential point was that the Labor government had split over the issue of conscription, and, given that Hughes had promised not to revisit the issue, there was little reason not to return to a Labor government: "The Hughes Government has been formed for no other purpose than that of winning the war," he said, "yet it has failed to show how it will do more than the Labor Party has done for the past two years, unless it has another referendum on conscription."

It was a reasonable, indeed powerful case that Tudor was attempting to make: either there was no difference of approach between the two parties to winning the war, in which case people could safely vote for the Labor Party, or Hughes was intending to renege on his promise of not revisiting the issue of conscription.

This reasonable argument had little chance of cutting through, with essentially every major newspaper in the country backing the re-election of the Hughes government. Hughes sprayed a cacophony of abuse and vitriol at his former Labor colleagues, accusing them of being unpatriotic, disloyal to Britain and in league with the International Union of Workers.

Tudor made another reasonable point in refuting these attacks in his Richmond speech, pointing out that:

> During the referendum campaign, the Labor Party was called pro-German, shirkers, disloyalists and members of the IWW and accused of having received German gold. Yet three months

afterwards the same Labor Party was invited to come and join the National Government. Either the men who made the charges did not believe them, or else they had no right to ask us to join the Government of this country.

Tudor wouldn't be the last leader of the Opposition to make reasonable and compelling points but get absolutely nowhere because all the political momentum was with the government of the day.

He used the substance of his Richmond speech as the basis for his stump speech throughout the country. He embarked on a train tour of the country, speaking to mass meetings in key electorates focused on the eastern seaboard. If crowd attendance and enthusiasm of the party's supporters were anything to go by, he was entitled to feel enthusiastic about his chances. Strong crowds (often larger than those Hughes was attracting to his mass meetings) and the enthusiasm of the audience was a theme to the press coverage of his campaign.

Three days after his Richmond speech, he arrived in Bendigo where the sitting Labor member Alfred Hampson was resisting a challenge from no less a candidate than the prime minister, who was not only changing electorates but changing states, seeking to transition from being the Labor Member for West Sydney to being the Nationalist Member for Bendigo. "The speakers were given a flattering reception when they appeared on the platform, the immense audience bursting into loud and prolonged cheering," *The Bendigo Independent* reported.

It was a long train journey from Bendigo to Toowoomba in the Queensland electorate of Darling Downs but the reception was similar in his next speech: Mr Tudor was given a "splendid reception", according the *Toowoomba Chronicle*. Brisbane was next on the itinerary, where although the hall was not packed, "The meeting was not lacking in fervour or enthusiasm," Brisbane publication *The Week* recorded. Then it was back on the long train journey to Melbourne so that he could address another mass meeting at Melbourne Town Hall on May 1, with *The Age* reporting that "the building was crowded to the utmost limits by an uproariously enthusiastic audience". After Melbourne, it was off to Benalla in an attempt to help sitting Labor member Parker Maloney hold onto the seat of Indi, where he was received to "loud applause" according to the *Benalla Standard*.

But as more than one future Labor leader would bitterly experience, the enthusiasm of the party base at rallies is a very poor guide to the mood of the electorate. The Labor Party was a weakened shell of its former self and in no fit state to win an election. Despite Hughes having been repudiated in the conscription plebiscite, the people still had confidence in his abilities to win the war and accepted his solemn promise not to revisit the conscription issue. The torrent of abuse that Hughes hurled at his former comrades, questioning their loyalty and patriotism, also had an effect.

The result was not a pretty one for Labor. A 7% swing against the party saw 20 of its MPs lose their seats, an effective halving of the size of the Caucus. Hughes had the biggest working majority of any prime minister since Federation. Despite the enthusiastic response to Tudor's campaigning in Bendigo, a 12.5% swing saw Hughes easily snatch his new electorate. In Yarra, Tudor had been so dominant in 1914 that he had been elected unopposed. Three years later he polled a still solid 71% of the vote, which was a reduction of 4% on his last contested ballot in 1913. This was the first big reverse in the seemingly inexorable rise of the size and power of the Labor Party in the Federal Parliament. Every other federal election except 1913 had resulted in an increase in seats for Labor, and 1913 had been a very minor setback in comparison. In the circumstances, it is doubtful that any potential Labor leader could have performed much better electorally than Tudor, despite the fact that the Australian people did not see him as a particularly credible candidate for prime minister against Hughes. All the momentum was with Hughes, and, by promising not to revisit the issue of conscription, he had neutralised the most potent political weapon that Tudor had at his disposal. Tudor had managed to keep the Labor Party as a viable, though much diminished, political force. This was the first time, but far from the last, that some commentators would question whether the party would survive. As leader, a considerable degree of the credit for its survival must go to Tudor. It wouldn't be long before the party had to gird itself for battle again.

The Second Plebiscite

It didn't take long for Hughes to renege on the most important commitment he had given the Australian people in the election campaign: not to revisit the issue of conscription.

Having been safely re-elected in May 1917, he announced on 7 November of the same year that in fact a second referendum would be held. Hughes' majority in both houses was now big enough that he could have introduced conscription by parliamentary means. But this level of repudiation of his commitment was too much even for Hughes.

The second referendum, like the first, was widely expected to be carried. Hughes clearly had the confidence of the people as expressed at the election and the press was just as willing to support him this time as the first. He could claim that he had tried volunteerism, and it was now more certain than ever that conscription was necessary.

It wasn't to turn out that way, however: the referendum was lost, despite the most outrageous manipulation of the voting system in Australian history. The ramifications would be substantial, not least of which for Tudor; for within the 1917 plebiscite campaign lay the seeds of what was in effect the first leadership challenge in the history of the Australian Labor Party.

Hughes decided on a slightly less ambitious request of the Australian people, proposing that conscription be introduced only for men between 18 and 44 and by ballot in months when voluntary recruitment fell below 7000 men a month. This was a minor concession, given that in 1917 the average rate of voluntary enrolments was under 4000 a month. The question put to the people was a leading one, in a very loaded fashion: "Are you in favour of the proposal of the Commonwealth Government for reinforcing the Australian Imperial Force overseas?"

A loaded question wasn't the end of Hughes' attempt to ensure a Yes vote. The electoral roll was closed to new voters just two days after the plebiscite was announced. And in an outrageous attempt to manipulate the electorate, all voters who were born in an enemy country or whose father was born in an enemy country were removed from the electoral rolls. It was a special combination of racism and sexism which led to the conclusion that if your father was born in a belligerent country then you were unfit to vote, but if your mother was German (for example) that was fine.

Later, in parliament, Tudor would point to the offensive absurdity of such electoral manipulation, citing the example of a man who had been denied the vote despite having volunteered for service himself, because his father had been born in Germany but emigrated as a small child, and even more outrageously a woman in Adelaide who was denied the vote due to her ancestry despite having five sons at the front, three of who had been killed.[10]

In the first plebiscite, Tudor had been just one of the many Labor politicians and ministers opposing conscription. Now, as Labor leader, he was to take the lead, although he was soon to find he had a rival as de-facto leader of the No campaign.

Just as during the recent election campaign, Tudor opened the No campaign with a speech in his electorate with an estimated four to five thousand people in attendance. He concentrated his argument on the numerical case: that enough volunteers were being provided and there was no need for conscription. By all reports, the audience response was enthusiastic but as historian Denis Murphy argued, "Statistics and figures in a hot and crowded hall can make dull listening and can confuse as easily convince."[11]

While Tudor was firmly and warmly welcomed by the anti-conscription crowd at the rally, the second speaker would hit a more emotional and emotive tone. It would have been the first time most of the Victorians in the crowd had laid eyes on the Queensland Premier Thomas Ryan, but there can be little doubt that many were impressed with his charisma and rhetorical power.

Known to all as TJ Ryan, he had actually been born at Port Fairy, 280 kilometres south-west of Tudor's birthplace of Williamstown in 1876, making him 10 years younger than his federal leader. Despite both being born in regional Victoria to working-class Celtic immigrants (Welsh and Irish), Ryan and Tudor could scarcely have had more different career paths to the most senior echelons of the Labor Party. They were also very different men: Tudor was slim with a reputation for good administration and Labor values rather than charisma; Ryan a fuller figure who was charismatic and his found his way to Labor only after a dalliance with the Liberals. Tudor had the more traditional path of the time: leaving school (by today's standards) early, entering a trade and being politicised by the trade union movement. The Catholic Ryan had a much more unconventional path for the era, mainly due to one person: his teacher at Pretty Hill State School, Mr Carmody, who recognised something special in young Tom and encouraged him to apply for a scholarship to the exclusive Saint Frances Xavier College at Kew.

This was a golden ticket for the son of an illiterate Irish farm worker in the middle of a Depression, and young TJ made the most of it. Even with the scholarship, the cost of attending Frances Xavier eventually became too much for the Ryan family and he was transferred to the cheaper South Melbourne College, a private school that still provided a far more thorough education than was normally available to a son of the working class. His access to this schooling enabled him to matriculate to the University of Melbourne to study Arts and Law, becoming the first in his family to go to university generations before it became more common in the latter part of the twentieth century.

He graduated from Arts before his finished his Law degree and worked as a Classics teacher at various schools in Melbourne and Tasmania. The course of his life was changed when he accepted a position as Classics master at Maryborough Boys Grammar in Queensland. While teaching was his occupation, law was his passion. While teaching, he studied for the Queensland Bar and was admitted in 1901. He based himself in Rockhampton and developed a substantial practice as a barrister.

While Tudor was already a Labor federal MP by 1901, Ryan's political involvement hadn't begun. He became involved in the Rockhampton Political Association, a non-Labor group, and contested the 1903 election for Capricornia as independent, on a Deakinite Liberal policy agenda (although the Labor candidate accused him of "coming forward on practically the Labor platform").[12] Regardless of whether his policy agenda was more Deakinite or Labor, it didn't take long after his defeat in the 1903 election for Ryan to complete his transition, becoming a member of the Labor Party in 1904. This perhaps wasn't as big a transition as it seems in retrospect, given the Queensland Government at the time was a coalition of Labor and Deakinite Liberals.

He entered the State Parliament as a Labor MP in 1909 as Member for Barcoo (covering remote south-west Queensland) and had a quite meteoric rise, being elected Labor leader in 1912 and leading the party to victory in 1915, forming the first Queensland Labor government with an outright majority on the floor of the Legislative Assembly.

His government's reforming ethos (price controls, improved rights for workers and an aggressive establishment of state-owned enterprises) was popular, but perhaps his biggest service to the party was devoting his leadership skills to ensuring that the Queensland branch didn't split over the issue of conscription. As JJ Cahill showed as Premier of New South Wales in another great Labor split four decades later, while a split might appear inevitable, a charismatic and sensible approach to leadership meant that the worst elements of a split could be avoided, as it was in Queensland in 1916 and 1917 and in New South Wales in the 1950s. In April 1916, Labor had controlled six out of the seven Australian jurisdictions, but by July 1917 Ryan was the only surviving Labor head of government.[13]

Tudor, Ryan and the No Campaign

While Ryan had played a minor role in the 1916 plebiscite campaign, as the only surviving Labor premier, and as charismatic foil to the more workmanlike federal leader, he would play a much larger role in the 1917 campaign, which would soon parlay into leadership tensions.

Ryan began his address to the No campaign launch by pointing out "no free people in the world have ever voted away their freedom" and he doubted that Australians would on this occasion. He warned that it wouldn't be long before married men also received the call-up, that Hughes was untrustworthy and that it was unfair to conscript manpower but not wealth.

While Ryan didn't concentrate on mathematic arguments at first, he did eventually warm to the theme that Tudor had set out. He used his skills as a barrister to build the case methodically and effectively. It would be Ryan's arguments about numbers that would lead to what Murphy would call "the most amazing sequence of events of the whole campaign".[14]

Ryan told Brisbane journalists that there were 209,000 men available for the five Australian divisions which only needed 100,000, meaning there were already 109,000 men available for reinforcements. Therefore, he argued, the case for conscription had collapsed. Hughes was clearly worried about this line of attack. Instead of refuting it (because all the evidence pointed to it being true), he promulgated a regulation under the War Precautions Act that any person who made a false statement designed to influence a vote in the plebiscite would be required to appear in a court within 48 hours and, if found to have committed a breach, no newspaper could publish the claim. Government censors were very actively policing comments and Hughes was increasingly desperate to silence the argument about numbers. Whereas Tudor's speeches were scantily covered in non-prominent positions in the newspapers, censorial pressure ensured that Ryan's speech at the Queensland No campaign launch was doctored so much that it implied Ryan was actually in support of conscription.[15] This censoring was the direct cause of an extraordinary stand-off between the federal and Queensland governments, a testing of parliamentary privilege to its outer limits and a significant increase in Ryan's profile across the country.

Attempting to censor the Queensland Premier was a massive own-goal for the Hughes government. Ably advised by his astute Deputy Premier Ted Theodore, Ryan knew he had parliamentary privilege and the resources of government at his disposal. He proceeded to the Legislative Assembly chamber and, as Murphy described it, "On 22 November, a packed gallery heard Ryan deliver a speech which was to change the tone of the whole referendum campaign."[16]

In fact, what Ryan did was to read into the Hansard the arguments about recruitment and the available volunteer force that had been censored out of the reporting of his previous comments. Thousands of extra copies of the Hansard were ordered, with the elements of Ryan's speech which had been previously censored this time printed in bold. No respecter of the rights of parliament any more than he was of free speech, Prime Minister Hughes was not to be deterred. In fact, he would rather spectacularly and personally intervene.

On 26 November, the Prime Minister personally led a small group of soldiers in a raid of the Government Printing Office in Brisbane. Hughes seized 3300 copies of the Hansard and instructed (on what alleged authority it is unclear) the state government printer not to print any further copies of the Hansard. It is difficult to imagine a more erratic act or action outside the law by any Australian prime minister before or after Hughes' midnight raid.

Hughes succeeded in doing two things: he played into the hands of the anti-conscription campaign, which was able to make Hughes' determination to silence dissent the issue, and he also managed to elevate Ryan to the effective leadership of the No campaign instead of Tudor. Murphy was accurate in saying, "Thanks to Hughes, Ryan had become the outstanding figure among the anti-conscriptionists and de facto Leader."[17] At the time, the conservative Attorney-General of

New South Wales David Hall complained that Hughes' heavy-handed treatment had massively boosted Ryan's profile and set him up for a tilt at federal politics.

Ryan astutely ordered the printing of a special government gazette which had explained what had happened, minus the figures on recruitment which meant Hughes had no grounds for censoring it. He convened a cabinet meeting which adopted a policy of "direct confrontation" with the Commonwealth, with the posting of armed police at the Printing Office to resist any raids by the army (or indeed the prime minister). It's not too much to say while World War One was raging on the other side of the world, the Commonwealth and Queensland governments went to war.

Much like in 1916, the Yes vote had expected to win. But this series of missteps by Hughes and the combined efforts of Tudor, Ryan and the labour movement meant the result was very different to what had been confidently predicted: 53.8% of Australians voted No, a swing of just over 2% to the No campaign.

Hughes had been defeated twice at plebiscites but retained a big majority in the House of Representatives and the reputation as Australia's most cunning politician. He would continue to dominate Australian politics. Hughes and the Governor-General, his friend Sir Ronald Munroe-Ferguson, conducted what can be fairly called a harmless enough constitutional charade when Hughes submitted his resignation as prime minister as a result of the electoral repudiation of the plebiscite loss. Absent of any alternative, Munroe-Ferguson then invited him to immediately return as prime minister. The question of who was best placed to lead Labor against Hughes would dominate politics for several years.

Tudor, Ryan and the 1919 Election

The Allies would of course go on to win World War One without the help of any Australian conscripts a little more than 12 months after the second plebiscite. Tudor seconded the motion of the Acting Prime Minister William Watt that the House welcome the Armistice two days after it was signed, on 13 November 1918. Tudor was not alone in assuming it was the war to end all wars, assuring the House that the conditions of the armistice against Germany were so stern that "it is practically impossible for war to break out again. Those conditions are more than stern; they are extraordinarily severe." Approaching eloquence, he said:

> Civilisation rejoices after four years of terror and horror; and agony and suffering on the part of all classes of people. Those who have had to carry the sad news of loved ones lost in the field have gone into practically every class of home in the community. In every class of home there have been tears and anguish.

And while the power of hindsight leads us to the conclusion that Tudor may have been naive, he was hardly alone or lacking in moral compass as he proclaimed:

> I hope that the one great lesson we shall have learned from this terrible war will be that all nations, small as well as great, will be able to work out their own destinies and that a League of Nations or a permanent Peace Conference may be evolved to render it impossible for a few individuals to again cause such wholesale destruction of human life as has taken place during the past four years.

As Australia recovered from the Armageddon of the war and the Labor Party contemplated the massive task of regaining government from its weakened position, it did not do so from a position of unity.

Radicals in the party thought they had the solution: a massive merger of all trade unions into "One Big Union", the OBU. Inspired by the International Workers of the World (a bogeyman that Hughes liked to invoke as secretly controlling Labor), the OBU movement began in the United States but had not inconsiderable support in Australia. However, the parliamentary leadership and existing unions, most importantly the Australian Workers Union, knew what a dangerous concept it would be and what a propaganda boost to the conservatives it would provide. While the OBU had considerable support in Queensland, it was in New South Wales that the battle was most hard-fought and would give Tudor the biggest headaches. To this day the NSW State Conference has a reputation for robustness, but the 1919 Conference, staging a dispute between the parliamentary party and the AWU on the one hand and supporters of the OBU on the other, was intense even by NSW Conference standards. The AWU/parliamentary group narrowly held the day. This led supporters of the OBU to walk out on the conference. Tudor despaired. He wrote to his predecessor as Labor leader, Andrew Fisher, that Labor had "only twenty-three members in our house and eleven in the Senate, and in some respects we are not solid as a party. At the last State Conference in Sydney, nearly half the delegates left the conference (and the irony was they sang Solidarity Forever as they broke away)." At least he could find some gallows humour as he went about the task of saving the Labor Party.

In the same letter to Fisher, Tudor despaired that, as well as the militant breakaway within the party, he was also dealing with the creation of a new farmers party (which would emerge into the Australian Country Party) making Labor's task in rural seats harder. Tudor predicted he had little chance of leading the party to victory.

Tudor wasn't the only one to be pessimistic about the party's chances. But some of his colleagues thought they had a plan that would increase the party's chances of success: the drafting of Queensland Premier TJ Ryan into the Federal Parliament and the leadership of the party.

This plan would become evident at the October 1919 federal special conference of the party. The conference was called to discuss taxation policy but in in the lead-up to the conference the Queensland Executive suggested to other states that their state leader should transfer to the Federal Parliament at the next election and be appointed campaign director. While the leadership of the party wasn't mentioned in the resolution, few could miss the ramifications of such a move. The push to draft Ryan into the House of Representatives had some support. The Tasmanian Executive voted to support the idea and it clearly had some parliamentary support because the Caucus Secretary and Member for Cook Jimmy Catts was instrumental in getting the NSW branch to also support the move, as well as invite Ryan to move to New South Wales and take a Sydney seat. The charismatic King O'Malley was also campaigning for Ryan to replace Tudor, despite (or perhaps because of) his defeat in the 1917 election. He was active in getting the Tasmanian Executive to endorse the proposal. It is not clear whether the federal leader was consulted about the move, but the Victorian branch did not reply to Queensland entreaties, suggesting that Tudor and his supporters were less than impressed.

In fact, when it was moved at the conference that Ryan be prevailed upon to transfer to the federal scene, the Victorians pointed out that such a resolution could not be considered, as the conference had been called to consider taxation alone. The leader of the Victorian delegation, EJ Holloway, the Secretary of the Victorian Trades Hall, conceded that he admired TJ Ryan, but he and his fellow Victorians couldn't countenance the disrespect being shown to their leader by shoehorning such a prominent figure into the parliament without Tudor's imprimatur. Even Murphy, Ryan's very sympathetic biographer, could see the problem in the way some were trying to push Tudor out of the leadership: "Tudor may not have been the greatest leader, but he had sacrificed his place in the cabinet over conscription; he was personally well-liked throughout the Labor movement and had served the party faithfully and well since 1901."[18]

The other strong opponent to Ryan's transfer was his fellow Queenslander, the Member for Capricornia William Higgs. This former treasurer saw himself not unreasonably as the most viable alternative to Tudor within the Caucus, and did not welcome Ryan upsetting the Caucus equilibrium.[19]

What did Tudor and Ryan think about all this?

Tudor had not been ambitious for the leadership, but, having received it, there is no evidence that he was prepared to contemplate giving it up, or at least certainly not for someone who wasn't even in the Federal Parliament, regardless of his abilities. Tudor was a regular correspondent with his predecessor Andrew Fisher who was ensconced in Australia House as High Commissioner to London. Tudor wrote of wanting to discuss with Fisher the travails of the party, which some have interpreted as a willingness on Tudor's behalf to stand aside for Fisher if he could be convinced to return to politics. This isn't clear, but even if he was prepared to resign to make way for a beloved former leader, it does not mean that he was willing to stand aside for anyone else.

Ryan was, according to his biographer, a somewhat reluctant recruit. At the same time as he was being approached to transfer to Melbourne as Labor leader, there was also an attractive option of resigning as Premier to take over as Chief Justice of the Supreme

Court of Queensland.[20] Ryan was alive to the logistical and political difficulties and risks that go with the very complicated manoeuvre of changing parliaments and taking over the party leadership. There is a reason that only two of Australia's 30 prime ministers have been former premiers: it is a hard transition to make, as such talented premiers as Neville Wran have found when contemplating such a change.

Ryan of course was perfectly entitled to make himself available for the federal leadership. Indeed he and his supporters had an obligation to do so if they genuinely felt that he had a better chance of leading the party to victory than Tudor. Norman Makin, who was sympathetic to Tudor, also concluded that "it must be emphasised that Premier Ryan did everything correctly".[21]

The Party Conference was held against the background of speculation that Hughes would call an early federal election for 1919, in part to capitalise on Labor's disarray. Preselections were underway. Tudor defeated two challengers for Labor endorsement for Yarra (the only time a sitting Labor leader has been challenged for preselection). Ryan's window for decision was closing.

The manoeuvring in the lead-up to the October 1919 conference was played out in public. The positions of Queensland, New South Wales and Tasmania were known. Victoria had made its disdain for the proposal clear by declining to even reply. South Australia and Western Australia had replied to the Queenslanders, but those replies were not recorded.

Catts, as Secretary of the Caucus, strained the authority of the office by declaring publicly that there existed "no member of the Federal Labor Party who would not wholeheartedly welcome Mr Ryan into Federal politics".[22]

Ryan responded publicly with a carefully worded statement:

> The request that I should enter Federal politics is not of my seeking. Since the matter was first mentioned I have had my attitude abundantly clear. The only reason which would induce me to resign the premiership of Queensland and enter the Federal fight would be the fact that an unequivocal desire was expressed by the workers of Australia that I should do so. The expression of that desire on the part of the workers should reach me in a form that would leave no doubt that my services were wanted.[23]

In other words: I'll do it, but I've got to be drafted. Actually, the support to draft Ryan was strong.

The special conference met in Sydney on 2 October. There were 33 delegates present. Tudor as leader (and a leader under challenge) was strangely passive. He wasn't a delegate and wasn't present.

True to form, Catts was quick to strike. He asked the chair of the conference, the NSW President William Lambert, if any business other than the agenda the conference had been called to consider (the party's policy on land tax) could be debated. Lambert ruled that it could not.

Catts was not to be deterred by a trifle like a ruling from the chair, however. He raised the question again and asked that the question of whether further business could be considered be put to a vote of the conference. There was a clear portent of the will of the conference in the resulting vote: by 16 votes to 13 it was ruled that new business could be introduced.

A New South Wales delegate, John Bailey, who was also the state Member for Monaro, moved a suspension of standing orders to allow him to introduce a resolution to endorse the wish of the New South Wales, Queensland and Tasmanian Executives that Ryan be invited to enter Federal Parliament.

Ryan absented himself from the room at this point. It was clear from the debate that the delegates were under no illusion that this was no mere resolution about a potential new backbencher. There was little regard for Tudor's feelings or the optics of a Federal Conference commenting that there were leadership options superior to the incumbent, although Victorian Senator John Barnes opposed the resolution, noting that it "might throw a reflection on the present leader". Indeed.

The South Australian MP Tom Butterfield cared little for any reflection on the present leader when he argued that "while Frank Tudor was one of the cleanest and whitest men in the Labor movement they must realise it and even Frank Tudor realised it – that one man stood head and shoulders above everyone else and that was Tom Ryan". Defenders of Tudor argued not so much that he was the superior option, but that the conference had no role in determining federal candidates and the process was out of line.

This constitutional argument clearly held little truck with the delegates, with the conference voting 19 votes to 10 to invite the Queensland Premier into the Federal Parliament. The voting was largely on state lines, with all of the delegates from New South Wales, Queensland (except for Ryan himself) and Tasmania voting in the affirmative. All Victorians voted against the motion and Western and South Australian delegations were split.

This was the first time, before or since, a Federal or National Conference has ever invited an individual to enter federal politics. That this was done against the wishes of the federal leader is all the more extraordinary.

The pro-Ryan faction wasn't content with their win, however. Having just won the vote that he be invited to join the federal Caucus, they also moved he be appointed the party's federal campaign director. This was carried by 20 votes to 12.

This level of overreach, in effect the organisational wing appointing a co-leader of the parliamentary party, was too much for the Victorian delegates, who threatened to walk out on the conference, risking another split so soon after the party had been so badly riven. Here Ryan showed the leadership that made him such an attractive option to so many, re-entering the conference room after having absented himself and declaring that he needed time to consider the requests made of him by the conference. He told the delegates that:

> it was imperative that there should be unanimity and harmony in anything that took place. In the interests of all he did not think they should come to a hurried decision in the matter. It would be unfortunate if he accepted the position and it should lead to any difference of opinion.[24]

This statement of indifference was almost certainly an artifice as opposed to a genuine reflection of his views. But it was an effective one that took the heat out of the issue, and was indicative of Ryan's skills as a manager of people and difficult issues.

It is unclear what Tudor thought of this course of events. His taciturn nature means there is no record of his response. Clearly the Victorian delegation would not have resisted the efforts at the Federal Conference without his imprimatur. But nor did he put his leadership on the line by publicly resisting the move or insisting that it be stopped if the party wished him to continue as its leader.

When Ryan publicly accepted the party's request to seek to transition to the Federal Parliament and serve as campaign director a day after the conference's completion, Tudor simply commented that "We will be glad of all the help we can get in the great fight."[25]

As it was, the sitting member for the safe seat of West Sydney, Con Wallace, agreed to stand aside for Ryan, who was quickly endorsed as the Labor candidate by the NSW Executive. However it had come about, both Tudor and Ryan had the maturity to handle well what in effect was a co-leadership, with Ryan twice travelling to Melbourne to confer with Tudor, and the party's policy document for the 1919 election being co-signed by both of them as well as the party's Federal President Holloway.

The 1919 election followed a similar pattern to the 1917 poll: frenetic travel and big crowds welcoming Tudor, followed by bitter disappointment on polling day.

Tudor again kicked off his campaign with the release of Labor policy with a well-attended speech at Richmond Town Hall. The policy was more economically radical in 1919 than in the war year of 1917, which may also have reflected the input of Ryan with his experience of a strong reform program in Queensland and touches of populism. Tudor decried the profiteering occurring during postwar shortages (which was a legitimate concern) and flagged that a Tudor Labor government would use the still extant war powers for price setting to give cost-of-living relief. Ryan's influence in Tudor's policy speech was probably at its clearest when Tudor pointed out that "As an instance of what can be done in the direction of making food available to the people at reasonable rates, the Queensland Labor government during the year from November 1915 to November 1916 reduced the cost of living by 12.6%." While the policy settings were more radical than 1917, Kim Beazley Senior pointed out that Tudor had done the party a service by resisting even more radical policies that were floating up, given most of the more conservative or cautious elements had followed Hughes out of the party. There were moves in the party to call for a more accommodative stance towards Germany rather than demand unconditional surrender from the enemy, and for a much more radical foreign policy. Tudor judged these policies would make the party unelectable and used his leadership to successfully resist them.

He promised a comprehensive public housing scheme and an increase in the old age and invalid pensions of 1 pound per week. A quarter of a century before the British Labour Party established the National Health Service and a little over 50 years before Whitlam established Medibank, Tudor announced that "We shall organise a National Medical Service, charged with the prevention, as well as the cure, of disease. As part of our policy, we shall provide for free medical and dental attendance for persons in necessitous circumstances." In keeping with the rural focus of many Labor seats (and with the fact that this was the first election that Farmers Associations would field candidates, in what would be formalised the next year as the Australian Country Party) there was a heavy emphasis on the rights of primary producers, especially of sugar and wool.

Tudor was honest in recognising that his program would be expensive and would have to be paid for, noting that "A considerable increase of revenue will be necessary during the forthcoming years" with a review of taxation leading to a tax increase on "the well to do", although an incoming Labor government would remove the hated "amusement tax" which controversially applied to theatres and cinemas.

Again, he proceeded on a train tour of the nation, reprising his policy speech to large and enthusiastic audiences in capital cities including, in this campaign, Adelaide. But unlike 1917, his health was not robust. He twice had to interrupt campaigning to recuperate from illness. The Melbourne *Age* reported on 8 November that "Mr Tudor who has had two attacks of haemorrhage within a fortnight, hopes to be able to leave for Sydney today in connection with the election campaign."

The campaign director Ryan also crisscrossed the country addressing large audiences. Interestingly, the government targeted Ryan, not Tudor, in their negative onslaught. Tudor was unexciting, but respected and regarded as safe. Hughes and the Nationalists decided that targeting Ryan was more fruitful, both to remove the positive of a popular premier as part of Labor's campaign team and as an effective bogeyman. "RYAN SPELLS RUIN" ran the Nationalist Party campaign posters and, in a not very subtle dig at Ryan's Catholicism in a time of rampant religious bigotry, "RYAN AND ROME". Hughes spent a lot of time in his speeches attacking Ryan's record as premier and alleging big increases in taxation under his influence.

While Ryan was campaigning loyally for Tudor, one piece of evidence exists that suggests he was planning to usurp the prime ministership from Tudor should Labor form a majority. While campaigning in Tasmania, Ryan caught up with his old friend and supporter King O'Malley. O'Malley wrote to a friend (and future Queensland Premier William Forgan-Smith) that Ryan expected to take the leadership and be commissioned as prime minister if Labor won. O'Malley warned him that he had served in parliament with Tudor for 17 years and he should not expect Tudor to lightly stand aside.

It was a hypothetical scenario that wouldn't be tested. Neither Tudor nor Ryan would be called upon to form a Labor administration after the election. While the Nationalist government suffered a 9% swing against it, the Labor vote fell by around 1.5%. It was the nascent Country Party that was the beneficiary. Labor won several new seats (Hindmarsh, Angas, Calare, Kalgoorlie, Hume and Gwydir), but lost Swan, Brisbane, Ballarat and Adelaide, meaning a net gain of just four seats off a low base. The Nationalists again swept the Senate with only one Labor senator being elected. The various farmers associations won 11 seats. At this stage the Country Party was somewhat of an unknown quantity. Some in Labor had hoped that Labor and the Country Party voting together on confidence might come close to bringing about the end of the Hughes government. While the Country Party would eventually force the removal of Hughes as prime minister as the price of a coalition agreement with the Nationalists, there was little prospect of the Country Party presence being Labor's ticket to office.

This was the first election with preferential voting, meaning that the Nationalists and the nascent Country Party could swap preferences and the informal vote increased significantly, costing the Labor Party seats. The government came through the election with 34 seats and the support of one conservative independent.

Labor Tragedy

Tudor was re-elected unopposed as leader of the party in the aftermath of the election. While a challenge from Ryan might have been expected, none was forthcoming. Despite the strong support for Ryan in the broader party, the numbers weren't there in the Caucus for a leadership change. As Ryan's sympathetic biographer Murphy noted: "There was some feeling in the caucus against the manner of entry into Federal Parliament and against his having overshadowed Tudor during the campaign."[26] In fact, Catts, the main and most vocal organiser of the Ryan operation, paid a price for disloyalty to Tudor when he lost the position of Secretary of the Caucus by one vote to the Member for Darling, Arthur Blakely.

Instead, Ryan was elected to the Caucus Executive under Tudor's leadership.

It wasn't long, however, before Tudor's ill health began to rear its head again and he missed parliamentary sittings in August 1920. Matthew Charlton, the Member for Hunter, took over as acting leader as the ranking member of the House of Representatives.

Tudor managed to return in late August and in September it was decided to appoint a formal Assistant Leader in the House. (In keeping with the practice at the time, Senator Gardiner was the deputy leader of the party as the most senior – in fact only – senator.) Tudor having seen off moves to replace him, the rivalry was now between Charlton and Ryan as to who was the next most senior member of the Caucus and heir apparent for the leadership. In a ballot for the position of House deputy, Ryan defeated Charlton by 14 votes to nine.

By May 1921, Tudor was again absent from parliament due to illness. The Caucus thoughtfully carried a resolution that "We sincerely regret the indisposition of our Leader Mr Tudor and are of the opinion that he should take a two or three months holiday if possible in the shape of a long trip."

In keeping with the practice of the time that Royal Commissions be run by serving members of parliament, Ryan was absent in Sydney serving on the Royal Commission into the mismanagement of Cockatoo and Garden Islands. The Caucus resolved that Charlton be acting leader of the party until Ryan could return. These three men, the titular deputy leader Senator Albert Gardiner and Charlton and Ryan, effectively shared the leadership while Tudor recuperated.

Tudor's absence must have forced Charlton and Ryan as well as their other Caucus colleagues to contemplate the post-Tudor leadership scenario. However, the party was to be denied its best option as a replacement. On 28 September 1921 the federal Caucus convened with Charlton in the chair, "in the absence through serious illness of

Mr Tudor", and a still shell-shocked Caucus than carried a resolution that "We place on record our deep regret on the loss of our Deputy Leader, the Hon TJ Ryan KC MP, realising he was one of the greatest exponents of the Australian Labor Party. His passing away is not only a severe loss to the Australian Labor movement but a distinct loss to Australia." Ryan had been suffering a long bout of influenza as the Spanish influenza pandemic gripped the world. In July, despite not having recovered from the flu, he journeyed by train from Melbourne to the seat of Maranoa in outback Queensland to campaign in the by-election brought about by the death of the Labor member Jim Page. Despite the entreaties of colleagues who could see he was seriously failing, Ryan insisted on continuing to campaign. On Saturday 30 July, as the voters of Maronoa rejected Labor and gave the Country Party its first Queensland seat, Ryan's condition, which had developed into pneumonia, was worsening. By Monday, he was dead, aged just 45. Labor had been robbed of the best hope for its future.

A week after the Caucus recorded its regret at the loss of Ryan, it resolved that:

> This Party places on record its appreciation of the services rendered by the Hon FG Tudor to the Australian Labor Movement and in expressing our gratitude to and confidence in him as our Leader. Further we desire that he should continue to occupy that position. We also express the hope that he will be sufficiently recovered in health to soon take up his political duties.

Tudor had sent message to his colleagues indicating that he was prepared to resign the leadership if his colleagues felt it to be desirable due to his ill health. The Caucus was old fashioned and loyal enough to believe that he should be allowed time to recover despite his ongoing health troubles and his defeat in two elections. The same meeting gave a clear indication of the likely succession plan, however, electing Charlton as the new deputy leader in the House to replace Ryan.

Regardless of the hopes of the Caucus that Tudor would return to the leadership, it wasn't to be. He had attended his last Caucus meeting. On 10 January 1922, Frank Tudor died of heart disease in his beloved Richmond. Hughes offered a state funeral to the first major party leader to die in office and acted as pallbearer at the funeral.

It was June before parliament would sit to consider a condolence motion on Tudor's death. Hughes, who had hurled abuse and questioned the patriotism of the party that Tudor led, was generous: "He was my friend and our friendship was close and unbroken for a period of twenty years. He was my fellow member of the Labor Party over sixteen years, and our friendship survived, and was unaffected by the political cataclysm which rent the party asunder."

Conclusion

Labor celebrates the heroes that delivered government and the chance to implement its agenda. But those who served in the most difficult of times also deserve to be recognised in history. Frank Tudor was a man of principle. He was right about conscription and right to stand up for his beliefs. He inherited the leadership of the party in the most difficult conditions imaginable. Kim Beazley Senior said of him that he "held the Labor movement together in the face of massive forces of disintegration, and he did it by his dignity and his absence of bitterness, hate or rancour… Tudor batted on the worst wicket of any Labor leader. Revaluations will enhance his standing in Australia's social history." I hope his inclusion in this book contributes to that revaluation of the life of Frank Tudor.

Chapter 4

JOHN DEDMAN

A Man Curtin and Chifley Could Rely On

John Johnstone Dedman only served in parliament for nine years. Many have served for much longer. But few could claim a more substantial record of achievement.

Almost all of his time in parliament was spent as a minister, and in the most consequential cabinets in Australian history: those of Curtin and Chifley. These cabinets had two overriding goals: to ensure Australia's contribution to World War Two was maximised and to build a better peace. Historian Stuart Macintyre has accurately described these twin endeavours as "Australia's boldest experiment"[1]. In each case Curtin and then Chifley looked to Dedman as the key minister to handle the task.

The names Curtin and Chifley dominate the history of the era but a close examination of the record of their governments leads to the conclusion that John Dedman can regarded as a hitherto overlooked key member of their team.

There were, of course, other important members of the cabinet. HV Evatt was a brilliant jurist, historian and very significant voice for Australia overseas, but his ministerial responsibility wasn't as central to the domestic priorities of the Curtin and Chifley governments as Dedman. Arthur Calwell was important in the field of immigration.

Eddie Ward was a volatile and radical force. Jack Beasley was important in reintegrating the former Langite forces into the Labor government. Norman Makin was an important player. But only Dedman ranged across the government and played a key role in the two vital tasks that fell to Labor: winning the war and building the peace.

The key public servants of the era, led by the talented Herbert Cole ('Nugget') Coombs have also rightly received much praise and attention for their role, particularly in imagining a more prosperous and economically stable peace. Again, Dedman worked closely with them and provided the political heft and management necessary to take their ideas through the processes of cabinet and parliament.

He was a loyal and steady lieutenant to the two giants of the government, but not an unquestioning one. He would stand up for his beliefs even if it meant disagreeing with Curtin or Chifley. He was the public face of difficult and tough war austerity measures that led to him being personally unpopular for much of the war. However, his colleagues knew his worth: Chifley had intended to make him treasurer if Labor won the 1949 election and he was a potential strong rival to Evatt for the Labor leadership in the post-Chifley era. There is credible evidence that Chifley preferred him over Evatt as his successor as Labor leader. But losing his seat in the 1949 election put paid to what might have been.

Dedman did not have a traditional Labor background. He was on the outer with the organisational wing of his home branch of Victoria for much of his career and had difficult relations with several trade unions. But he had the confidence of those who knew him best and needed him most: his colleagues.

His work has stood the test of time. He was a vital part of the war effort, but it was in mapping out the postwar era that he really made his mark. He saw science and education as the two keys to a better society. The CSIRO he engineered into existence has the same structure today, 70 years later. He revolutionised federal Labor's approach to education, promoting federal involvement in education for the first time, encouraging Labor away from its traditional distrust and misunderstanding of university education and shepherding the important Australian National University into existence.

While controversial and at times unpopular, he won the praise of many who understood his worth. Journalist and commentator Don Whitington regarded him as the only one of the cabinet members loyal to Chifley and Curtin with "outstanding ability"[2]. Kim Beazley Senior recorded that he was one of a handful of truly talented ministers in the Chifley government.[3] Andrew Spaull concluded that in the post-Curtin era he graduated to become one of the "Big Three" of the government (along with Chifley and Evatt).[4] Chifley's friend and biographer Fin Crisp wrote that "Chifley liked Dedman and trusted him implicitly for his tenacity and high sense of duty"[5] and Labor historian Ross McMullin noted his "commitment and considered, intelligent contributions".[6]

He was somewhat of an enigma. A champion of austerity, but a strong supporter of federal expansion into education and the importance of liberal studies; an advocate of cutbacks in war but a lonely voice in support of federal assistance to the arts in peace; and originally a member of the Country Party who came to support bank nationalisation and other radical interventions.

Dour, with a Scottish burr, he wasn't likely to strut the world stage or promote his own achievements unduly. But he imagined an Australia renewed after victory in the war and he was prepared to undertake big, difficult and unpopular tasks to bring it about.

While a competent and respected administrator, he was no middle-of-the road, risk averse politician. His views were in a way as radical as the left-wing firebrand Eddie Ward, but he had a much more steady and determined modus operandi to make his dreams a reality.

He lost his marginal seat in Labor's landslide 1949 defeat and wasn't helped in that election by having been the man who had undertaken many difficult tasks. He encountered some tough times after parliament but his resilience saw him eventually make further contributions to the cause of social justice. John Dedman was a good Labor man of great achievement.

Early Years

Dedman was born in 1896 in the Scottish township of Knowe, very close to the residence of the founder of the British Labour Party, Keir Hardie.

His father was the schoolmaster in the elementary school at which young John was enrolled. Although being a schoolmaster was a profession of reasonable status, it wasn't well-paid and the family was quite poor. His parents, James and Mary (nee Johnstone) were strict Presbyterians and John maintained a serious Christianity throughout his life, noting in his later years that "my parents were deeply religious and whatever character I may have developed, it owed to them".[7]

As well as being the local schoolmaster, James was an active supporter of the British Liberal Party and was elected to the local council (the Liberal Party in this era was home to many adherents of radical reform, especially in its Celtic wings). On the council he became a champion of the local hospital movement and poor-law reform (movements to extend the coverage of hospital care to more people in Scotland and reform the haphazard system of poverty relief).

John was bright enough (he was dux of Ewart Boys High School) to overcome his parents lack of wealth and he gained entry to the University of Edinburgh to study science. The advent of World War One, however, saw him cut his studies short to enlist in the Officer Training Corps. This was the first of several aborted attempts to gain a tertiary education. He would not succeed in finally attaining a university degree until 50 years after this initial attempt in Scotland.

Following his officer training, he was posted to Gallipoli where he had his first exposure to Australians. He was not there for the fateful dawn landing, but did make it in time for the masterful evacuation.

His intelligence and scientific bent led him to experiment with weaponry: coming up with improvements to the design of guns and suggestions for better new weapons. His suggestions must have been worthy because he was transferred to the Divisional Headquarters in Egypt to concentrate on his design projects. It was in Egypt that he met the then Prince of Wales (the future King Edward VIII) who was also serving at Divisional HQ.

As Dedman later recorded, "My experiments eventually ended with my meeting with an accident"[8] and he was sent back to England to recuperate before being sent with so many others to the killing fields of the Somme where he was injured again.

As the war moved to a close, he applied for and received a transfer to the British Army in India, in which he served as a captain in the British war with Afghanistan.

The terrible Armristar massacre disillusioned him about a military life. He wasn't involved in this massacre of hundreds of Indian civilians by the British Army, but he was repulsed by it, noting that "it was this incident that made me decide to give up soldiering as a profession".[9]

He faced a fork in the road. On return to Scotland, he found that a young woman with whom he had a love interest had moved on from him and the chance of a life together had evaporated. It was then that he received a letter from an old school friend, Walter McEwen who had emigrated to Australia with the hopes of starting a dairy farm. He invited Dedman to join him. Having found that his brothers and sisters had left Scotland for various places, and with his heart broken, he found a dramatic move like going to Australia attractive.

Hence he booked his passage to the Southern Hemisphere. He arrived in Fremantle on 26 January 1922 and received a quick introduction to the Australian lack of regard for class. Used to Indian porters providing full service, he asked an Australian porter for assistance carrying his baggage down the gangway. "Carry your own bloody baggage" were the first words uttered to the new arrival in Australia. Such bluntness didn't put him off his new country.

He travelled to Melbourne to see Walter McEwen. They set about inspecting potential dairy farms, eventually buying at the small town of Launching Place about 50 kilometres east of Melbourne. He soon bought out McEwen's share of the farm, but did so on good terms, as the transaction was timed with him marrying Walter's sister Jessie. They enjoyed more than 50 years of marriage and would have three children together.

It was dairy farming that set Dedman on the route to politics, even though it was a circuitous one. The relationship between the dairy farmers of Victoria and the men of Melbourne who were the wholesale buyers of milk and milk products was an antagonistic one. Dedman joined various dairy farmer groups, but they were utterly ineffective in bringing about a change of circumstances for farmers. Showing signs of later political and organisational skills, he was instrumental in forming a new, more militant group, the Dairy Producers Association of Victoria. He became the first president of the Association, which he later described as "a kind of union".

The producers advocated that a milk board be established to provide for more fairness in the negotiations between the farmers and bulk purchasers. The key was to get the main political parties in Victoria to sign up to the policy. Dedman hatched a plan. One of the other dairy farmers in the association was Tom Houlihan, a prominent member of the Labor Party. Knowing it would require more than one party to advocate against the interests of the powerful buyers' cartel, Dedman said to Houlihan, "Tom, you get the Labor Party pledged to a milk board and I'll join the Country Party and get them pledged to a milk board."

Entering Politics

He joined the Country Party (still then officially called the Victorian Farmers' Union) and began organising a large and successful local branch. It is not as jarring as it might seem from the distance of 100 years that this future giant of a Labor government would first join the Country Party: both believed in economic interventions on behalf of the less powerful, and in those nascent days of the Country Party it was far from clear that they would settle into a consistent pattern of supporting the conservatives (indeed Victoria was the state in which the Country Party and Labor had the closest relationship, forming a coalition government from 1935 to 1942). In any event, Dedman's political views were still quite undeveloped and he was mainly interested in one issue.

His involvement in the Country Party saw him become the candidate for the state seat of Upper Yarra in the 1927 state election. He did not do well, gathering just 596 votes compared to 4002 for the victorious Nationalist James Knox. But Dedman's most bitter disappointment in the Country Party was not his electoral defeat. It was the later betrayal of his cause by the party which was established to promote the interests of farmers.

Houlihan had fulfilled his part of the bargain by convincing the Victorian Labor Party to support the establishment of a milk board. Dedman also successfully moved at the Victorian conference of the Country Party that such a board become party policy.

Labor supported the establishment of a milk board not only to improve the price paid to farmers, but also on the basis that better regulation would eradicate the problem of impure milk being sold in Melbourne and better prices for farmers would better enable farmers to invest in equipment to eradicate more bacteria from milk. The election of the Hogan Labor government in 1927 saw legislation for a board introduced into parliament.

When the legislation came before the upper house, however, the Country Party, whose support was required, decided to side with the interests of the wholesalers over the farmers and defeat the legislation. Dedman was bitterly disappointed, so much so that he resigned from the Country Party.

While ceasing involvement in that party, he became more involved in the community, becoming an Elder of the Presbyterian Church and being elected as a (non-partisan) councillor on the Upper Yarra Shire.

Also, as part of lobbying efforts on milk, he increasingly came into contact with Labor politicians like the future Victorian Premier John Cain Senior and his future cabinet colleague Reg Pollard. He was impressed with them and, as he would later record, "I began to feel the Labor Party was doing more for the primary producers than the Country Party."

Pollard, who was then in the Victorian Parliament, set about recruiting Dedman to Labor. They had much in common. Both were World War One veterans and dairy farmers, and Pollard showed Dedman there was place for someone like him in the party.

It wasn't just rural issues and impressive Labor personalities that were drawing Dedman towards the Labor cause. He started to read intensely about economics and was developing a keen interest in Keynesianism. He had long been an avid reader of scientific journals but transferred his inquisitiveness to the dismal science. Reflective of his growing interests at the time are the magazines he subscribed to: *Labor Call*, *The Messenger* (the newspaper of the Presbyterian Church) and the *New Statesman* (a British left-wing magazine). He enrolled in due course at the University of Melbourne to study economics.

All these forces drew him to the Labor Party and he not only joined in June 1928 but became a dedicated activist, putting his considerable organisation skills to good use. He visited Labor branches around Victoria, lecturing on the benefits of Keynesian economics and what he called "social control" or social democracy.

The Labor Party latched onto this enthusiastic organiser with strong rural links and he was soon the Labor candidate for the state seat of Upper Goulburn. Presaging his interest in financial matters, in this campaign he ran on the platform of abolishing the gold standard which was controversial at the time, and his conservative opponent railed against his irresponsibility. History would judge him correct on the gold standard, but history would also record him losing the election.

His involvement in local government continued and he became President of the Upper Yarra Shire in 1931. Given it was the height of the Great Depression, this was an opportunity to add a practical element to his growing belief in Keynesian intervention, personally championing and managing local public-works projects to stimulate economic activity and create employment.

Two years later he was asked by the party to be the candidate for the seat of Polwarth in a 1933 by-election. This rural seat, then within the division of the federal seat of Corio, has never been won by the Labor Party (it still exists) and nor was Dedman a realistic chance.

This unsuccessful campaign was very significant for his political career, however. The campaign was launched by the federal leader James Scullin who was impressed by Dedman and "henceforth would take a healthy interest in Dedman's political career".[10] Trade unions based in Geelong lent assistance to his campaign and were also impressed – so impressed that they invited him to contest the preselection for the federal seat of Corio the following year, a preselection that he won.

He received a 4% swing against the sitting member Richard Casey, but this was nowhere near enough, with Casey comfortably re-elected with 59% of the vote to Dedman's 39%. Casey would be federal treasurer within a year.

Dedman's big break came in 1940 when Prime Minister Menzies appointed Casey to become Australia's first Ambassador to the United States. The stakes were high. A loss in Corio would see the Menzies government lose its majority on the floor of the House of Representatives. Casey had opposed Menzies' installation as prime minister and Menzies had removed him as treasurer as a result. The fact that Menzies was prepared to risk the stability of his government by removing Casey from parliament shows how much enmity there was between the two men.

First, Dedman had to win preselection. This was no easy task. He had sat out the 1937 election (which Casey had won with 56% of the vote). He and Jessie had, however, moved their young family to

Geelong, in a sign that he was serious about being the Labor candidate for Corio again.

In fact, he had considered nominating for the state seat of Geelong when the sitting Labor member Bill Brownbill passed away. He withdrew from the race in deference to Brownbill's widow Fanny who went on to win the seat and become the first female Labor member of the Victorian Legislative Assembly. This generous act would pay off for Dedman as Brownbill threw her considerable support behind him in the hard-fought preselection for the Corio by-election, in which he took on eight other candidates.

It was a field of strong contenders and Dedman did not have the support of the ALP Central Executive. He was competing against Leo Carmody who had been the candidate in the 1937 election and two former state MPs among others. However, the combined support of the Brownbill local machine and some trade union support saw him win 574 votes of the around 1000 votes of local Labor members cast.

The campaign itself was also hard-fought, with Menzies claiming that "Hitler has his eyes on Corio". The concept of the Führer lifting his gaze from the maps of the battlefield to check on the progress count in the Corio by-election was, to say the least, far-fetched. There was a ready media market for such hyperbole, however, with the Keith Murdoch owned (Melbourne) *Herald* breathlessly warning that a Labor win in Corio would shake "the foundations of the Empire".

Despite Menzies' pride in his Scottish heritage, the United Australia Party was happy to draw not so subtle attention to Dedman's Scottish birth, with the slogan "Vote for Vinton Smith, the Australian born returned soldier."

This was a serious by-election campaign, with Curtin visiting the electorate four times and officially launching the campaign at a large meeting in Geelong Town Hall. Dedman actively campaigned every day except for the Sabbath. The *Herald* campaigned strongly against Labor throughout the campaign, reviving the old trope that Labor was less than patriotic and not fully committed to the war effort.

Any chance the Menzies government had of holding the seat disappeared in the final week of the campaign when a major corruption scandal broke. The Minister for Trade and Customs John Lawson (who had defeated Chifley in Macquarie in the 1931 election) had secretly issued Australian Consolidated Industries (ACI) a five-year monopoly to become the only car manufacturer in Australia, and had not allowed alternative manufacturers a fair opportunity to bid. Curtin received this information and exposed it at the beginning of the campaign, but during the campaign it was also revealed that Lawson had a secret stake in a racehorse with the General Manager of ACI. When this was exposed, Lawson resigned in the last week of the by-election campaign. In the words of Andrew Spaull, "The tide, which was running towards Dedman, turned into a flood."[11]

Despite or perhaps partly because of the shrill conservative campaigning, the people of Corio turned their backs on the Menzies government and embraced John Curtin's candidate. Dedman achieved an 8% swing to snatch the seat with 51.8% of the vote.

In Parliament

The ramifications of Dedman's win were substantial not only for him but for the entire country. Menzies was forced to invite the Country Party back into his government to protect his majority. It was a clear indication that there was a mood for change in the community and frustration about the war effort of the Menzies government. It encouraged, for example, High Court judge HV Evatt to act on his inclination to leave the court and enter the House of Representatives, as a Labor government was looking increasingly likely.

However, the general election held a few months after the Corio by-election did not deliver that – not quite. While Curtin's Labor Party won 50.3% of the national two-party preferred vote, this was only enough to deliver 32 seats in the House of Representatives compared to 36 for the incumbents. Menzies was two seats short of a majority due to the presence of four "Lang Labor" members of parliament and two independents. The two independents (Arthur Coles and Alex Wilson) pledged support for Menzies, but when the four Lang Labor MPs rejoined the official Labor Party shortly after the election, the numerical and political pressure on the government increased dramatically.

Meanwhile, Dedman had been re-elected at the general election with another small swing towards him, seeing him garner 52.6% of the vote. He was making an impression in Canberra, particularly with his leader. His speeches on the economy were well-crafted and confidently delivered. He had discontinued his Melbourne University studies in economics but put his training to good use. Given he and Evatt (now in the Caucus as member for Barton) were the only two Caucus members with any university education, his knowledge stood out. "When I went up to Canberra, I worked hard and made not very many speeches but every one carefully prepared," Dedman would recount years later. He also showed a willingness to make cutting political arguments in his speeches condemning the performance of the Menzies government.

His inaugural speech in the House of Representatives was a strong showing of his credentials. Speaking on the Address in Reply to the governor-general on 19 April 1940, he showed a willingness to take the fight to the government and a strong grasp of financial concepts and language. "First, I compliment the Government upon its conversion to a fundamental principle of sound finance which has been advocated by the Australian Labor Party for many years," he told the House. It was a backhanded compliment, as he went on to say, "It is true that the Government has not openly stated its conversion. It has not had the guts to do so." While Dedman claimed the Labor Party had long championed sound finance, he was actually advancing a comparatively new economic argument, because by "sound finance" he was actually advancing Keynesian full-employment policies, pre-empting the postwar policy he himself would come to implement. Indeed, he was also pre-empting the Modern Monetarist theorists, arguing that "everyone knows it is a fact that the private banks can, and do, create credit money every day of the week".

Following Dedman's opening parliamentary contribution, Harold Holt paid him a partial compliment, congratulating him "on the self-confidence and easy assurance of his delivery" but noting that "I cannot congratulate him with the same enthusiasm on the subject matter of his talk… We have always been brought up to believe that dead men tell no tales, but I fear that this Dedman is going to repeat on many future occasions the financial fairy tale which he has just told us."

Curtin also noticed that Dedman was a much needed loyalist in a fractious Caucus. While he was loyal, he was not unquestioningly so, and despite being a new arrival was willing to respectfully express his views. The Caucus was a riven one, with contention over how Labor should handle an ailing conservative government tottering in the House of Representatives during the war. Menzies extended repeated invitations to join a government of national unity in the mould of the Churchill–Attlee coalition in the mother country, but Curtin was adamant that this was the wrong model for Australia, and was concerned that Labor would be drawn into the government with little real power but with shared responsibility for the errors and defeats. The strong willed HV Evatt was equally determined that Labor should join a national government, either under Curtin as leader or, if he were unwilling, under himself.

Curtin also faced pressure from his Caucus to be more proactive in bringing the government down. Curtin, while willing to apply pressure, also measured his timing carefully, knowing that there was much at stake in a gamble made and lost.

It is a sign of Dedman's quick elevation to the status of a senior operative that he played a role in these deliberations as somewhat of an honest broker.

Arthur Calwell, who had a difficult relationship with Curtin, recorded in his autobiography that in August 1941, as Menzies was being replaced as Prime Minister by Arthur Fadden, Evatt asked him to move in the Caucus that steps be taken to defeat the government on the floor of the House. Curtin knew that it wasn't the right time and that the two independents, whose support they would need to prevail, were not ready to move. He wanted to wait until the budget. Curtin asked Dedman to convince Calwell to withdraw his motion. Dedman carried out the task, but he actually agreed with Calwell that the pressure should be applied to the government. Calwell declined to withdraw his motion.

To Calwell's surprise, Evatt voted against the motion despite having asked him to move it. Evatt was prepared to agitate against Curtin, but not openly defy him. Dedman on the other hand had the courage of his convictions to vote for the motion and Curtin in turn had enough confidence in him to withstand a disagreement. Calwell's motion was lost, but no damage was done to the relationship between Curtin and

Dedman, and Calwell also appreciated his honesty and willingness to stick to his position unlike Evatt.

It was increasingly clear the Fadden government's days were numbered. Jockeying for positions in cabinet was beginning.

A very telling conversation occurred between Curtin and Calwell on the lawns of the Kurrajong Hotel, the accommodation of choice for Labor MPs. Calwell, noting that it was increasingly likely that Labor would form an administration, asked the leader who he thought would likely be elected to the ministry from Victoria. "I want Scullin," Curtin replied. When Calwell indicated that Scullin would not be a candidate for the ministry, Curtin cut off Calwell's ambitions by replying, "Oh, well therefore it will be Dedman."[12]

Calwell, who had been a party operative since his early adulthood and had been president of the Victorian branch, was entitled to be surprised that Dedman was on track to beat him to the cabinet. His memoir noted that "Dedman became a very great Minister for War Organisation."

Another sign of Dedman's preferment by Curtin came a few months later. When the budget was brought down, Curtin moved an amendment of a one-pound change in the budget, which in accord with parliamentary precedent would amount to an expression of no confidence by the House if carried. This was Curtin's moment to strike. When the debate came, which was one of the most important debates on the floor of the House in the history of federation, he asked Dedman to be the second speaker in favour of a change of government. True to form, Dedman based his argument for a change of government on the argument that Labor had superior plans to finance the war effort.

And so, on Friday 3 October 1941, the House voted on Curtin's motion. The vote was not a surprise. Coles had told the House that he was voting with the Opposition, ironically enough to provide stability. He had decided that the coalition government was so unstable that the best way to provide the certainty and leadership that the country so desperately needed was to change to a Labor government. And hence, when the House divided at 4.15 p.m., there were 33 members sitting in support of the coalition government and 36 expressing no confidence. Fadden advised the governor-general that evening to send for Curtin as Prime Minister.

The next step was for the Caucus to elect the new ministry. The Caucus meeting on Monday lasted three and a half hours as the ballot ensued. There were to be 19 ministers and it was decided to conduct the ballot in two lots. Calwell alleged that Curtin ran a formal "Leaders ticket" which excluded him, while others thought that Curtin had simply indicated some preferences to those who asked him his preferred cabinet. Either way, a combination of Curtin's implicit support and the respect he had built up quickly in the Caucus led to Dedman being elected in the first ballot.

Curtin wanted Dedman close to him but also responsible for an important area of the war effort. So, aged 45 and in parliament for a little over a year, he became Minister Assisting the Prime Minister, Minister for War Organisation of Industry, and Minister in Charge in the Council for Science and Industry Research (CSIR).

Curtin and Dedman both soon realised, however, that if Dedman was to have the authority necessary to bring about a step change in the domestic war effort, then this ministerial arrangement wouldn't do. And so, on 16 October, less than a fortnight into his new government, Curtin approved the establishment of the "Production Executive" under Dedman's chairmanship. It would consist of Dedman, the Minister for Munitions (Norman Makin), the Minister for Supply

(Jack Beasley) and the Minister for Labour and National Service (Eddie Ward).

This was clearly a mechanism designed by Curtin to give Dedman more seniority over his fellow ministers, some of whom (Ward and Beasley in particular) he had an uneasy relationship with. It is a telling insight into the confidence that Curtin and Chifley had in Dedman that neither chose to impose themselves as Chair of the Production Executive, as either would have had the authority to do. Evatt opposed the creation of the Production Executive and then argued that a more senior minister (his friend and ally Jack Beasley) should be the Chairman. Curtin prevailed on both questions.

Frederick Shedden, the Secretary of the Department of Defence Co-Ordination (and the public servant Curtin relied upon the most) called the creation of the Production Executive "a feat without parallel in Australian history". As John Edwards noted, this hyperbole probably had something to do with the fact that the creation of the Executive was Shedden's recommendation.

Curtin completed Dedman's elevation to the most senior ranks of the government when, two months later in December, he appointed him to the War Cabinet, alongside Curtin himself, Chifley, the Deputy Prime Minister Frank Forde, Evatt, Beasley, Makin and the Minister for Air Arthur Drakeford. Edwards would accurately characterise this as "the heart of government".[13] The War Cabinet functioned as an inner cabinet, the true decision-making body in a fast moving and difficult environment.

Dedman needed all the support and seniority he could get as he endeavoured to turn around what was a lethargic domestic war effort. Although Menzies and Fadden had had a minister for defence industry organisation, they did not have the departmental heft to get anything of any note done. Dedman said that he inherited an empty office, with no departmental staff, systems or processes in place. In effect, two years into the war, he had to start from scratch to get Australian industry on a footing to make a contribution to the war effort.

There was no Australian precedent for an agency of government to have such far reaching responsibility for organising Australian industry. Dedman's combination of economic understanding, a belief in government intervention and organisational capacity would prove very effective. He would use the Commonwealth's constitutional defence powers to great effect in the most interventionist and innovative period of industry policy in Australian history.

He saw his role in two key parts: more efficient allocation of the resources of production focused on materials vital for the war effort, and reducing non-essential consumption of luxuries and other goods that weren't adding to the effort. The first element had difficulties in a capitalist society that wasn't regarded as being in imminent danger of direct attack, and the second element saw him soon become arguably the most unpopular man in Australia.

In order to arrange for available labour resources to be allocated to war-related production, Dedman convinced the Production Executive to recommend to cabinet the creation of a Manpower Directorate under the control of a Director-General of Manpower which would be responsible for enforcing strict provisions. "In effect," historian Jan Beaumont would write, "Manpower imposed industrial conscription. It issued identity cards to all Australian adults, had the sole power to decide who worked where and raided hotels and racetracks rounding up those evading war work."[14] Relying on the federal government's constitutional defence power, Curtin supported this very radical intrusion into the workings of the economy when Dedman took it to the cabinet, and it was implemented from January 1942.

If labour was going to be corralled into essential production, Dedman thought the next obvious step was to reduce consumer demand for non-essential goods by an equally radical intrusion into the retail economy. His first step was to successfully argue to his colleagues on the Production Executive that prohibition should be applied to the sale of radio sets, whitegoods, cars, metal furniture, guns and many toys. He deliberately chose an expansive list of goods to try to shock the Australian people into changed habits. Having won approval of the cabinet, he announced the new regime in his first radio address as Minister for War Organisation of Industry. He pointed out that, so far, those Australians who weren't fighting had not really experienced a reduction in their standard of living. "We are fighting for our homes, our wives and children. Sacrifices of non-essentials are demanded… if we are to survive and retain our freedom."

He knew the restrictions were a bitter pill, but he didn't believe in applying much sugar to help it go down. He said in a radio broadcast in March 1942 that "these economies might cause a little inconvenience to householders. Don't grumble about it."

Where possible, he would ask industry to come up with their own plans for product rationalisation, showing a flair for consultation backed up by industry knowing he had substantial war powers at his disposal if a more consultative approach failed. In this way, for example, the tobacco industry came up with a plan to rationalise 763 different products down to 17, and 46 varieties of garden shovels were reduced to 14. Also useful here was the Manpower Commission, because Dedman could and did intimate that the Commission would only guarantee a protected workforce for a particular sector if industry agreed to rationalise products.

The first round of austerity restrictions did not prove very unpopular, but by 1942 he needed to go much further, and became the subject of much angst.

His public standing wasn't helped by him taking on the newspapers of Australia, arguing that Sunday and sporting newspapers should be abandoned, that morning and evening editions of daily papers should be combined and that there should be restrictions on the size of pages and number of pages per edition – all to save paper and newsprint. This led to another type of war: war between Dedman and the media proprietors, who claimed that these restrictions would amount to an attack on freedom of the press.

The media barons found an ally in Evatt, who argued passionately in cabinet that they were right. Evatt's remarks, defending freedom of the press and castigating Dedman, were conveniently leaked to *The Sydney Morning Herald*.

Curtin decided on a compromise: a mandatory reduction of 40% in the male labour force of newspapers, with the newspapers to decide themselves what to cut to cater for this dramatically reduced workforce. Dedman was to find that from this point forward he was the subject of regular attacks from the nation's newspapers.

These attacks came into their own when Dedman tackled a particularly controversial issue. He ordered that cuffs be banned from trousers and pockets be abolished from pyjamas to save material. He also ordered that only one, very efficient, style of men's suit should be produced (he named this the "Victory suit", which was single breasted to save material and had no buttons on the sleeve). He later (semi-) joked that his plan was to make the suit so unpopular that no-one would want one.

He also declared that only three sizes of dress should be produced for women. Tails were to be removed from men's shirts, leading to the allegation that Dedman was bringing about lower-back pain in winter and earning him the nickname "Lumbago Jack". At first, at least, the restrictions had the opposite effect to the one Dedman intended, with a rush to the stores to beat the new rules coming into effect and get the last of the old varieties of clothes. In a rare mistake, Curtin had accidentally announced tougher restrictions than had actually been agreed, using more stark language than Dedman had recommended employing in his Friday night radio address.

The Saturday morning of 9 May 1942, the morning after the announcement of the new restrictions, was called "the Battle of Bourke Street" in Melbourne and "the Battle of George Street" in Sydney as bedlam ensued. The (Sydney) *Sunday Sun* of 10 May described the situation breathlessly, but not unreasonably: "Like hordes of locusts, the crowds swarmed through every department of retail stores, stripping stands and counters bare in the biggest orgy in Sydney's history."

Dedman was able to tell parliament that "There have been achieved not only large savings in respect of materials and manpower previously absorbed in unnecessary frills but also important gains in industrial efficiency resulting from the avoidance of frequent change overs in production, and the necessity to handle and stock many different varieties."

The Opposition attacked him strongly over the scale of the restrictions and found plenty of willing newspapers to support their argument. Dedman ploughed on. He took out government advertisements (complete with his picture) in December 1942 asking people to reduce Christmas spending and used his powers to limit Christmas advertising by retailers. The response from retailers and newspapers (who had a symbiotic relationship, with retailers supplying newspapers with substantial advertising revenue) was harsh. Cartoons parodying "Deddy Christmas" accompanied editorials condemning his heavy-handed approach. It was the *Sydney Morning Herald* editorial of 9 December 1942 that coined the term "Dedmanism" to encapsulate austerity – a term the Opposition was only too happy to adopt. In Perth, the owner of the *Guardian* newspaper and perennial conservative candidate for parliament, Carlyle Ferguson, took Dedman's restrictions on Christmas advertising to the High Court. But the court backed the minister, finding that "The waging of war involves a large measure of control over economic matters, including control over expenditure."

He also decreed that only white or pink icing was allowed on cakes, that two gallons of petrol a month be allowed per car, and that tea, butter and sugar were all to be rationed.

While Curtin and Chifley publicly and privately supported these restrictions, it was Dedman who wore the public opprobrium. His dour demeanour added to his austere image. The conservative Opposition felt no obligation to support a need for austerity in the spirit of bipartisanship. Nor was the criticism of Dedman confined to the media or the Opposition. Calwell, bitter at his defeat in the Caucus ballot for the ministry, was active in his criticism, as was former New South Wales Premier Jack Lang who was at this stage still a Labor member of the New South Wales Parliament. Dedman had a university education, which made him suspect in Lang's eyes. Lang ran an ongoing campaign through his newspaper *The Century* against Dedman and argued for Calwell's elevation to the cabinet. Lang argued through the pages of the newspaper that the talented bureaucrats at the Department of War Organisation of Industry were a "bunch of crackpots who owe no allegiance to Labor".

Historian Stuart Macintyre explained the trade-off between the success of Dedman's policies and the price paid in terms of his public standing: the policies "released half a million workers for war activity by the end of 1942, but at the cost of turning Dedman into a pettifogging killjoy".[15]

While Lang and supporters of Calwell argued that Dedman was impure of Labor pedigree, the attacks from the conservatives were at the other end of the spectrum, arguing that Dedman was abusing his war powers to introduce socialism by stealth.

The other regular opponent of Dedman was Evatt. Evatt never got over Curtin's rapid promotion of Dedman (although this was a rather hypocritical thing for Evatt to resent, given that Dedman had actually been in Federal Parliament slightly longer than Evatt). He regularly opposed Dedman's measures and on more than one occasion his opposition in the cabinet leaked into the public domain. The most spectacular example of this was the argument between Dedman and Evatt about restrictions on domestic servants. Dedman judged that the 90,000 workers in domestic service in late 1942 was impossible to justify given the drain on the war effort. He proposed that domestic servants should only be legally employable if a permit was issued in cases where genuine need had been established. Predictable howls of protest emanated from the Opposition and newspapers about "class war". Curtin, keen to maintain stability and harmony in the government, decided on a compromise in which one domestic servant per household was allowed automatically, but the employment of any further domestic help would need a permit.

Talented in policy, a friendly outward-facing image wasn't Dedman's forte; "public relations were a closed door to him," Ross McMullin would write.[16] It's been argued by some that he was not worried about the attacks on him or his unpopularity. Few people, however, let alone politicians, relish unpopularity. Dedman would tell parliament, "Like everyone else, I want to win the war. Unlike some other people, I'm prepared to take the action which is necessary if we are to have a chance of winning it." He also told the House in September 1942 that "Restrictions are not imposed for their own sake, or from sadistic delight in imposing hardships upon civilians. They are imposed only in cases where restrictions will make a clear and positive contribution to the war effort."

If anything, many informed observers thought that Dedman could have been stronger in defending himself and the government against the coalition of convenience that was the retailing sector, newspapers and the coalition. The head of the government's Directorate of Research and Civil Affairs, Alf Conlon, argued that "there are times when the Minister should have gone on air and denounced the newspapers which were guilty".[17]

Despite the significant criticism of Dedman, there was a growing (if grudging) respect for his commitment and the necessity of his policies. By 1943, he was able to say that, despite the "obstruction, direct opposition and not a little misrepresentation from vested interests", Australians had responded well to the changes made necessary by war and that a total of 300,000 people had been transferred from non-essential production to war-related industry.

While he may have shrugged off the personal effects of unpopularity, he knew that they might have a political impact. He did not take re-election to Corio for granted in 1943, despite the fact that the Curtin government was receiving widespread support for its success in turning around the war effort. Corio was a marginal seat and Dedman had been away in Canberra for swathes of the term, and so he threw himself into active local campaigning in the lead-up to the August election.

His campaign was helped by two things: the local conservatives were split, and many supported an independent, the retired Brigadier Neil Freeman, over the official United Australia Party candidate Rupert Curnow. Another fillip came when Robert Menzies, having been ousted from his party's leadership, launched his re-election campaign for Kooyong. Menzies chose to deliver some mild criticism of Dedman's methods, but conceded he had done what was necessary to boost the domestic war effort, an endorsement that Dedman was quick to deploy in a pamphlet he distributed throughout the electorate.

In a landslide win for Labor across the country, Dedman copped a tiny 0.3% swing away from him, probably as a result of his controversial ministerial job. The UAP vote collapsed to just 17%, however, with Curnow falling behind the independent Freeman on 27% of the vote.

Following the election, Dedman easily won re-election to the ministry and Curtin confirmed him in his important roles.

It wasn't until 1945 that he received his next ministerial challenge. In February Curtin transferred the Post-War Reconstruction portfolio from Chifley to Dedman, and subsumed the Department of War Organisation of Industry into the Post-War Reconstruction portfolio.

Just as Curtin and Chifley relied on Dedman as their key domestic minister when it came to organising the war effort, so they also entrusted him with great responsibility when it came to the other great priority of Labor in government: building a better peace.

On coming to office, Curtin had created the Department of Post-War Reconstruction and appointed Chifley as minister together with his responsibilities as treasurer. With the war clearly drawing to a conclusion, there was no point having one of the cabinet's most effective members concentrating on the war effort. It was a better use of his abilities to have Dedman focused on the government's other great project. Separating the portfolio from the Treasury was also an indication that rebuilding was going to be such an increased focus for the government that it needed the concentration of a stand-alone minister. And finally, it is possible to surmise that Curtin, who was ailing by this time, was reshuffling his cabinet as a bequest to Chifley and the Labor movement, and ensuring that one of his favourite ministers was elevated as part of the process.

The tasks of war organisation and postwar reconstruction were similar: both required a massive rethinking of the role of government in the economy. Dedman would bring the experience of his instructive time as Minister for War Organisation of Industry to the designated task of creating a new Jerusalem.

It was a wide-ranging portfolio which enabled Dedman to involve himself across the entire government. However, there are two areas where he made such a mark that those who look closely can see his fingerprints still, 75 years later: education and science. Here, he used both his portfolios to reshape the federal government's approach.

Minister for Education?

There was no federal Department of Education until 1966. However, Dedman didn't allow such constraints to stop him having an indelible mark on our education system. As minister, he was prepared to push the constitutional envelope to expand Commonwealth involvement in education, telling parliament that "The extent of the Commonwealth's educational activities is in fact much wider than is generally recognised. It stands in marked contrast to the belief that under the Constitution, the Commonwealth Government has no power or responsibility at all in the educational field."

There is merit in Andrew Spaull's argument that Dedman could be regarded as our first federal Minister for Education despite not officially holding the title.[18]

He was passionate about education, telling parliament, "We are prone at times to say that this or that subject is of paramount importance, but in actual fact all other problems are secondary to that of better education." He was speaking as the son of a schoolmaster who had twice had to discontinue university studies (once because of World War One and then because he was elected to Federal Parliament).

His achievements in education were even more remarkable when you consider that not only was there no precedent for an interventionist federal minister, but there was also very considerable scepticism in the Labor Party about universities: they were seen (not unreasonably at the time) as places of elitism and privilege. Less flattering in the eyes of history was the view of some in the party that working-class kids going to university would simply take them out of the working class and turn them into conservative voters. Dedman allowed none of this to hold him back, although a less enthusiastic cabinet did mean that he did not achieve everything he set out to do and had to wait decades for the election of the Whitlam government, just before his death, to see more of his agenda implemented.

His strong involvement in education pre-dated his appointment as Minister for Post-War Reconstruction. He had a heavy role in university policy as Minister for War Organisation of Industry. And he used that role to promote the controversial view that more students from poorer families should be admitted to university and that university entry should be based on merit instead of wealth.

In 1942, universities were understandably confused about their role in the war effort and vice-chancellors approached Dedman for clarification. Obviously men of university age were prime candidates for recruitment or work in essential industries, but how could universities balance their obligation to continue educating young Australians with the necessity of ensuring all available manpower?

Dedman acted decisively, framing a request to the Production Executive to issue a regulation that would enable the Minister for Labor and National Service to direct a university to limit the number of students in any course and, very importantly, that the availability of these limited places must be determined solely on academic merit.

He was shocked to learn that universities could and constantly did re-enrol failed students, which he regarded as a waste of resources. He was also passionate that young working-class kids should have access to university, driven in part by his experience as a "struggling low income student at the University of Edinburgh".[19]

He saw the war as an opportunity to expand the Commonwealth's role in university policy. He used the Production Executive to establish a Universities Commission to administer Commonwealth financial assistance. His appointments were interesting. He rejected departmental advice and appointed Lloyd Ross (then an official of the Australian Railways Union), the Labor Member for Maranoa Frank Baker, and the principal of the exclusive Geelong Grammar JR Darling, whom Dedman knew from his electorate.

Despite the austere nature of Dedman's policies and utterances when it came to the need for a total war effort, his views of the need for a broad, liberal education, even in the dark days of war, shone through. In announcing the formation of the Universities Commission, he stressed that he wanted the universities to maintain all courses, including those not linked to the war effort but holding intrinsic value.

Used to being blamed for shortages and restrictions, he was aware of the good news that federal funding of universities and merit-based selection brought: "For once, I can be Deddy Christmas," he said, the closest thing that can be found as a John Dedman joke on the public record.

He had an eye on postwar reconstruction even before he took the portfolio, asking senior high school students to consider a university education as national service to build the skills necessary for a massive government-led effort for peacetime renewal.

University students responded warmly to Dedman's interest and his policies. The National Association of University Students conferred honorary membership on him. I'm sure future ministers for education would be astonished that the peak body representing students would be so lauding of their minister.

Not everyone was happy though. John Drummond was a young man who wanted to be a medical student at the University of Sydney, but, while his family could afford the fees, he could not qualify for entry on academic merit. His family took the Dedman rules insisting on merit-based entry to the High Court – and won. The court ruled that there was a flaw in the regulation because if someone was denied university entry there was no guarantee they would end up working on the war effort, hence the government's use of its war powers was misplaced. Dedman got around this by changing the regulation to comply with the High Court requirements.

In his period as Minister for Post-War Reconstruction, he was interested in extending support to low-income school students. In a crowded government agenda, however, he reached the view that he wouldn't receive enough cabinet support to make this a priority. He must have taken soundings with Chifley and other ministers to reach this conclusion. He was convinced that such an intrusion into school education would be seen as endangering other priorities like housing and the Snowy Mountains Scheme. Dedman would live just long enough to see Whitlam oversee greater Commonwealth involvement in schools but wouldn't live to see Hawke and Keating lift the school retention rate from 30% to 90% or Rudd and Gillard introduce needs-based funding, reforms he would have wholeheartedly approved of.

He had more success in shepherding into existence the Australian National University (ANU). The ANU has become such a valued part of the tertiary education landscape in Australia that it would be easy to assume its creation was inevitable or uncontroversial. That would be an erroneous assumption.

There had been a university presence in Canberra since 1929, with the University of Melbourne establishing the Canberra College. What was proposed by Dedman and the Chifley government was much more than a university to service the young people of Canberra. It was proposed that the new university be an institution of national significance, with research capacity in areas important to the national interest.

Senior government and academic figures such as HC "Nugget" Coombs, Alf Conlon and Sir Robert Garran had long championed the concept of a significant university in Canberra. In fact, as ANU historians Margaret Varghese and Stephen Glynn noted, "Ideas about a national university for Australia... can be traced back to the 1870s."[20]

The reason it hadn't been brought about was because no federal government had been of a mind to establish a national university, and existing universities were adamantly opposed to its creation, fearing it would attract students, resources and attention.

But the time was right. Coombs, as Director-General of Post-War Reconstruction, was a strong and longstanding supporter of the concept. Dedman began the process towards a national university when he was still Minister for War Organisation of Industry. In 1943, he appointed an inter-departmental committee to consider the possible establishment of a university. He appointed as chair the deputy head of his department, Ronald Walker. Other members appointed by Dedman were Coombs, RC Mills (Professor of Economics at the University of Sydney) and Sir David Rivett (head of the Council for Scientific and Industry Research). These were wise appointments. Mills, in particular, was close to Treasurer Chifley and "the only person to whom the treasurer's door was always open"; hence with a combination of Coombs and Mills making the case, Chifley as treasurer was more likely to approve the necessary (significant) resources for a new university.

The committee reported to Dedman in October 1944 and unsurprisingly, given its makeup, found that there was an urgent need for a national tertiary institution based in Canberra. The report recommended the new university focus on Pacific affairs, international relations, government, and Australian history and literature.

Dedman took the committee's recommendation to cabinet unamended and suggested that a small committee of ministers be delegated to progress the recommendation. Shortly afterwards, Curtin appointed Dedman as Minister for Post-War Reconstruction, absorbing the Department of War Organisation of Industry into the new department and thus giving Dedman clear responsibility for education.

The cabinet subcommittee continued to work with the committee of bureaucrats and academics. The main addition which came about as part of this process was the addition of medical research to the list of key aims of the new university. This addition was led by the winner of the 1945 Nobel Prize in Medicine, Howard Florey, who saw an Australian-led medical research institute as being essential for the new university. The cabinet subcommittee chaired by Dedman accepted all the recommendations of the working group bar one: it rejected the name "University of Canberra" and, in keeping with the national sweep of ambition of the university, recommended to the full cabinet that it be named "National University". When Dedman took the recommendation of the subcommittee of ministers to the full cabinet, the cabinet in turn made one further change: at the instigation of Arthur Calwell, it decided the name should be "Australian National University".

Dedman was helped by the fact that Evatt was absent for the key cabinet meeting which accepted his recommendation for a new national university. Evatt, with his long and intimate ties with the University of Sydney, was uncomfortable with the concept of a rival to his alma mater as the principal prestigious university in Australia and would certainly have resisted the naming of the new institution which implied a certain superiority to the other universities. While Dedman almost certainly would have prevailed anyway, his path was easier due to Evatt's absence.

Dedman progressed the development of the university through the government and the parliament, moving the legislation to establish the ANU. The ANU historians noted that he spoke "with conviction of a Scottish Presbyterian whose own efforts to gain a degree had been twice cut short by world wars".

Menzies, speaking for the Opposition, supported the legislation but opposed the name "Australian National University" and questioned why the medical and science schools would be located in Canberra. But he began his speech with generous praise for Dedman's commitment to expanding higher education.

Dedman's contribution to bringing about this important institution was also ultimately recognised by the university itself. The John Dedman Building at ANU would host the teaching of mathematical sciences until its demolition in 2018.

The Creation of the CSIRO

The Commonwealth's scientific research body was something Dedman had ministerial responsibility for through his entire eight years in the federal cabinet.

The Council for Scientific and Industrial Research (CSIR) had been established in 1926 by the Bruce government. However, after 20 years in operation, the organisational and legal structure of the CSIR was no longer appropriate.

The Council was a federation of state appointments. However, every single staff appointment, including the most junior, had to be approved by the minister. This rather amateurish and cumbersome arrangement did not fit what Dedman had in mind as one of the world's premier scientific research organisations playing a key role in an enlightened period of scientific and social progress in postwar Australia. And so he turned his mind to modernising the structure of the CSIR and transforming it into a new, professional body.

There was also another reason for him to consider reform. In this Cold War period, the CSIR was coming under attack from the Opposition for harbouring secret communists. The parliamentary attack was led by the Liberal Party's Eric Harrison and the Country Party's Arthur Fadden. Historian CB Schedvin would years later write of this attack on the integrity of the CSIR that "This episode is one of the most unsavoury in the history of the Commonwealth Parliament."[21]

Regardless of the unsavoury nature of the attack, it was further reason for reform. Dedman felt particularly exposed. Required by the Act to personally sign-off on every appointment, he was of course not involved in the recruitment process. When the officials of the CSIR turned up at Parliament House to ask him to sign appointment forms, he began asking them "What assurance have I that I am not indeed appointing a communist?"[22] In addition, the British and American governments had expressed disquiet over the suggestions that communists had infiltrated the CSIR and change was necessary to ensure continued intelligence sharing on scientific developments.

One option available to Dedman was to "departmentalise" the CSIR, create it as a department and bring it under the Public Service Act. But Sir Frederick White, who was intimately involved in the discussions around restructuring the CSIR, would later write: "Looking back, I believe that both Chifley and Dedman so genuinely appreciated CSIR's work and so admired [Chief Executive, Sir David] Rivett that they refrained from the action immediately available of bringing the whole staff within the public service proper."[23]

Bringing Australia's primary science organisation into the public service would have robbed it of the autonomy and agility it needed to function. Dedman was originally open to the option of departmentalisation but Coombs was opposed and Dedman ultimately found those arguments convincing. Still, he thought reform was necessary, although it was resisted inside the CSIR itself. Chief Executive David Rivett recommended simply removing defence research from the remit of the CSIR so as to reduce the sensitivity of the work to allegations of communist infiltration. This was hardly going to be enough, as

Dedman knew, and so he set about urgent reforms although "few of the senior scientists on the council shared Dedman's sense of urgency".[24]

And so, in August 1948 he asked the Chair of the Public Service Board Sir William Dunk and Coombs to report on the best basis to reorganise the CSIR. Dunk and Coombs recommended that a new organisation be legislated for, to be called the Commonwealth Scientific and Industrial Research Organisation (CSIRO) which would have more autonomy on hiring and firing, a more modern management structure, enhanced security provisions, with the minister having the power to direct the CSIRO as to what areas to research without interfering in the research itself.

Dedman accepted this as a good model, sought cabinet's agreement, overcame resistance from the management of the CSIR, and then shepherded the legislation through the parliament before the government's defeat in 1949.

The organisation that Dedman legislated for remains in place today, having stood the test of time. The CSIRO has served Australia very well in the decades that have passed, and those who shepherded the reorganisation through, led by John Dedman, deserve considerable praise.

1946: Deputy Labor Leader?

The 1946 election saw the Chifley government re-elected with a reduced majority, but saw Dedman increase his margin in Corio with a healthy 56.4% of the vote.

The election saw the defeat of the party's deputy leader Frank Forde in his seat of Capricornia, opening up a vacancy for which Dedman decided to run. His competition was stiff. The Attorney-General and

Minister for External Affairs HV Evatt was the front runner but the left-wing firebrand Eddie Ward was in no mind to give him a free run and could not be underestimated. Arthur Calwell was also keen to stake a claim on a leadership position.

Chifley, however, supported Dedman running and gave him his vote. Chifley's support was an indication that he saw Dedman as his preferred successor.

Under the party rules at the time, the position was filled by exhaustive ballots with the worst-performing candidate eliminated each round until one candidate could claim an outright majority. In the first ballot, Evatt scored 28 votes, Ward 20, Calwell 13, Dedman 12 and competent but dour Arthur Drakeford 3. On Drakeford's elimination, all his votes went to Dedman, putting him ahead of Calwell. On Calwell's elimination, all those 13 votes went to Ward, meaning the tally was Ward 33, Evatt 28, Dedman 15. Dedman and his supporters were not about to see Ward, who had created trouble for Curtin, rewarded with the deputy leadership, and they all voted for Evatt, giving him a winning margin of 43 to 33. This was a creditable result for Dedman, outpolling Calwell who would of course go on to eventually claim the deputy leadership and then the leadership.

Dedman was entitled to feel he had a reasonable chance at a leadership position in the future based on the result and was to note of the 1946 election that "It was at this stage that I began to think that I might be prime minister of Australia."[25] The electoral gods were to intervene to ensure that he wasn't given the chance, but he was not alone in thinking it was a possibility. His rival in this ballot, Calwell, noted in his memoirs that Dedman "could have filled the highest office in the land with distinction".[26]

Postwar Rebuilding

While education and science were the two key areas that Dedman could focus on through both his portfolios in government, the rebuilding of Australia from 1945 onwards was much more wide-ranging. The core element of the government's postwar vision was full employment. Keynesian intervention to ensure full employment and a better society than the one that followed World War One was the leitmotif of the Chifley government.

The first attempt at a policy dealing with postwar employment was the Re-Establishment and Employment Bill. This bill was important because it created the Commonwealth Employment Service, the first time a federal instrumentality had been created to help match the unemployed with jobs. The CES would exist until its abolition by the Howard government 50 years later.

However, the bill was extremely controversial within the Labor movement because of the provision for preference in Commonwealth employment for returned servicemen. Dedman had actually opposed this provision when it was discussed in cabinet, but being a cabinet loyalist had then defended it in the Caucus and publicly. Ward launched a bitter attack on the policy in the Caucus (Ward was still in cabinet, but the vital principle of cabinet solidarity had not yet been entrenched in Labor governments, and wouldn't be until the Hawke government). Preference for returned soldiers was bitterly opposed by the union movement as being divisive and undermining worker solidarity. Dedman defended the policy at ALP conferences, which did little to endear him to already suspicious union leaders. The government prevailed although it conceded that the policy would only be in place for seven years after the cessation of hostilities.

When Dedman was defending preference for returned soldiers, he emphasised that unions should see the context of a government committed to full employment, although it was not enshrined as official government policy until the release of the Full Employment White Paper. The White Paper, issued in May 1945, was the defining document of economic policy under the Chifley government, but it would also come to define and set economic policy of all Australian governments until the 1970s. The White Paper represented the full and official embrace of Keynesian intervention in Australian policy. While vitally important, it was more a working document than an erudite expression of principles. It was dense and detailed, although the crux of the new ambition was in the introduction:

> Full employment is a fundamental aim of the Commonwealth Government… The policy outlined in this paper is that governments should accept responsibility for stimulating spending on goods and services to the extent necessary to sustain full employment.

While Dedman had not drafted the White Paper (Coombs could claim primary authorship), he was intimately involved in it and it was his job to steer it through the cabinet, which was no easy task. While Chifley kept a close interest in the paper, his biographer Fin Crisp noted that Chifley and Dedman shared "joint parental concern" for the important document.[27] It was criticised internally as not being radical enough and containing too much bureaucratic language. While Dedman had to endure a two and half day cabinet meeting to steer it through, he did so without substantial amendment.

Just as important as the policies contained in the White Paper was the sentiment it represented. As Fin Crisp put it, "by contrast with the

1931 Premiers Plan of bitter memory for Labour men, the White Paper represented the authentic, forward looking reformist tradition of the ALP. It was the product of Labour united and in the ascendancy."[28]

While Dedman was usually far from a flowery communicator, he did draw on his passion for full employment when he tabled the White Paper in parliament, declaring to the House:

> I make for my colleagues on this side of the House this declaration, paraphrasing Blake –
>
> I will not cease from mental fight
>
> Nor shall my sword sleep in my hand
>
> Till we have built Jerusalem
>
> In Australia's pleasant land.

These lofty words and this noble sentiment were laudable, but he was responsible for a wide array of detailed plans to achieve it, including retraining of returned servicemen, housing construction and the Snowy Mountains Scheme.

Inevitably with such an ambitious and complicated agenda, Dedman experienced both successes and setbacks. The Commonwealth Reconstruction Training Scheme (CRTS) managed to retrain 128,000 returned servicemen but squabbling between employers and unions and concerns that not enough jobs would exist in industry to cater for the newly minted retrained workers meant that his ambitions for greater numbers would be frustrated.

The Snowy River Scheme provided no such frustration for him. Like so much of the Chifley government's postwar agenda, the scheme wasn't Dedman's brainchild, but he provided the political leadership and determination necessary to make it a reality.

Using the vast Snowy River for irrigation and hydro-electricity had been a long-held dream of many in New South Wales. In 1944, Curtin had commissioned a study of the viability of the proposal. The report, which eventually came to Prime Minister Chifley, was very positive about the potential of the scheme.

Chifley asked Dedman as Minister for Post-War Reconstruction to chair a conference between New South Wales and Victoria to progress the plan. It required considerable skills to bridge the rivalries and differences between the two states and make the scheme a reality. Each state jealously guarded their interests and protected their rights and both were unimpressed with the Commonwealth's idea that the scheme could provide energy for the ACT.

It was in his capacity as Minister for Defence, however, that Dedman played a pivotal role in bringing the Snowy Scheme to fruition. With the states and the Commonwealth unable to reach agreement, he proposed to the federal cabinet that the project would generate electricity vital to the nation's defence, and therefore, using the Commonwealth's defence powers, a federal commission should take control to build and run the scheme. The cabinet agreed and, while Dedman and their colleague the Minister for Works Nelson Lemmon needed Chifley's help to get the New South Wales Premier Jim McGirr over the line, that's what transpired.

Dedman reminded the House of Representatives in the debate about the legislation to set up the Snowy Mountains Hydro-Electric Commission that developing reliable electricity supplies that would be difficult for enemies to bomb was regarded as a vital piece of the nation's defence planning. The Liberal and Country parties opposed the legislation as being an insult to states' rights and part of the creeping socialism of the Chifley government. Although Menzies and his colleagues boycotted the ceremony to begin construction, they couldn't stop the legislation or the scheme from getting underway.

Taking Our Place in the World

In his capacity as Minister for Post-War Reconstruction, Dedman was also to become Chifley's vital lieutenant in his bid to see Australia join the new international economic bodies being established in the wake of World War Two. While it now may seem inevitable that Australia would have joined the International Monetary Fund (IMF), the World Bank and the delayed (for 50 years) International Trade Organization (ITO), this was far from the case. Joining the IMF and World Bank required Chifley to deploy all his prime ministerial authority and political skills, ably assisted by Dedman.

Always a Chifley loyalist, but never a sycophantic one, Dedman actually opposed Chifley's first attempt to convince the cabinet to join the IMF in early 1946, but his reasons for doing so were pragmatic. Whereas Ward and big swathes of the labour movement had deep-seated antipathy and suspicion of international finance, Dedman was more concerned that the new body would be overly influenced by the United States, which was inward looking and not committed to the principles of full employment. He was also concerned that the case for joining had not yet been convincingly built and that Chifley might receive a humiliating rebuff at the hands of the Caucus.

Dedman was always willing to listen to expert advice, however. And over the course of 1946 the eminent economist Leslie Melville convinced him that the benefits of joining outweighed any risks. He was converted to the Chifley cause. (The draft constitution of the IMF had also been revised to allow constituent nations to devalue their currency to support full employment, assuaging a lot of his concerns.)

When Chifley again recommended to cabinet in November 1946 that Australia should join the IMF, Dedman's support was crucial as Chifley stared down a sizeable group who were viscerally suspicious of international finance, led by Ward but also containing Calwell, Labour Minister Jack Holloway and the usual ally of Chifley and Dedman, Arthur Drakeford.

Convincing the cabinet was only half the battle. Despite an attempt by Dedman to introduce the principle of cabinet solidarity on the issue, no such principle had been established. Thus seven cabinet ministers actively opposed the cabinet recommendation when it came to Caucus. These cabinet votes were vital in forming the Caucus majority (29–26) that rebuffed Chifley by insisting that the matter should be referred to a special Federal Conference of the ALP before proceeding.

Chifley had previously arranged agreement from the ALP Federal Executive to Australia's joining but was a lot less sanguine about his chances of convincing a Federal Conference. Hence, Chifley engaged in a strategy of encouraging state branches not to call for a special conference, rendering the Caucus resolution without effect. Dedman was an active supporter of the Chifley campaign and engaged in a high-profile defence of Australia joining the IMF. In fact, he became the leading cabinet advocate in public and an extraordinary spectacle ensued of two cabinet ministers engaging in a public duel with Ward mounting the public campaign against the prime minister's position.

In a display of cabinet disunity unthinkable today, Ward published a pamphlet entitled "The Case against the Bretton Woods Financial Agreement" and Dedman responded by publishing "The Case for Bretton Woods". He ran the basic argument that Australia had a choice between isolation and cooperation and that cooperation was the much better of the two options. He even agreed to debate Ward at the Melbourne Trades Hall, but this public disunity was too much for Chifley who asked Dedman not to attend.

The Chifley and Dedman campaign succeeded and no special conference was requested by a state branch, hence the motion was returned to Caucus. Six ministers insisted on maintaining their opposition to Chifley in the Caucus. This time, however, Chifley and Dedman carried the day 33–24. Unbelievably for a cabinet minister, Ward abstained from the final vote on the ensuing legislation in the House.

Following victory on the IMF issue, Chifley chose Dedman as the government's chief negotiator at the international conferences to establish the ITO at Geneva and Havana. On his way to Geneva, Dedman visited London and was received for a private audience with the King, and also took the opportunity to visit his brother and sister for the first time in decades.

He led difficult negotiations with the US delegation to the Geneva conference and successfully managed to procure a hard-fought 25% reduction in the US wool tariff. The Geneva Conference also developed a draft charter for the ITO which Dedman was by and large satisfied with and publicly supported.

The charter would be put to a larger conference in Havana later in 1948 and he also led that delegation. (Typically frugal, he was horrified by the palatial nature and cost of the hotel for the Australian delegation. He ordered they all move out to a rented house and he sacked the delegation chauffeur, instead buying a car for the delegation to use. The car was sold for a profit when they departed.)

The Havana Conference was acrimonious, with the less developed countries which had been unrepresented in Geneva complaining the interests of the developing world had not been properly considered. Dedman successfully inserted full-employment references into the charter. Despite the acrimony, a charter was eventually agreed. It was all a wasted effort, however, as the US Congress refused to ratify the creation of the ITO, and it lay abandoned and unimplemented until the creation of the World Trade Organization in 1995.

Bank Nationalisation

It was while he was in Geneva that Dedman heard the news that the Chifley cabinet had decided to nationalise the banks. He was delighted but shocked. He had long supported bank nationalisation as an integral measure to give the government more control over monetary policy. He had opposed Chifley's 1945 banking legislation in cabinet because it didn't go far enough. But he was incredulous that the cabinet had made such a decision as it had always been so reluctant. The last time the cabinet had discussed the option of bank nationalisation it was only the highly unlikely pairing of Dedman and Ward who were in favour.

Dedman's support for it was longstanding; it predated his election to parliament and stemmed back to his study of economics at the University of Melbourne. His view was that the federal government should have an active monetary policy, and the way to enable this most effectively was bank nationalisation. He was, of course, correct in his determination that an active monetary policy was necessary, but wrong in his view that bank nationalisation was the way to achieve it.

However, the High Court had declared the 1945 legislation unconstitutional, leading Chifley and the cabinet to decide that they had no choice but to go further and nationalise the banks. On return, Dedman threw himself into the task of publicly defending the measure with a "sense of deep elation and high enthusiasm". He addressed public meetings in support of the case, arguing that nationalisation, far from being a radical socialist plot, was a sensible measure to give the government the control it needed to bring about financial stability, given the government's more modest 1945 legislation had been declared invalid.

The rhetorical efforts of Chifley, Dedman and all their colleagues were not enough to win the argument for such a radical change implemented without the mandate of an election policy and against the combined efforts of the private banking sector. Bank nationalisation would be a significant, perhaps the most significant, factor in the defeat of the Chifley government in 1949.

1949 and Beyond

With responsibility for the Chifley government's most important priority, postwar reconstruction, Dedman was responsible for more legislation in the 1946 to 1949 term than any other minister. But he also had to hold a marginal seat.

As well as defending bank nationalisation, another electoral negative was Chifley's decision to reintroduce petrol rationing from November 1949, a decision motivated to ensure Australia was providing maximum support to the British economy. But the Anglophile Menzies was not above railing against the measure. Chifley's 1949 budget contained no electoral sweeteners despite the fact the Australian budget was in a relatively healthy situation. Dedman did not argue to Chifley that the government should be providing a dividend to the Australian people after so many years of austerity, something he later regretted as "we could afford it". Andrew Spaull argued with some justification that "If anyone could have persuaded Chifley to bend to electoral opinion in 1949 it was Dedman, but he remained silent."[29] Chifley, supported by Dedman, thought that the Labor government could successfully run on its record of having invigorated Australia's war effort and rebuilt for the peace. This was a miscalculation.

In Corio, the challenge for Dedman was elevated by the Liberal Party preselecting the famous and popular bicyclist Hubert Opperman. This move was the brainchild of Dedman's old nemesis, Richard Casey. Casey was by now Federal President of the Liberal Party. He was to return to the House at this election, but wasn't going to risk running in Corio: he ran in LaTrobe instead. But it he knew that "Oppy" would be popular in Geelong. Menzies wasn't in the loop and showed an uncharacteristic political tin-ear by not recognising the salience of Opperman's candidacy, telling Dedman's staffer Leo Warton, "They have made a present of Corio to your Minister. They have put a cyclist in."

Dedman was also at a disadvantage because the government had decided to significantly increase the number of seats in the House. As a result, Corio was effectively split in two, with the new seat of Lalor taking the strongly Labor voting areas of Werribee, Altona and Sunshine. He could have run for Lalor, and been guaranteed re-election, but his old friend and mentor Reg Pollard needed to vacate his seat of Ballaarat,[30] which would be difficult to hold and Dedman would never have contemplated running against him, so stayed in Corio.

Like 1940, the campaign was bitter. Opperman's campaign director was the Secretary of the Geelong ALF Club, Ivo Gibson. As well as being a Liberal, Gibson clearly had a strong personal dislike of Dedman and authorised flyers pointing out that, while Opperman had moved to Geelong, Dedman was always in Canberra or travelling. The Liberal campaign also pointed out that Opperman loved sport, whereas Dedman didn't even come to Geelong Cats games. The campaign reached a bitter nadir when Liberal advertisements alleged Dedman did not support private home ownership. Dedman was personally affronted and knew the damage such an allegation could do. He issued a radio broadcast denying the allegation and saying he believed that "no society could properly be described as socialist until not only some but every head of a family owns his own home". He even began legal proceedings for defamation against Gibson, but the Liberals kept repeating the claim.

The campaign was hard-fought and close, with Dedman falling just short with 49.7% of the vote, a tantalising 234 votes behind Opperman. His defeat has been described as "the greatest single surprise of the defeat of the Chifley Government".[31] He was bitter at his defeat and unfortunately gave a less than gracious concession speech at the declaration of the count. This did not serve him well when he later tried to regain the seat. In political circles, giving a bitter concession speech became known as "doing a Dedman" for several years.

Given the seat had always been marginal, and the defeat of Labor across the country was heavy, it shouldn't have been so surprising. But Dedman was so senior and high profile that commentators thought he had made Corio impregnable. And while the fall of the Chifley government now looks somewhat inevitable, it is important to remember that in those days before ubiquitous polls it was actually widely expected that the government would be returned with a reduced majority.

Just as his rise had been meteoric, so his fall was sharp. One of the government's most important members, the man Chifley had planned to appoint treasurer if they were returned to office, was now unemployed. He was considered to be appointed as the first head of the United Nations Children's Emergency Fund (UNICEF) in Asia, a position for which his experience in India and his considerable organisation skills and experience made him very well suited. However, in an act of deeply distasteful spite, the Menzies government vetoed his appointment on partisan grounds.

He had difficulty finding work and so had little choice but to return to farming for an income. Burnt from his tumultuous time as a dairy farmer, he turned to wool and bought a farm at Apollo Bay. This was a well-timed decision as wool prices were about to soar due to the Korean War.

He still had unfinished business in Canberra, and made two attempts at returning to parliament, challenging Opperman in both the 1951 and 1954 elections. A sign of how keen Chifley was to see Dedman's return to parliament is that Chifley, who had on doctor's orders agreed to campaign only in capital cities, made an exception to campaign for Dedman in Geelong in 1951. But he won only a tiny swing to take him 49.8% of the vote (he led Opperman on election night, but eventually lost by 134 votes).

Dedman attended Ben Chifley's funeral in Bathurst in the same year. In keeping with the widespread view that he had actually been Chifley's preferred successor, senior party figures approached him at the funeral about re-entering parliament as blocker to Evatt whom many regarded as temperamentally unsuited to the leadership. But even if a majority of the Caucus could have been persuaded of Dedman's merits, there was no seat available (running for Chifley's seat of Macquarie was not really viable) and the furtive plan came to nought.

In 1954, he again contested Corio. In many ways this was a more serious effort than 1951. He (any many others) felt Labor had a real chance in 1954 because of the state of the economy. He sold his farm and campaigned full-time, but his vote fell back slightly to 48.6%.

The 1954 defeat was to be his last and he took up the position of Director of Refugee Resettlement with the Australian Council of Churches, a position he was well-qualified for, with his organisational skills complementing his serious dedication to the Presbyterian Church.

The World Council of Churches was involved in the settlement of around 50,000 European refugees in Australia and Dedman was responsible for the Australian reception and settlement arrangements.

"I am very grateful that this period of my life, when I might have had a nervous breakdown from a sense of frustration of not being able to find something worthwhile to do, the churches gave me the opportunity to do something which was very close to my heart,"[32] he honestly and touchingly said towards the end of his life. He retired from that role in 1962 and he and Jessie decided to move to Canberra.

The ANU honoured his role in its inception with the award of an honorary doctorate in law in 1965. It was the next year, however, that he was to finally achieve an ambition that had been burning away in him for more than 50 years. The man who had his first attempt at a university degree stymied by enlistment in World War One and his second attempt derailed by appointment to the ministry in World War Two used his retirement to enrol at the university he helped found, and graduated with a Bachelor of Arts in 1966.

In 1967, he collaborated with Arthur Calwell, Frank Forde and Arthur Fadden on the rule which at that point forbade the release of cabinet documents for 50 years to be relaxed to 30 years in the case of World War Two documents, to enable historians to better research this important period. Also, as the Vietnam War escalated, he became involved in the moratorium movement.

Interviewed in 1967 for an oral history project at the National Library, he noted in his usual methodical fashion that "Actuarially, they tell me that my expectation of life is six or seven years yet."[33] This dry prediction proved to be prescient.

He lived long enough to see Labor's long period in the wilderness come to an end with Whitlam's election in December 1972. The incoming prime minister was good enough to invite Dedman and other Labor veterans Frank Forde, Sir William McKell, Reg Pollard and Cyril Chambers to lunch at Parliament House to celebrate. For lovers of Labor history, this would have been quite the lunch to be at. The main topic of conversation was Sir William's controversial decision as governor-general to grant Menzies a double dissolution election in 1951. "At the time some Labor people had been very angry with McKell's decision," historian Ross McMullin recorded. "But the lunch guests all agreed that McKell had been correct, since it was axiomatic that in such matters the Governor-General must always comply with the wishes of the elected government."[34]

This was an ironic conversation for such a group of luminaries to be having at the outset of the Whitlam government, which would end with a governor-general disregarding this axiom. Dedman wasn't to live long enough to disapprove of the Dismissal, however. He passed away in Canberra in November 1973. His state funeral occurred at St Andrews Presbyterian Church in Canberra, where he served as an Elder. Prime Minister Whitlam was a pallbearer. The House of Representatives carried the obligatory condolence motion, but the sentiments expressed by members on both sides of the House were clearly genuine. Whitlam, moving the motion as Prime Minister, said that "I believe the word 'great' is an epithet we should use judiciously on such occasions as this; I believe it can justly be used of John Dedman." The Liberal former treasurer Les Bury, who had worked at the Department of Post-War Reconstruction under Dedman, spoke the truth when he said, "the amount of ridicule to which he was subjected and pillorying over many years by the mass media over many years would have deterred a lesser politician, [and] were withstood by him in a very solid and brave fashion". Bury's party participated enthusiastically in that pillorying, but his tribute was heartfelt nonetheless.

Conclusion

John Dedman wasn't your typical politician. He was determined to do what he saw as right, regardless of popularity or consequences. He certainly wasn't your typical Labor politician. Not from a traditional Labor or union background, he rose near to the top and had some of the most important jobs in the most consequential cabinet in Australian history. Curtin and Chifley couldn't do it all alone. They needed reliable partners, allies and competent hands in cabinet. When in need of such a person, they usually turned to John Dedman. He wasn't perfect, he wasn't charismatic, but he was solid, loyal and passionate. He served Australia and Labor well in some of our darkest days. He deserves an honoured place in the pages of Labor history.

Chapter 5

GERTRUDE MELVILLE

A Tough Pioneer

When the Labor Party chose Gertrude Melville to become the first woman elected to the oldest parliamentary chamber in Australia in 1952, they were bowing to growing pressure from female party activists to have women finally represented in parliament and rewarding a stalwart of the party for five decades of activism and loyalty.

They imagined she would continue to advocate for the causes she had devoted her life to: better social services, support for migrants, education and more support for women's health. Little did they suspect they were picking a woman of principle who would use parliamentary privilege to make a stand for victims of police brutality and corruption in a way that would cause great discomfort to the longstanding Labor government and set her on a highly charged and public collision course with some of the government's senior ministers. Gertrude Melville would not abandon her principles in the face of the machine and pressure from the cabinet. But there was one thing she would not contemplate: crossing the floor or betraying her beloved party.

If the powers that be had closely examined her record in the party before her preselection, they would have found signs of the gritty determination in the face of adversity and willingness to stand on principle that would mark her parliamentary career. Hers was a truly remarkable political career. Although it was her husband who convinced her to join the Labor Party soon after their marriage in 1903, it was she who became the party activist.

She was not content to fulfil the stereotypical role of women in politics at the time of providing sustenance to the campaigning men and confining her activism to encouraging fellow women to support the cause. The New South Wales Labor Party in the first six decades of the twentieth century was a rolling battle for control of the party. Melville was a very active participant. And in the judgment of this author, she was consistently on the right side of history: staying loyal to the party in the conscription split, opposing the corrupt Executive of the 1920s, supporting Chifley and "Federal Labor" against the state leader and breakaway "Lang Labor", and actively opposing the Industrial Groups and breakaway Democratic Labor Party in the 1950s.

This is no small thing. While Melville was in tune with the great majority of the party in resisting conscription, plenty of people followed Hughes out of the party during World War One, never to return. Melville was an active and ardent supporter of Chifley and Federal Labor when Jack Lang dominated the state branch in the 1930s. Following Lang was the course of least resistance for someone interested in state politics, but she was never tempted to do so. In the split of the 1950s a Catholic like Melville may have been tempted by the work of the Industrial Groups and to follow them into the Democratic Labor Party. But not only was she not tempted, she actively worked against the groups, in support of federal leader Evatt.

Melville was not a "bit player" in these great Labor fights. She was an active participant in the arguments of the time as a member of the State Executive of the party between 1922 and 1926 and again between 1950 and 1952.

She was the first woman to be preselected by the Labor Party for the New South Wales Parliament although decades would come between her first preselection and her eventual entry into parliament.

She was one of the first women elected to local government in Australia, representing the Labor Party on the Cabramatta and Canley Vale Council in the 1940s and pursuing an agenda of promoting investment in social services and women's health at the local level. Her time on the council was also marked by controversy. She would not take a backward step when she considered that her honour had been impugned or her rights as an elected official had been compromised.

In keeping with the activist ethos of the times, she was involved in many organisations. Along with Kate Dwyer, Annie Golding, Millicent Preston-Stanley, Edith Glanville and 56 others, she was a member of the group of first female justices of the peace appointed in 1921. She was a vice-president of her local Country Women's Association and an executive member of the New Settlers League and its successor body the Good Neighbour Council, which was set up to encourage British migration to Australia and provide material support for new migrants.

And yet, this remarkable woman has been forgotten.

Early Life

Gertrude Mary Day was born in October 1884 at Port Macquarie on the New South Wales north coast, to Australian-born parents Joseph Day, who worked as a sawyer at the Hamilton Saw Mills, and Mary Ann (nee Dunbar). The family moved to Sydney while Gertie was an infant and she attended St Peters convent school in Surry Hills.

Not very much is known of her early adulthood, and the first significant recorded event of her adult life was her marriage to a New Zealand-born labourer, Arthur Melville, at St Patrick's Catholic

Church in The Rocks in Sydney in 1903 at the age of 19. Young Arthur was a member of the still-nascent Labor Party. A year after their marriage, Gertrude joined the party and they were both active members of the Paddington branch.

A motion moved by Gertrude at the Paddington branch calling for the introduction of child endowment in New South Wales was the catalyst for the Holman Labor government seeking to legislate for the endowment in 1919. The government passed the legislation through the Legislative Assembly, but it failed in the upper house, which Gertrude would enter four decades later. (Holman's successor as premier John Storey would also attempt and fail to introduce a child endowment. Premier Jack Lang would finally prevail in 1927.)

Battles for Control

To this day, the NSW branch of the Labor Party has a reputation for a certain toughness when it comes to internal battles for dominance. The modern branch, however, is a sedate affair compared to raging battles between the forces competing to shape the nascent Labor Party in the early decades of last century. Increasingly, Gertrude Melville was key combatant in those battles.

Any consideration of the battles for control of the New South Wales party has to begin with the 1916 Annual Conference. This is the conference that changed everything. For the first 25 years of the party's existence, no one group had been in control. Conferences and party fora had been a genuine contest for majority support from members based on the merits of the issue under consideration, with shifting majorities and uncertain outcomes. This changed in 1916, with a group of unions deeply dismayed by the support of the Labor Premier William Holman for Prime Minister Hughes' support for conscription and equally dismayed by what they saw as a lack of progress on industrial legislation. These unions, led by but not confined to the Australian Workers Union (AWU), organised and established institutional control via a majority on the floor of the 1916 conference. The takeover was in no small part orchestrated by the controversial and divisive AWU President, Jack Bailey. Bailey became the most powerful person in the party following the 1916 Conference. In the words of former New South Wales minister and Labor historian Rodney Cavalier: "Before 1916, the Labor Party was controlled by its members. After 1916, it was under the control of affiliated trade unions, which meant that the party was in the hands of whatever coalition of union officials could command a majority of the Annual Conference."[1] From 1916 on, the governing faction would change from time to time, but there would always be one.

By 1923, the dominant unions' control was strong, but it was then that they overreached. Gertrude Melville was by now a senior rank-and-file activist and she played a strong role in defeating the Executive, which was by then widely regarded as corrupt.

She was elected to the State Executive in 1922, but she was a member of an ostracised rump in alliance with a few other disaffected representatives of the rank and file and unions that were not part of the governing group. There were eight minority members, out of an Executive of 32. Her position on the Executive would give her a prominent vantage point for the 1923 conference.

New South Wales Labor Party Conferences are known for their robustness and the 1923 one was arguably the most robust in history. Whereas today's conferences last a weekend, this was no quick affair: it lasted for a fortnight, dragging on between June 2 and June 13. In the words of Jack Lang, it was "the most turbulent and dramatic in the history of the Labor Party. For thirteen days and nights, the battle raged."[2]

Some brief background to the battle is necessary. Following defeat in the 1922 federal and state elections in which allegations of corruption against the NSW Executive had played a role (especially in the state election), the federal and state leaders Matthew Charlton and James Dooley issued a statement calling for the NSW branch to be cleaned up. The Executive was not going to accept such an insult from the parliamentary leaders. They were limited in what they could do about the federal leader but they believed they had the measure of the state Opposition leader. They did not believe in half measures. The NSW Executive simply carried a resolution removing Dooley as leader of the party and expelled him. However, even this Executive would not remove a leader simply for criticising them. They needed another reason. They found it in Dooley's appointment of his friend JB Suttor to the Legislative Council when he had been premier earlier. The party rules required all Legislative Council appointments to be party members. The Secretary of the Mount Victoria branch asserted that he had faked Suttor's membership to enable his appointment. This was enough for the Executive to remove the premier from the party.

The Caucus might just have accepted the Executive removing their elected leader, but it was a bridge too far for them to also name his successor. The Executive appointed Member for Yass, and Bailey ally, Greg McGirr as leader. This arrogance was too much and galvanised support for Dooley in the Caucus. Dooley now had majority support.

With a stand-off between the Caucus and Executive, it was the Annual Conference which became the flashpoint, with the leader being forced to ask the conference to re-admit him to the party and affirm his leadership.

As a member of the small minority on the Executive, Melville played an important role, bravely authorising, with her fellow eight Executive members, a "Minority Report" of the Executive which was released on the first day of the conference, to set the tone for effort to wrest control of the party from the Executive. "Comrades!" the document began, "We, the undersigned members of the state executive… desire to place before you our views on recent happenings". There followed seven tightly framed and well-argued accusations against the ruling junta, under headings such as "Muzzling free speech" and "Treatment of the parliamentary party". The report mounted a defence of Dooley (and Charlton): "On December 21, 1922, the federal and state leaders, inspired no doubt by the allegations of corrupt ballots, issued a circular to branches and unions making suggestions whereby the movement might be strengthened and cleansed… We consider that the leaders acted within their rights and had every reason to be dissatisfied with the existing state of affairs."

Dissatisfied with the state of affairs the delegates certainly were. Luckily, delegates didn't need to wait the full 14 days to find out who would prevail. A combination of a strong majority of rank-and-file delegates, parliamentarians and unions which defected from the majority group (the Miners Union, Timber Workers and Municipal Unions and others) joined to form a new majority, forcing the AWU out of control.

Melville was re-elected to the Executive, but went from being a minority member to a majority member. She would continue on the Executive until 1926.

A Labor Candidate

Women won the right to stand for election to the New South Wales Legislative Assembly in 1918, but by 1925 the Labor Party had yet to field a female candidate. This was to change in that year. Labor fielded three female candidates in the 1925 election. The sequence of preselecting them meant that Gertrude Melville could claim the honour of being the first female preselected by Labor for the New South Wales Parliament. She was preselected for the seat of Eastern Suburbs, the seat in which she and Arthur were then living.

The electoral result for her was not impressive, however: 1057 votes, giving her 2% of the vote, putting her fourth among the five Labor candidates in the multi-member electorate (including behind the magnificently named Septimus Denbigh Alldis who polled second of the Labor candidates). The Eastern Suburbs division would provide the Legislative Assembly with its first female MP, but it was not to be Melville. Nationalist candidate Millicent Preston-Stanley polled 7958 votes, making her the last MP elected from the seat with two Labor, two Nationalists and one independent representing Eastern Suburbs.

The other Labor women contesting the election, Kate Dwyer in Balmain and Florence Ewers in Cumberland, also failed to win seats, although Dwyer did better with 7.8% of the vote and Ewers polled less than Melville with just 1%.

Melville would claim that the impact of the women running was not so much in electoral success, but rather in shaping policy; specifically, the policy commitment of Lang to introduce widows' pensions. With Labor still shut out of office federally thanks to the split of 1917, much of Labor's experimentation with improved social policy came at the state level.

Although Lang and Labor didn't emphasise its policy of a widows' pension until late in the campaign, it was a very significant element of Labor's policy. Melville would posit that it was lobbying by the three women candidates that brought it about.

A general commitment to widows' pensions and a child endowment had been part of Labor's New South Wales platform during the 1920s, but Lang for some reason had not highlighted the pensions commitment during the campaign. As Melville remembered it, the party's Women's Central Organising Committee demanded to see the leader before a public rally to demand that he commit the Opposition to a widows' pension and highlight it in the campaign: "Mrs Dwyer, leading the delegation, was very indignant, and after threatening to ask questions from the floor of the meeting, he (Lang) agreed to make a statement, which was that he would bring in legislation to help women and children."[3]

Lang's memoirs make no mention of such a delegation. He noted his own commitment, saying, "I was determined that the State must recognise its true responsibility to family life." He was not a fan of Melville because of her consistent opposition to him and may have been reluctant to give her and her fellow female campaigners any credit. He certainly recognised the centrality of the promise to his election win, judging that the poster which advertised the commitment to widows' pensions "did more than anything else to win the elections".

And win the election Lang did, with a 7.7% swing towards Labor. Following the election, his government legislated for a widows' pension and thus, as Lang noted, "New South Wales was the first government in the world to provide widows pensions on a non-contributory basis". Regardless of whether Melville and her colleagues were correct in thinking that they convinced Lang to make the pension a specific commitment, their long advocacy in the party for such measures played a big role in Labor's progressive approach to welfare for women.

The Lang Split and the 1932 Election

Melville sat out the tumultuous 1927 and 1930 elections which saw the Lang government defeated and then re-elected. This probably had much to do with the fact that she was otherwise occupied as a new mother, giving birth to Arthur junior in 1927 and Leonard in 1928.

By 1932, she was ready to re-enter the fray as a candidate in the district of Hurstville, which covered the suburb of Arncliffe to which she and Arthur had moved their young family.

Much had changed between 1927 and 1932 when it came to New South Wales elections. The state had changed from multi-member electorates elected on proportional representation to single-member electorates elected by compulsory preferential voting. Much else had changed as well.

In between Melville's two electoral forays, the Labor Party had again been rent asunder, split in two between supporters of the state leader, which formed Lang Labor, and supporters of the existing party, which became known as "Federal Labor" and for which Ben Chifley was the senior operative in New South Wales. There was no question where Melville stood in this fight: she was with Federal Labor and against Lang.

To understand this split, it is necessary first to have an understanding of Lang. He became leader in 1923. Having been vindicated in his fight with the State Executive, Dooley then resigned as leader. Lang, who had been a loyal lieutenant to Dooley, was elected by the Caucus in his place. His ascension to the leadership would mark the beginning of the arguably the most tempestuous and fraught 15-year period of the party's history in New South Wales.

Difficult to pinpoint on an ideological spectrum, Lang would best be described as a left-wing populist. He was fiercely and genuinely anti-communist and very passionately for government activism to assist the working class. His governments introduced worthy social and economic reforms. It wasn't his policies so much that brought about such turmoil, but his personality.

While he was elected leader by the majority of the Caucus, this was never to be his power base. Lang was a passionate, headstrong, determined and arrogant leader who paid his Caucus colleagues little in the way of consultation or regard. For much of his leadership he was at war with a majority of his parliamentary colleagues, state and federal. He did not care. His power came from elsewhere. Graham Freudenberg summarised well the dynamics of the power struggles that Lang engaged in with the federal and state parliamentary parties:

> These struggles lasted so long because Lang understood better than any of his opponents how to tap the sources of power in the Labor movement... The key to his conduct in the twenties was his vulnerability in the Caucus, and his recognition of its main cause: his appalling personal relations with most Caucus members... The main source of Lang's strength always lay in the Labor branches and unions. For two decades, he focused his skills and energies, with a singleness of purpose never before or since matched, to gain direct personal support from branches and key unions... By the mid twenties, Lang had created a hard core of as many as twenty thousand personal supporters ready to go to the barricades for him.[4]

This singlemindedness and stubbornness was to lead to the first of several party splits at Lang's hand in 1931. The genesis of the split was the by-election for the seat of East Sydney caused by the death of sitting member John West. The year 1931 was a very difficult one for the Scullin government to be facing an electoral test. However, the headache for Jim Scullin from the East Sydney by-election was not to come from his conservative political opponents. Preselected for Labor was the left-wing firebrand Eddie Ward. This was a time of competing economic plans. Treasurer Ted Theodore had a plan for fiscal stimulus and the creation of a Reserve Bank. This came up against fierce criticism and was derailed when Theodore had to stand aside to face corruption allegations. The conservative approach of austerity and deflation, which was recommended by the visiting British econocrat Sir Otto Niemeyer, was eventually known as the Premiers' Plan. Lang proposed his own prescription which involved the suspension (unilaterally if necessary) of government loan repayments to overseas creditors and the expansion of public works financed by an expansion of bank finance.

The sudden death of the Member for East Sydney John West would have political reverberations well beyond what would have been imagined when news of the worthy member's demise spread. The preselection of the left-wing firebrand, boxer and tramway worker Eddie Ward was one thing; the insistence of Lang that Ward campaign in the by-election in support of his plan, and therefore in direct repudiation of the policy of the government he was seeking to join, was quite another.

Lang was not constrained by any respect for the constitutional niceties of economic and fiscal policies being the responsibility of his federal colleagues. Such was his approach to politics that he demanded total control.

The Lang-controlled NSW party Executive resolved that Ward would campaign in the by-election in support of the Lang plan, that Lang and not Scullin would launch the campaign and that any federal MPs opposing the Lang plan would be expelled.

No self-respecting federal government or Federal Executive could accept such an affront. And nor did they. The Federal Executive in turn resolved that debt repudiation would contravene federal Labor policy and that if Ward campaigned in support of the Lang plan, he would not be admitted to the Caucus.

The moment of irrevocable break came when Ward won the by-election and Scullin made good on his intention of refusing Ward admission to the Caucus. Six Labor representatives in parliament then formed a breakaway party they termed "Lang Labor". Ben Chifley later recorded that "I decided then and there to fight Lang until I had seen him out of the Labor Party."

A special Federal Conference was held in March 1931. It fell to John Curtin to move the remarkable resolution: "That the Executive of the NSW Branch, having refused to acknowledge and accept the Federal Platform, Constitution and Rules is hereby declared to have automatically placed itself outside the Australian Labor Party."

Branches and individual party members had to decide: were they with the federal party or with Lang? Melville was in no doubt: she was loyal to the federal party. Unlike in the conscription split, her decision to stay loyal to the established party put her in the minority. Those activists who eschewed Lang showed the bravery which goes with making a conscious decision to be in a minority.

The split in Labor was to have the inevitable electoral consequences at both the state and federal level, compounding the electoral difficulty the Scullin government faced as a result of the Depression.

The federal election of December 1931 was precipitated when Lang Labor voted with the Opposition on an adjournment motion, denying the government its majority on the floor of the House and obliging Scullin to advise the governor-general to call an election. It was in this action that the leader of Lang Labor, Member for West Sydney Jack Beasley, won himself the lifetime sobriquet of "Stabber Jack". In the ensuing election, Federal Labor was reduced to 19 seats in the parliament of 75. In New South Wales, the supremacy of organisation and support for Lang Labor over Federal Labor paid results, with four Lang Labor MPs being returned but only three Federal Labor MPs surviving.

Not long after this federal drubbing, the people of New South Wales went to the polls in the most tumultuous circumstances in the state's political history. In the first of (so far two) vice-regal interventions to remove elected Australian governments, the Governor Sir Philip Game dismissed the Lang government on 13 May 1932 on the basis that a directive to state public servants to circumvent federal law was illegal. He commissioned the leader of the Opposition, Bertram Stevens, to form a caretaker administration on the understanding he would call an election. This the new premier duly did, with the election held on 11 June.

This was the context for Melville's second tilt to enter State Parliament, this time under the banner of Federal Labor. She contested Hurstville, against the sitting member Walter Butler who was Lang Labor and the United Australia Party candidate James Webb.

Like much of the rest of New South Wales, Hurstville was a disaster for both Labor parties. There was no fraternal cooperation between them. Federal Labor supported Game's vice-regal intervention as an appropriate response to Lang's irresponsibility and opposed Lang's debt repudiation as "immoral".

Lang's populist policies were more popular than Federal Labor's fiscal prudence, and the strength of Lang's support among Labor branches was clear. Federal Labor did not win a single seat in the Legislative Assembly, and Melville's performance in Hurstville was a mere 873 votes, giving her the support of 4.6% of the electorate. Lang Labor received a 20% swing against it in Hurstville, with Butler's vote crashing from 63% at the 1930 election to 43% in this poll. James Webb enjoyed a 15.6% swing to him. Federal Labor had decided not to recommend preferences for either Lang or the UAP, leaving its voters to decide which was the lesser evil. In Hurstville, this was a moot point. Webb's 51.6% of the primary vote meant that Melville's preferences were not distributed.

The two parties would keep their separate identities until 1936 when federal Labor recognised the ongoing superior strength of the state Labor Party and the necessity for unification if there was to be any chance of electoral success. The Australian Labor Party (New South Wales) was recognised as the official Labor Party and the Langites were re-admitted to the Caucus. Graham Freudenberg records that "The last official act of the Federal Labor Party took place on 2 April 1936. On the motion of Mrs Gertrude Melville, Chifley's staunch ally, the Executive posed for a photograph 'to mark the closing of the page'."[5]

The page was closed, but would eventually reopen in 1940 with another two splits with Lang in 1940 and again in 1943. Lang would have a lot less support in these subsequent fractures.

Melville would not seek to enter State Parliament again until her elevation to the Legislative Council almost 20 years later. Her level of involvement in the (federal) Labor Party would not wane over those years, however.

Into Local Government

With her very strong involvement in community groups and having seemingly been passed over for State Parliament, local government was an almost inevitable attraction for Melville. Women on local government were still a rarity in the 1940s. Local government in New South Wales had existed for a century, with the first council being incorporated in 1842. In that century, only six women had been elected to local government across the state, with the first being Lilian Fowler in Newtown in 1928.

And so it was the topic of much commentary and tittering when Melville sought and won election to the then Cabramatta–Canley Vale Council in 1944, becoming the first woman to serve on the council (the council would be amalgamated with Fairfield in 1949, making her the only woman to ever serve on the council). "The Knitting Alderman" ran the headline in the local Fairfield newspaper *The Biz* when profiling her. "Can any other Council or Shire boast an alderman who knits her municipal problems into a handsome cardigan while heated discussions on drains (and bus routes) never cause her to drop a stitch?" the paper gushed in appreciation of the novelty of a woman civic leader.

Melville was no token female on the council, however, and she was to show some of the same determination to pursue issues important to her that would later mark her term in parliament.

She focused her attention on social services, in which local government had an important role in both service provision and lobbying the state government for better resources. While her first act on council was to call for a new railway platform for Canley Vale, which was the ward she represented, it was maternity and health services she focused on in her motions and speeches. She pushed for a maternity ward for the local Fairfield Hospital, opining that it was disgusting that babies were being born in ambulances on the way to Liverpool Hospital. The McGirr Labor government was not forthcoming with a maternity ward with the alacrity that Melville wanted. A dismissive response from the Minister for Health, Labor's Gus Kelly, led her to declare she was "disgusted with the Health Minister", a sign that she would prioritise advocacy for issues over a blind loyalty to Labor ministers.

While some books reference her as having been the Mayor of Cabramatta, this is incorrect. Perhaps this misunderstanding arises from the request to her by the Mayor, Alderman Adams, to serve as his "Mayoress", an undertaking that involved hosting civic receptions and representing the mayor when he was unavailable. Although usually undertaken by the mayor's wife, Adams asked the council's only woman member to undertake the role because his wife was too ill to fulfil the duties of the job which was, in that era, a fairly onerous one.

It was a debate that would usually be regarded as an innocuous "bread and butter" issue which became the centre of the most controversial element of Melville's tenure on the council. During a debate on the distribution of new footpaths throughout the municipality, she interrupted the contribution of a conservative alderman, RA Light, in a way which the minutes of the meeting do not record but which Light took offence at. She was asked by the mayor to withdraw the remarks, but she went further and said, in relation to Light, "You could not put anything into your dumb head." Asked to apologise, she again declined. A motion was carried requiring her apology. A motion by her male colleagues was hardly going to persuade her, however. Instead of apologising, she took the rather drastic step of resigning from the council and immediately re-nominating. "I desire to tender my resignation," she wrote to the mayor, adding that "I much prefer to wait for the ratepayers' endorsement of my action." Whether or not it was an endorsement of her insult of Alderman Light, the ratepayers appeared happy enough with her performance as an alderman, because she was re-elected unopposed in the by-election triggered by her resignation. There was no requirement for her to apologise to Light on her triumphant return to the council chamber. He had had a glimpse of the determination of spirit that her parliamentary colleagues would witness a few years later.

The McGirr Labor government was engineering a program of council amalgamations to try and get more efficiency in local government. Sensibly, Melville supported the concept of Cabramatta amalgamating with neighbouring Fairfield, but opposed Bankstown joining the new conglomeration. Her popularity in her former ward wasn't enough to see her elected to the newly constituted Fairfield Council in 1949. The unpopularity of the Chifley government probably didn't help the prospects of Melville as a well-known and proud Labor activist. She probably thought her political career had come to an end with her defeat.

In 1952, when she and her husband Arthur left Cabramatta to move to Randwick, a well-attended farewell was held at the Soldiers' Hall in Canley Vale. The local state Member for Liverpool, Jack Mannix, presented Arthur with a gold tobacco pouch and Gertrude with a "wallet of notes". The local newspaper reported that "He spoke in glowing terms of the work done by Mrs Melville in the district and that she would be missed by the many people with troubles who were able to approach her." He also commented that she had been an "unpaid member". In fact, by this time, Melville was a member of parliament, having been elected to the Legislative Council earlier in the year. Mannix would have a part of the biggest controversy of her time in parliament.

Legislative Council

The scene for Gertrude Melville's election to the upper house was set at the Labor Party's NSW Annual Conference in 1952. The NSW Annual Conference was, and is, a political spectacle. Sometimes claimed to be the biggest political conference in the Southern Hemisphere, debate is usually rugged. The 1952 conference was the scene of a rare event in the state's political history: a change of management in the branch. Political historian Ken Turner described the conference as "the most sweeping defeat of an executive since 1939". Control was taken by a coalition of the Australian Workers Union and the Industrial Groups, formed to fight communism in the trade unions. This conference was the beginning of the right-wing dominance of the NSW branch which continues to this day (although the formal "Centre Unity" faction wasn't established until 1979). The Legislative Council played a significant role in the changing of the guard in the branch. The AWU's National Secretary Tom Dougherty (described by Graham Freudenberg as "huge in his physique, ambitions, arrogance and grudges") moved that members of the Legislative Council be regarded as ineligible to sit on the party's Central Executive. This change meant that eight members of the existing Executive were ineligible to serve any longer, and the AWU–Industrial Group majority used its numbers to fill those positions and take control of the party.

As part of the new broom and as an anecdote to the previous Central Executive's iron grip on Legislative Council preselections (in which the Central Executive often chose members of the Central Executive), the conference resolved that women and country members of the ALP should receive "adequate consideration" for Legislative Council preselections. The voting system for the Legislative Council was also opened up.

Having pledged that women should receive "adequate consideration", the preselection of a Labor woman in the not too distant future became a lot more likely. The opportunity came with the death on 16 June 1952 of Ernest Farrar. Like a number of active Liberals of his generation, Farrar had started his political life in the Labor Party, but followed Hughes and Holman out of the party over conscription. He had been appointed a Labor member of the Legislative Council in 1912. The rest of his career in the Legislative Council was spent in the various iterations of the conservative party and he became President of the Legislative Council 1946. On his death, Labor had to preselect a candidate.

By 1952, the Legislative Council was elected, not appointed – but not popularly elected. Until 1934 it had been wholly appointed by the governor, on advice of the premier of the day. Lang had made three attempts (in 1925, 1926 and 1929) to appoint enough new Legislative Councillors to form a majority. The first act of the newly formed majority would be to vote the Council out of existence, fulfilling longstanding Labor policy of abolishing this appointed house that was seen (correctly) as a handbrake on reforming Labor governments. Lang's attempts were frustrated, with governors resisting and delaying the appointments. In the end, Lang had appointed 25 new members of the Council when 35 would have been necessary, and the abolition had failed (Labor would keep trying to abolish the Council until 1960 when enough of its new members decided on balance that the upper house was rather a good place to be, and voted against abolition).

In order to stop future Labor governments "stacking" the Council with appointees pledged to its abolition, the Bertram Stevens Nationalist government in 1933 changed the method of choosing Legislative Councillors to election by members of both houses of parliament. Legislative Councillors were elected for 12-year terms with a quarter of the Council retiring every three years.

Ironically, given this system was designed to stymie a Labor majority being appointed to the Council, the existence of a long-term Labor majority in the Legislative Assembly gave the government a chance to build a majority by gradually replacing conservatives with Labor members. The Labor government elected in 1941 had engineered a majority in the Legislative Council by 1948, making the New South Wales upper house one of the very few state houses of review with a Labor majority.

And so Farrar's death gave the government (led by the new Premier Joseph Cahill since April 1952) a chance to extend its majority. The preselection of a woman for this vacancy would mean that she would receive the honour of being the first female elected. The two previous Labor women in the Council, Catherine Green and Ellen Webster, had both been appointed in 1931 and both had left by 1934 without making much of a mark.

Five women and 52 men nominated for the Labor preselection. Melville, with her years of service, was the favourite.

The Labor majority in both houses meant that once Melville had won preselection, her elevation to the Council was not in doubt. As it was, there were seven nominations including Melville and the Liberal candidate Laurence Farrar, the son of the departed member. Premier Cahill and the government's Council leader Reg Downing nominated her and she won along party lines with 43 votes to 30.

The novelty value of an older woman entering parliament is what most of the media focused on when she was elected: "A Grandmother as MLC" was one headline. "I am delighted," Melville told the media. "I'm glad that the Labor Party has shown its appreciation of the need for a parliamentary spokesperson for the women. I will do my best to put the women's point of view. I believe that the Labor Party's policy fully considers this viewpoint, when the policy is carried out in its entirety."

1953 was an election year, with the new Premier Joe Cahill seeking and receiving a mandate in his own right. So it was August 1953 before Melville rose in the chamber to deliver her first speech, which was to second the Address in Reply to the governor's opening of the parliamentary session. The Address in Reply gives members the opportunity to range across topics and not be limited by relevance to a particular bill. Melville celebrated the elevation of two women in her remarks to the chamber: her own elevation to the Legislative Council and Princess Elizabeth's elevation to the throne:

> I should like to say how delighted are the women of New South Wales at the Coronation of Her Gracious Majesty, Queen Elizabeth II, and I hope that all realise what a wonderful job she is doing as Queen of our country. I hope that it will be realised also that more women should join me in this chamber. My election to this chamber has been a great experience to me. I was a little afraid that a woman's entry would be resented, but soon discovered that my fears were groundless. I am very thankful for the warm welcome I have received from both sides of the chamber.

She went on to talk about the importance of home ownership, noting that "A man who is buying his own home becomes a better citizen. He is a contented man, and a contented man is a good citizen." She supported the government's health spending, and emphasised the importance of maternity services in particular. She continued her campaign from her time on Cabramatta Council, calling for the provision of a maternity ward at Fairfield Hospital.

Towards the end of her speech, she made a powerful case for equal pay for women (which would not become a legal requirement until 1969). "No one can deny that equal pay for equal work is only common justice, but again the cry of cost is raised. Why must it be the women who always suffer?"

Over the next few years, hospitals and health funding would be a common theme of her speeches to the Council. She also spoke on education and child welfare. She was very supportive of government policy, saying in 1956 for example that "The Minister for Education [Bob Heffron] will go down in history as the greatest reformer in the field of child welfare this State has ever had." (Heffron had been Education Minister since 1944. He presided over a large expansion of public education and significant reforms to the syllabus.)

Her socially conservative (although very mainstream at the time) views came through in her speech on the Publications Bill of 1955, in which she argued that "We are a Christian people. We ask God each day in this House for grace to do what is right. How can we deliberately shut our eyes to the soul-destroying effect of the ever-increasing flow of obscene, indecent, vulgar and sordid literature on our young people?"

Leading Loyal Labor Women through the Tumultuous 1950s

Although she resigned from the State Executive of the ALP on her ascension to parliament as she was obliged to do under party rules, she continued as President of the Women's Central Organising Committee, an office she had held since 1947.

She was the chair of the committee's Jubilee Conference in 1954, a fitting coincidence given she had been active in the committee for all of its 50 years. This conference, unlike the one to follow in coming years, was a happy and harmonious affair. The Executive noted in their report of the year's activities that a welcome-home reception had been organised by the committee to honour the wives of the Premier

(Cahill) and Lord Mayor of Sydney (Pat Hills) on their return from the coronation of the new Queen.

The Executive also reported that:

> Our President, Mrs Melville, visited Gilgandra Branch of the ALP in connection with the formation of a women's auxiliary. She reported that there were seventy-eight women in the Branch… Subsequently, Mrs Melville visited Broken Hill by invitation where interest in a women's organisation was stimulated. As a consequence, Broken Hill is now entitled to six delegates to the conference.

The conference also noted that "The year 1953 was rounded off by a very pleasant Christmas Party held at the President's home in Arncliffe." There was a very nice touch to finish the Executive's report to the delegates, with it being noted that "The Committee has purchased the portrait in oils of the Hon. GM Melville, MLC, which was entered in the last Archibald Prize portrait competition. Financial assistance for the purchase has been forthcoming from members of parliament and permission has been given for the portrait to be hung in the vestibule of the Legislative Council." The commissioning of the Melville portrait was to be the high point of harmony, for soon the Women's Organising Committee would be beset by the same ructions that would beset the Labor Party more broadly from 1954 to 1957 – the split.

By way of background, the 1945 Annual Conference of the party had established Industrial Groups to organise within trade unions in the party's interests and battle the Communist Party for control of the unions – a laudable goal. The Communists alleged "that the Groups would do the work of the Catholic anti-Communist campaigners".[6] While that wasn't entirely the case in the beginning, it was true that by the early 1950s the Catholic Social Studies Movement had come to dominate the activities of the Industrial Groups. Jim Hagan and Jim Turner explain that the Movement's origins "seem to go all the way back to the days of the United Front and the Spanish Civil War, but which was formally established in Melbourne in 1942".[7]

By August 1954, the Movement was supporting a challenge to HV Evatt as federal leader. Evatt dramatically denounced the Movement in October 1954, issuing a press release which asserted that:

> In the election, one factor told heavily against us – the attitude of a small minority group of Labor members, particularly in Victoria, has, since 1949, become increasingly disloyal to the Labor movement and the Labor leadership. Adopting methods which strikingly resemble both Communist and Fascist infiltration of lager groups, some of these groups have created an almost intolerable situation, calculated to deflect the Labor movement from the pursuit of Labor objectives and ideals. Whenever it suits their real aims, one or more of them never hesitate to attack or subvert Labor policy or Labor Leadership.

It was in this context that Melville wrote to her friend Edna Roper, the Secretary of the Women's Central Organising Committee (WCOC), on 9 January 1956:

> Dear Mrs Roper
>
> I desire to tender my resignation as President of the WCOC. I do so with regret. But I feel I am doing nothing to advance the Labor movement by remaining in office.
>
> The Committee seems to have got right away from the purpose for which it was formed; viz organising and helping build the Party.
>
> I have repeatedly told members that coming along in large numbers to vote is not the only function of the Committee.

It is impossible to get assistance at elections. No canvassers. Few speakers, and very prepared to give an hour or two a night for hospital votes.

At a recent by-election an appeal was made for helpers – four volunteered. Three of them old women.

My association with this Committee is fifty years this month, and I can honestly say it has never been so little use to the Labor Party.

With Best Wishes

Fraternally Yours.

She may well have had her frustrations with her comrades, but there was a context for her resignation that her letter did not express. Her close friend Edna Roper was more forthright when she sent her resignation letter two days later: "Recent happenings on the committee have convinced me it is no longer functioning for the purposes for which it was established." The "recent happenings" to which Roper referred were the development of warring groups with the WCOC, with one loyal to the Evatt and the other promoting the "Grouper" (i.e. Industrial Groups) cause. Melville and Roper were in no doubt where they stood: they were with the leader.

The WCOC met on the night of Roper's resignation. She was present, while Melville stayed away. The typed minutes of the meeting, while not being a verbatim account of all that was said, still show the tension in the air on the night of the meeting, even when being read nearly 70 years later.

There was a dispute about the minutes and questions about Melville's reasons for her resignation. Roper was asked to reconsider her resignation, but the minutes record that "Mrs Roper said she had definitely made up her mind." A motion to request Melville to reconsider was carried. There were motions to refer the dispute within the WCOC to the Federal Executive, and, when it was pointed out that the WCOC was a New South Wales body, to the State Executive. But the motion wasn't put to a vote, the chair declaring the meeting closed in exasperation at the arguments.

"House Divided" was the headline in the *Daily Telegraph* two days later. "Labor's internal troubles are too grave, too fundamental, to be covered up. The split manifested itself again at the Trades Hall on Wednesday night. Members of the ALP Women's Central Organising Committee put on what looks to have been a first-class row."

This first-class row was a minor skirmish compared to what happened at the WCOC Annual Conference in April. This was a row for the ages.

It would be hard to piece together the events of the conference by reading the official minutes and the correspondence on file in the Labor Party's records. But almost 70 years later, this author is very grateful to two of the delegates to the conference for their very detailed account, which has lain seemingly undisturbed in the bowels of the State Library of New South Wales for many years. Mrs S John and Mrs S Hoban were the delegates to the conference from the Broken Hill Women's Branch, which Melville had helped establish a couple of years earlier. Mrs John felt the obligation to provide a copious written report to her branch to explain what had happened at the conference. This account will draw heavily on John's detailed report.

Mrs John reveals that the conference seating had the supporters of Melville and Evatt on one side and the pro-Grouper dissidents on the other. Proceedings were civil while Premier Cahill delivered his annual address to the party's female activists. It was to be a short lived peace. "After Mr Cahill left," John reported to the good members of Broken Hill, "Mrs Melville addressed the conference. It was a wonder to us that she even got half way through because of the shouts and abuse which was hurled at her without ceasing. By this time we knew we were sitting on the wrong side of the hall and we quickly changed to the right side of the hall. As I said, the interjections were loud and insulting and cruel, but stout hearted Mrs Melville carried on."

This was an inauspicious start to the conference. The catalyst for its implosion was (not for the first or last time at a Labor conference) the credentialing of delegates. Mrs John explains:

> There were forty delegates from the Branches and Unions who were disqualified on the flimsiest of pretext and, as they were known supporters of the Leaders of the ALP, were forbidden to take part in the conference… Mrs Melville said "when I have read the correspondence, I am going to rule that they come onto the floor of conference – as fully credentialled delegates". That was the end of Conference – virtually.

The most active organiser of the Grouper-aligned delegates was Mrs McCarney of Granville branch. Mrs John reported to the Broken Hill members that "Mrs McCarney reached for the microphone and screeched into it because bedlam had broken out and it was impossible to hear one-self speak. She screeched, 'I move a motion of dissent in the President's ruling'."

Melville was ready: "Mrs Melville said 'You cannot move a motion of dissent when I have not ruled anything yet. I said WHEN I have read the correspondence relating to the delegates, I will move. I did not say 'I move'."

The Groupers were not prepared to bide their time and wait for the ruling to test the numbers. A delegate by the name of Miss Nyham turned off Melville's microphone, meaning she could not be heard over the din.

Another Grouper delegate, Miss Josie Freeman, moved to a microphone that was still switched on and moved a motion of no confidence in Melville as president. "There was absolutely no hope of regaining control while the Groupers were determined to keep up the disturbance and thus force Mrs Melville to resign," John reported. "Mrs Melville saw this and knew that very soon the Press would get to hear of the 'brawl' as it was termed in the City papers. So to try and redeem the Labor Party from the mud into which it was trodden, she said 'I have no other cause before me but to adjourn his Conference'."

While bedlam and discord were the order of the day, there was one important tradition that the members of the WCOC would not neglect. One of the delegates pointed out that as the conference was being held on the Queen's Birthday, it was incumbent on them to conclude the conference in keeping with tradition with a rendition of 'God Save the Queen'. John reported to her members that all delegates, "Grouper and all", stood to sing the anthem.

It wasn't the only singing that occurred. The delegates loyal to Evatt followed Melville onto the Goulburn Street footpath and sang 'For She's a Jolly Good Fellow'. John told the Broken Hill members that "Mrs Hoban and I were proud to follow Mrs Melville out of the conference because we knew we were following truth, faith and loyalty to the Leader of the Federal Parliamentary Labor Party."

The members of the Broken Hill Women's Branch were impressed with the report from their delegates, carrying a resolution to commend their stand and send a letter of congratulations to Melville.

Of course, not everyone sent congratulatory notes to her. The Groupers were sending in charges against her under the party rules, accusing her of acting unconstitutionally and provoking discord. In fact, a draft resolution of the State Executive condemning her remains in the party records, but this appears to have been a draft by a Grouper-aligned member of the Executive and wasn't carried.

The next two annual conferences, which Melville also chaired, went more smoothly. In April 1957, the credentialing process rolled out uncontroversially and she was re-elected as president with 174 votes over the Grouper candidate, her old sparring partner Mrs McCarney, with 79. At the 1958 conference Melville did use her presidential report, however, to make her views about the Groupers clear:

> for years there has been a faction which has determined that we shall not function as we should; we spent years fighting the "Groupers" whose sole aim was to destroy the Committee… I know I have been subject to much criticism behind my back, but the experts at intrigue and smearing within our ranks have worked on women, who are vulnerable and do not realise they are being used.

She also reported on her trip to China and Japan (this may well be the only overseas trip she ever undertook). The trip turned her into somewhat of a peace activist:

> I went from the Peace Assembly but with the consent of the NSW Executive. And I make no apology for my peace activities since my return. I only wish you could all go to Nagasaki and Hiroshima and see the dreadful effects of the bomb victims' cancerous burns, such as you could never imagine. It would make you resolve to do your utmost to save the world from such horrors and I do regret that the ALP did not do what the Women's Conference advocated some years ago and set up our own peace organisation.

Police Brutality

It was presumably a quiet enough parliamentary sitting night on the evening of 27 August 1958, with the Legislative Council considering the Address in Reply to the governor's opening of parliament providing an opportunity for members to wax lyrical on topics important to them. Given Melville's track record of strong defence of government policies and focus on health and social policy, ministers had little reason for concern as she rose to speak. She began innocuously, welcoming old friend and ally in Labor disputes Edna Roper to the chamber. Roper had become the second woman elected to the Council in April and had just made her maiden speech.

But by the end of Melville's speech, she had made accusations that would shake the Cahill government to the core, put her on a collision course with two of the government's most senior members and dominate the media for days. In this McCarthyist era, allegations were even made of playing into the hands of communism.

In August 1958, the Cahill government had its eyes on the election due early in 1959. This was to be no easy ride. Historian David Clune has well summarised the challenges facing the government:

> Labor had been in power for eighteen years and Premier Joe Cahill for almost seven. The government's support had been eroded by years of allegations of corruption and by conflict within the ALP. The federal electoral tide was running against Labor. Also, the Democratic Labor Party was in the field for the first time, a factor that many felt would finally defeat Labor in New South Wales. In the 1956 poll, the government's majority had dropped from twenty to six. In 1959 it was fighting for its life.[8]

The last thing the government needed was accusations of systemic police brutality on its watch. But that's what it got from one of its most loyal members, Gertrude Melville.

She knew that what she was doing was significant:

> I intend to say something that will probably not make me popular, but I have done that all my life. If something needs doing and others are not willing to do it, I will do it. I am alarmed at the increasing number of complaints about police officers. There are many fine men in the police force, but unfortunately there are many who are not fitted for the job.

She then proceeded to use parliamentary privilege to outline a series of cases of alleged police brutality.

The New South Wales Police Force had been under the command since 1952 of Commissioner Colin Delaney. In many ways, he was a reformer, dramatically increasing the number of police stations and embracing modern technology to improve efficiencies. New South Wales' first Catholic Commissioner of Police, he was also deeply conservative. Historian Garry Witherspoon has written that "Regarding homosexuals as Australia's 'greatest menace' Delaney made their surveillance and prosecution a major priority… Police methods of entrapment (using good looking young CID officers) were ethically dubious."[9]

Her language made clear that Melville had no quarrel with stern action against homosexuality, her concern being the entrapment of innocents: "I have been told by a member of the legal profession that he personally refrains from using public conveniences at night, not because of perverts, but because he fears wrongful arrest. He has clients who have been victimised in this fashion," she told the chamber.

She then went on to outline five individual cases of alleged wrongful arrest or brutality. The most serious case was one in which she noted that "I knew the victim personally." A man had been drinking outside a hotel when the police told him to move on. The man was arrested. By the time a friend went to bail the man out, he was dead.

> The local member of Parliament saw the man and told me that he had never seen a man so shockingly beaten; he was bruised from head to toe and appeared to have been kicked to death. An inquiry was held but it was conducted by the police, who of course found that the police were not responsible.

The speech was not confined to individual allegations. She also touched on more thematic concerns. "No honourable member can pretend to be so innocent that he does not know that a lot of funny business goes on about starting price betting and that a considerable amount of money is paid to some police. These men should be out of the force." Given what we now know about police corruption in New South Wales in this era and for decades afterwards, there can be little doubt that Melville was close to the mark.

The method of appointing magistrates also came under fire that evening. Magistrates in New South Wales were appointed from among the public service, not from the legal profession more broadly (indeed legal qualifications had only been required since 1955). This narrow pool from which to choose magistrates came under fire from Melville: "A clerk of petty sessions, if he passes the prescribed examination and has reached the age of 35 can become a magistrate. Now clerks of petty sessions are no doubt conscientious people in their jobs and remain so when they become magistrates… but they have been associated with police – particularly in country towns – all of their working lives."

She was keen to ensure the parliament knew who her target was when she reached her concluding remarks: "I am not attacking the Government, which I believe has always given people a fair deal, but is being wrongly accused. I am not attacking the Commissioner of Police, but some members of the police force are ruining its fair name… they are not fit to be in the police force."

Melville was no doubt genuine in her belief that she had sought to attack corrupt police as opposed to the Labor government. But this veteran of Labor politics was being naive if she thought the political reverberations would not rebound around the parliament.

"Bitter Attacks on Police by Veteran Lab. MLC" screamed the headline of the *Sydney Morning Herald* the next day. The article spread over three pages and accurately reproduced Melville's arguments. Through the passage of more than 60 years, the article provides more context than the colourless Hansard does, the journalist noting that "Throughout Mrs Melville's long attack, the Minister for Justice, Mr R Downing, sat with his head in his hands." "No comment by Minister" was the government's official response, according to the paper. Comments from the government would certainly be forthcoming soon enough.

This story was not going away. Two days later on 30 August, the *Sydney Morning Herald* again contained a prominent article, with new material. "MLC Claims She Can Give Specific Evidence" was the headline. Now she was calling for a public inquiry into her allegations, and, while still not explicitly criticising government ministers, her comments were hardly designed to de-escalate the situation or win favour from the premier. Melville had told the *Herald* that she was willing to provide evidence to an inquiry into her allegations, "But I don't intend to make it available to the Premier, Mr Cahill, or anyone else, until an inquiry takes place."

While not taking a backwards step, some of the stress she was experiencing was evident in the article: "After making her statement, Mrs Melville, who is 73, left her Randwick home to spend the weekend with friends at an undisclosed address. She said she was exhausted and in need of a rest from the drain of congratulatory phone calls and interviews after her speech in the Legislative Council."

By now, the Opposition had got into the act. The ambitious and effective deputy leader of the Opposition, Robin (later Robert) Askin, was the Liberal Party's spokesman on the Melville accusations. He was more than prepared to make hay. "The Cahill Government has been indicted just as much as police officers by Mrs Melville's attack." He demanded a "full and open inquiry". Askin cannily attempted to avoid unnecessarily annoying the police, painting the Liberals' demand for an inquiry as an opportunity for the police to clear their collective name and restore public confidence.

While Melville was prepared to double-down in defence of her claims, not all her colleagues were standing by her. It was now clear that the young man who had died in police custody had been at Liverpool Police Station. The MP who Melville had asserted had witnessed the bruising was her old friend Jack Mannix, the Member for Liverpool who had given her such a warm send-off on her departure from Cabramatta seven years earlier. He wasn't backing up her claims. "My opinion is that the marks on his body did not suggest he had been kicked or bashed. They could have been due to a fall caused either deliberately or accidentally," he told the paper.

Regardless of whether the bashing had occurred, it is difficult to believe that Melville would have told parliament that another member of parliament believed bashing had occurred without that MP having told her that was the case. Perhaps she was withstanding the political pressure better than Mannix.

There was another development in this saga, broken in this *Sydney Morning Herald* article. One of the cases of brutality outlined in Melville's speech was very close to home. The victim was her son. Melville had mentioned:

> a man in a country town who was arrested for drunken driving and brutally assaulted by the policeman making the arrest. As a result he spent about two weeks in hospital. At one point he was in so serious a condition that his family was sent for. In a subsequent civil court action he was awarded considerable damages but later was convicted of the drink driving charges in a court of petty sessions. He then appealed. However the judge hearing the appeal, on the night before giving his judgement, attended a farewell party for the magistrate against who the appeal was lodged. At the party were the Crown Prosecutor, the local inspector of police and other witnesses for the prosecution.

This case bore a remarkable resemblance to the situation facing her son Brian, with Melville telling the *Sydney Morning Herald* that "a policeman had kicked her son 'nearly to death' at Orange. She said he had spent nearly a fortnight in the hospital after his treatment in the cells… Her son had been charged with drunken driving and convicted… Later he took civil action against the policeman responsible and obtained a 200 pound damages verdict for assault. The action for wrongful arrest failed."

What are we to make of this? By modern standards of accountability and transparency, a member of parliament raising a matter in relation to a member of their immediate family and not disclosing the relationship would be a serious breach of parliamentary standards. However, despite the fact that the debate about her actions became robust, there was no public criticism made of her on this point, indicating that it was more in keeping with the standards of the time.

She may well have been inspired by the treatment of her son to closely examine other claims made to her about police brutality. The fact that her son had, in her eyes, been mistreated by the police does not mean that the allegations she made were ill-founded or illegitimate for a member of parliament to raise.

Her call for a public inquiry, taken up with alacrity by the Opposition, put considerable pressure on the Cahill government. As the *Herald* noted on 31 August:

> Mrs Gertrude Melville's scathing indictment of police methods came at a moment when the Cahill Government was trying to put the best pre-election face on its record. The veteran Labour MLC was careful to say that her speech was not intended as an attack on either the Government or the Commissioner. Intended or not, it could not fail to be damaging to the Ministry.

Cahill and his cabinet had to consider how to respond to the allegations made by Melville. Broadly speaking, the options were to accept that the allegations from a member of their own side were serious and order a Royal Commission or similar inquiry, or double down. The political pressure was on, with Askin indicating that the Opposition would move a censure motion against the government if the reply wasn't satisfactory.

That reply came on 3 September with the premier indicating that the government would not be going to the expense of holding a Royal Commission which would be "some fishing expedition". While Cahill was obliged to give a broad response on behalf of the government, he was statesman-like in refusing to attack a member of his own parliamentary team and did not reduce himself to commenting on specifics. This was not the case for two ministers in particular. Melville was on a collision course with two of the Cahill government's most senior members: her leader in the Legislative Council and the Attorney-General and Minister for Justice Reg Downing, and the Minister for Health and former attorney-general Billy Sheahan.

As well as being cabinet colleagues, Downing and Sheahan were cousins. They were both products of the effort by former premier Sir William McKell to strengthen Labor by recruiting high-quality candidates. Sheahan became Member for Yass in McKell's 1941 landslide while Downing had been encouraged by McKell to enter the Legislative Council. They were both accomplished lawyers. While Sheahan had built a substantial private practice before going into parliament, Downing has entered the Labor movement. By 1958 they were among the Cahill government's experienced and senior members.

These cousin ministers had different personalities and approaches. Sir Robert Menzies said of Downing that he was "by instinct and training a negotiator and seeker of compromise".[10] Sheahan was a more forthright political brawler. The difference of approach showed in the details of their responses to Melville.

First came Sheahan, who dealt with the allegations in the Address in Reply in the Legislative Assembly. His approach was a robust one, declaring "I deplore the attacks that are now being made upon a body of men who are the guardians of the law and protectors of the people." He did not hold back about his upper house colleague, opining that "In these times, with equality of the sexes and the demand for equal pay, the privilege of members of parliament is equal for men and women when they become members of such a deliberative body. Nothing in parliamentary procedure provides that in these circumstances more chivalry shall be shown."

He told the chamber that "I do not want to refer to the Honourable Gertrude Melville's son." He then proceeded to refer to him at some length, revealing to the Assembly that Melville had approached him about the case when he was attorney-general but that the evidence against him for drink driving was substantial. "Asking a Minister of the Crown to take some action was not the proper action in the circumstances," he said. "I do not like to see a collective force damned by a member of another place, though she belongs to the same party as I do and though she is a woman, supported by some newspapers… It is all very well for [the leader of the Opposition] and the Hon. Gertrude Melville to say that they are not attacking the police force. If that is so, let them give the information so that any person who has been guilty of a crime might be prosecuted."

Downing was less personal, although he did assert that she had provided "meagre facts" to support her case. He was speaking on a motion to call an inquiry into the Melville allegations, which was moved by the Opposition. This was a shrewd but predictable move by the Opposition. It was a wedge between Melville and her party. Melville had called for an inquiry but the government which she supported had decided against it. What was she to do?

It was an emotional and defensive Melville who rose to her feet in the Legislative Council on 4 September. "First I want to make it clear that I had no intention of attacking the police force of New South Wales; certainly I did not intend to attack my own Government," she stated, adding self-deprecatingly that "I must say I am not a legal mind; I am an ordinary housewife, an ordinary member of Labor Party, and have spent all my life trying to do justice to the people… I came here in innocence and perhaps I took the wrong action in bringing these matters before the House."

Support from the other side was forthcoming: "No, you did not" came the interjection from the Opposition MLC, the Queens Council and future Supreme Court judge, Colin Begg.

Melville spent some time responding to Sheahan. She had clearly taken offence at his contribution, more so than Downing's. "A press report states that a Minister in another place has suggested… that my speech was written by someone else… Who does he think wrote it? I thought it was suggested that my speech had been written by the Liberal Party, but I have since been informed of the general idea that it was written by the Communist Party." In 1958, this was a serious allegation. She assured the House that she had written the speech herself, with some assistance from Edna Roper and Mannix.

Her attack on Sheahan went to a new level as she defended her son. Parliamentary niceties were put aside:

> A Minister in another place lowered the dignity of a Minister of the Crown further than it has ever been lowered in this community. I say deliberately – and I am prepared to go before the Labor movement or anywhere else and say – that that Minister had lied. My son certainly was charged, and I am not ashamed of him. I have five of the finest sons in New South Wales, Australia or the whole world.

She went on to outline specifically what brutality she alleged had been meted out to her son: "That policeman broke my son's nose in three places and ground a fingernail off his hand. He put him in such a condition that on the Monday night his people were sent for. They thought he was about to die."

The peroration of her speech is where she dealt with the nub of the issue. Would she vote for the inquiry that she had originally called for? Or would she vote with her party? The Opposition wanted to know. The Hansard records the exchange:

> **Melville:** "I say deliberately that I am going on with this fight, by every means at my disposal, within my own party, to get something done for these people. I do not intend to vote for the motion."
>
> **Colonel the Hon. HJR Clayton:** "Would the honourable member tell us why?"
>
> **Melville:** "Yes, because I still have faith in the Labor Government. I still have faith in my own party. I believe that once my party realises that these things are being done, that things are as I believe they are, justice will be done… I am not going to help any other political party which tries to make this a political matter."

Melville's approach was perhaps inevitable. The government had a solid majority in the upper house and she could have voted for the motion without endangering that majority. But this party veteran was not the floor-crossing type.

Liberal MLC Arthur Bridges followed Melville with the declaration that:

> Had it not been for the concluding remarks of the Honourable Gertrude Melville I should have said that her speech ranked with the greatest that have been delivered in this Chamber. It was fully in accordance with our highest traditions and I am sure we all feel very sympathetic with her and proud indeed to know that she had the courage to bring to this House in the presence of the Attorney-General and all those who criticised her matters that call out resoundingly for strong and resolute action.

As with her previous speech, it was the newspaper reports the next day that give us more colour and flavour for the atmospherics of the chamber, not conveyed by the factual verbatim record of the Hansard. *The Sydney Morning Herald* tells us that Melville was speaking to a "crowded, hushed House" with many Labor women in the gallery to support her and many members of the lower house having made the trek from one side of Parliament House to the other to listen to her. She was holding a "large bag crammed with documents" as she spoke "in a voice trembling with emotion". She "frequently leant across the Government benches to wave a handful of papers".

The defeat of the motion for an inquiry on the floor of the upper house was not the end of the matter. Melville's longstanding friends and allies from her 50 years of involvement on the Women's Organising Committee rode into battle in defence of their comrade. "Women to Back Mrs Melville's Fight in ALP Executive" announced the *Herald* of 6 September. A combination of support from her female colleagues and the veterans of the Pro-Evatt/anti-Grouper faction was at play:

> Women members of the ALP State Executive are expected to take up the fight for an inquiry into charges by 73 year old Mrs Gertrude Melville MLC against police… Whatever the women do in support of Mrs Melville, they are almost certain to have the backing of the pro-Evatt members of the Executive, and possibly some of the moderates, giving them a majority vote.

The same article saw an escalation of the battle between Melville and Sheahan, with him responding to her claim that he had lowered the dignity of his office with the response that "The truth hurts. I am not going to amplify and retract anything I said in the Lower House about Mrs Melville." She wasn't giving him the last word: "If the truth hurts, Mr Sheahan must be feeling very hurt," she told the paper. Her parliamentary colleagues also received a robust appraisal from her: "Mrs Edna Roper has been wonderful… I won't say anything about the rest. But you can say that the attendants, waiters and other staff at Parliament House have stuck to me magnificently."

The battle would rage on for a little while yet. The following day, another article followed. "Machine Threat," screamed the headline. Unnamed non-parliamentary players were now sharing their views: "While Mrs Melville was taking her enforced rest yesterday, some Trades Hall veterans branded her cause as a lost one. 'Whatever she does, Mrs Melville must be crushed by the machine.' A Labour veteran said… 'it's a great cause Mrs Melville is fighting for, but my money is on the machine'."

The article confirmed that Melville was receiving a lot of support from the party's rank and file, which is confirmed by the many letters to the party office from branches that are still in the historical files. Despite the claim by the unnamed operative, Melville wasn't "crushed", but nor did she prevail. With no support from the premier or cabinet, her quest to have police brutality investigated petered out. No inquiry into police corruption would be held until the Labor Party under Bob Carr forced the appointment of the Wood Royal Commission from Opposition in 1995. The Royal Commission would find serious and systemic corruption. The Cahill government went on to win re-election in March 1959 with the loss of only one seat, with the police brutality issue mentioned but not made central by the Liberal Opposition. Before the end of 1959, Gertrude Melville would be dead.

The End

There are numerous mentions in the media coverage of the police brutality saga of Melville having to rest to protect her health. There can be no doubt that the stress of the political crisis took its toll on her. We can of course not be sure if it was a direct contributing factor to her death, from coronary occlusion, just 12 months later in August 1959. Both Premier Cahill and federal leader Evatt attended her funeral at Holy Family Catholic Church at Maroubra. Cahill himself would be dead two months later, the last New South Wales Premier to die in office. Members of the Women's Organising Committee, which had been such an important part of her life, formed a guard of honour for the casket outside the church. She was survived by her husband Arthur (who would die a year later) and her five sons and multiple grandchildren.

None of the published obituaries captured the length or colour of her service to the Labor Party. *The Sydney Morning Herald* came closest to the mark, noting that she had been a party activist since the age of 19 and making reference to the police brutality saga of the year before as well as her opposition to the Industrial Groups. Premier Cahill remarked that "The death of such a vigorous personality as Mrs Melville will sadden all those who knew her inside and outside the Labour movement."

Perhaps the most important tribute to her years of lobbying for a greater role for Labor women in parliament came with the preselection of her successor. The party now knew they were obliged to choose a woman to replace her, and preselected Anne Press. Press was no Melville, however. Melville would not have been impressed if she had known her replacement was not a loyalist like her; being expelled from the ALP for breaking Caucus solidarity soon after her election and eventually transitioning to become a Liberal MLC.

Conclusion

In 1956, the Labor Women's Organising Committee raised funds to commission a portrait of Melville, which the then President of the Legislative Council agreed would hang in the Council's foyer, in tribute to the chamber's first elected female. While the portrait was hung, it was, at some point thereafter, removed. It sat unloved and forgotten in the basement of the parliament for decades, an allegory for the memory of Melville herself. In the course of writing this chapter, this author made enquiries about the portrait's whereabouts, leading it to be rehabilitated. It is now proudly displayed in the office of one of Melville's successors as a woman Labor MLC, the Hon. Rose Jackson.

Just as it is right that the portrait be rehabilitated, so it is right that Melville have a more prominent place in Labor history than she has so far attained. A trail-blazer; a feminist of her times; a passionate advocate for what she regarded as right, in spite of the costs. Gertrude Melville was a remarkable Labor woman.

Chapter 6

KEN WRIEDT

A Quiet Achiever

Every government tends to be dominated by big personalities. The Whitlam government was even more prone to this phenomenon, both at the time and in the telling of history.

Whitlam himself, Cairns, Connor and Murphy are big names in Australian political history. In different ways Hayden, Beazley, Barnard and Crean are prominent in the history of the Whitlam government. Even non-parliamentary figures like Khemlani and Morosi are associated with his government in the public consciousness nearly 50 years later.

One name you won't hear mentioned prominently in the retelling of those tumultuous years is Ken Wriedt. This is unfortunate. Wriedt was a substantial figure. He was erudite, thoughtful and, importantly, more than willing to stand up to Whitlam when necessary. He was the second and final Labor Senate leader of Whitlam's tenure and was responsible for the government's agricultural policy throughout almost the entire term. This was at a time when agriculture was a much bigger proportion of the economy and employment than it is today.

Like most areas of policy, the Whitlam government had a very active policy agenda in agriculture. Also like most areas of policy, the Whitlam government's agriculture policy was controversial. Their determination to wind back subsidies and protections which favoured large agricultural producers was inevitably unpopular with vocal sectors of the rural community. Wriedt's accessibility and common touch went some of the way (but only some) towards ameliorating the white-hot anger of agricultural producers towards Whitlam, who did not make much of an effort to empathise with "the man on the land".

To the extent Wriedt is remembered, it is often for something he didn't do: a phone call he didn't receive; a meeting he wasn't invited to. When Whitlam was dismissed by Governor-General Sir John Kerr, he retreated not to Parliament House to plan his fightback with key colleagues in both houses, but to The Lodge to have a steak for lunch. He then summoned key staff and House of Representatives parliamentary tacticians to inform them the government had been terminated and to set the strategy for the government-in-exile. No-one summoned the Senate leader, meaning Wriedt was blissfully unaware that he was no longer a minister. His counterpart in the Senate, the Liberal leader Reg Withers, was fully briefed on the situation and instructed his senators to finally vote for supply to be allowed. It had been the blocking of supply which had brought about the constitutional crisis.

Historians differ as to how materially different history would have been if Whitlam had briefed Wriedt and a decision had been taken by Labor to deny supply to the newly installed government. Wriedt for one didn't think that the error made a big difference to the course of history. Of one thing we can be certain: Wriedt was embarrassed and angered, even humiliated by the error. Whitlam's actions were unfair to him. This was reflective of Whitlam's general lack of regard verging on contempt for the Senate and senators.

In many ways, the relationship between Wriedt and Whitlam is a useful historical tracker of the rise and fall of Whitlam. Whitlam was a great man who dreamed of a better, more modern Australia and set about delivering it. But he could also be arrogant and dismissive of colleagues, was too willing to tolerate unconventional public administration by some of his more adventurous ministers and was not always an easy man to work for and with.

Wriedt was a strong supporter of Whitlam's leadership from even before his entry to parliament. He had been elected but had not yet taken his seat in the Senate for the 1968 leadership ballot between Whitlam and Cairns (brought about mainly by the expulsion of Brian Harradine. Whitlam and Wriedt agreed Harradine should not have been expelled). There is no doubt he would have supported Whitlam had he received a vote. Whitlam in turn supported his elevation to the ministry and eventual rise to the Senate leadership. However, the events of 1975 saw their relations strain. Wriedt disagreed with the government's most contentious decision in his own portfolio, the abolition of the superphosphate bounty. Wriedt was in a small minority of the Caucus who opposed Whitlam's tactics in the lead up to the Dismissal. He thought the "crash or crash through" approach Whitlam embarked upon was more likely to lead to a crash than the happier outcome. Again, historians can differ as to who had the more meritorious argument. In Opposition their relationship was rent asunder. Wriedt was shocked and appalled by Whitlam's role in the Labor Party's attempt to borrow money from the Iraq Ba'ath Party. He became an active opponent of Whitlam's leadership despite being a fellow member of the leadership team as Senate leader.

Wriedt knew Whitlam's flaws better than anyone. But he also knew his greatness. Despite their differences, he said in retirement that "It would be a travesty of history if Gough Whitlam was not assessed as one of the greatest figures of the Australian political scene."[1]

In 1980, Wriedt unsuccessfully attempted a transfer to the House of Representatives in an effort to add to Labor's tally in that house. This was brave act, which misfired. Although he regarded his political career as over in 1980, it wasn't to be. A second act in politics saw him notch up a number of political firsts. He successfully made the quite rare transition from federal politics to state politics, being elected to the Tasmanian House of Assembly in 1982. He also achieved the rare honour of walking into parliament on his first day not as a backbencher, but as leader of his party. Defeat in the 1986 election saw him achieve a less happy record: the first leader of Tasmanian Labor not to serve as premier.

Wriedt was a good man – competent, caring and respected. In his early days as Prime Minister, Whitlam would confide in Governor-General Hasluck as to which ministers he thought were performing well. Wriedt was on the list.[2] Paul Kelly wrote that Whitlam regarded him as one of the government's best ministers[3] and would later describe Wriedt to this author as "calm and level-headed with an enquiring and effective mind". Alan Reid, the most prominent political journalist of his day, regarded him as "a man of strong common sense [who] had established a rapport and secured the trust of the rural community during his term as Agriculture Minister and helped considerably in retaining for the ALP that portion of the rural vote which the ALP did retain".[4] Similarly Susan Ryan, who served under Wriedt in the Senate, wrote of the Whitlam government that "primary producers were relentless critics, despite their liking for their hard working minister Ken Wriedt".[5] *The Bulletin* magazine (no editorial friend of the Whitlam government) claimed on 23 February 1974 that, while most Whitlam government ministers were deeply unpopular with constituents in their portfolio, "there is scarcely a farmer with a harsh word to say about Ken Wriedt" and reported that he had a 71% approval rate among farmers. His successor as Agriculture Minister, John Kerin, said of Wriedt that "he was a principled, honest, straight-shooting and straight-talking former seaman with little detailed knowledge of agricultural production as a practitioner but with a keen knowledge of the general political, as well as rural, situation." His friend and one-time rival for the Labor leadership in the Senate, Doug McClelland, told this author that Wriedt was "an honest, competent man, very comfortable with his own company but also welcoming of the company of colleagues". Whitlam's speech writer and Labor historian Graham Freudenberg regarded him as one of the government's most successful ministers.

Wriedt was a complicated man and a deep thinker. He didn't fit neatly into a factional stereotype and never formally joined a faction. He was regarded as a right-winger because he was a fiscal conservative and because he had done things like oppose Brian Harradine's expulsion from the ALP, and move at the 1964 Tasmanian State Conference to replace the party's socialist objective with one focused on outcomes, not on means. And yet his views on foreign affairs, civil liberties and social reforms would have been shared by many on the left.

His complexity did not end at his political views. He was a polymath. A lover of classical music, and a passionate aficionado of Australian Rules Football (and loyalist of Geelong Football Club). He loved cricket, as well as poetry. He loved everything about the sea and had a deep understanding of navigation and shipping. He also had a deep and abiding interest in and respect for Buddhism, so much so that many of his colleagues believed him to be a practising Buddhist.

As tall as Whitlam, Wriedt was an imposing figure. His good looks were widely commented on (his Senate colleague Ron McAuliffe called him "Gary Cooper without the horse"). The wide respect with which he was held across the parliament was not because he pulled any punches though: he had an earthy vocabulary and deployed it willingly against his political opponents across the aisle.

Wriedt was a Labor loyalist. He stood up for what he believed in, even if that put him on a collision course with a strong personality like Whitlam. He sacrificed his federal career in 1980 because he thought it was in the best interests of the party. He came back for more politics in 1982 because he was convinced by others that he still had a contribution to make to the party. He can be counted as one of the quiet achievers of the Whitlam years and his story deserves to be told.

Early Years

Kenneth Shaw Wriedt was born in Melbourne on 11 July 1927. His father Frederick was a fitter and turner of Danish ancestry and his mother Ivy (nee Renfrey) was a schoolteacher. Frederick's strong trade unionism rubbed off on Ken, the youngest of three boys growing up in the Great Depression. Wriedt described his family life during the Depression as "one hell of a grind of unending poverty at the time". Frederick was adamant that, regardless of their limited means, the three boys would stay in education for as long as possible and not be forced into the workforce. This attitude saw Ken and his brothers attend the prestigious University High School.

While Ken's support for Labor was inherited from his father, his love of the sea doesn't appear to have been particularly inherited from either parent. His nickname at school was "Admiral" and he kept a scrapbook of newspaper clippings about anything associated with shipping. Coming of age during World War Two, the only question was whether he would join the Navy or Merchant Navy. He applied to join Flinders Naval College at age 13 (then the age of admission for naval training) but was rejected because his marks were not high enough. "They only took the cream of the cream," he later explained. In 1943, he was admitted to the Merchant Navy aged 16.

Being a mariner in World War Two was a dangerous occupation. Merchant ships were often attacked by the enemy and many merchant seamen lost their lives. His service took him all around the Australian coastline, into the Pacific and over to the Middle East. Victory in the war did not end his service and he continued on in the Merchant Navy, returning to more normal contours for companies as diverse as BHP, the Australian Shipping Board, the British Tanker Company and the Anglo-Iranian Oil Company.

This continued service would introduce him to some of the other loves of his life. He was introduced to classical music by one of the other sailors on one particular trip in 1945. This began a lifelong passion. Writing about his introduction to classical music more than 45 years later, his emotion is palpable: "the light was revealed to me in a dirty little iron carrier by the illustrious name of 'Iron Warrior'… it was a turning point in my life".[6] He became particularly fond of the Russian composers and nominated Alexander Scriaban and the French Francis Poulenc as particular favourites. Doug McClelland recounted to this author that when colleagues would go to Wriedt's Parliament House office for a meeting, a record player would always be playing classical music. He would turn the volume down to conduct a meeting, but not turn the music off.

Some Indian crewmates introduced him to Buddhism and thus began a lifelong fascination and affinity with that religion. Throughout his life his affinity with Buddhism would assist him in looking at things philosophically and taking the "long view". "The principles of Buddhism have been around for 2000 years and will be around in 2000 years time. The bloody Tasmanian forest debate won't be around in 2000 years," he said later in life.

Long sea journeys gave him plenty of time for reading and this helped with the development of his political consciousness and a growing interest in international affairs. The British left-wing magazine the *New Statesman*, the newspaper the *Guardian* and the international edition of the *New York Times* were his staples. These spurred an interest in international relations which stayed with him through his life. The reading material of the most influence on him in his political development was the book *The Martyrdom of Man* by Winwood Reade which he said opened his eyes to the "the enormity of injustice in the world" and fired his sense of social justice. Written in 1872, it has been described as a secular history of the Western world.

While his war service was dangerous, it was his postwar service that almost saw his life tragically cut short. In 1950, while docking his ship in Mackay as Ship's Mate, he fell off the bridge, hit his head on a girder and then fell into the water, unconscious. He suffered six broken ribs, a punctured lung and a broken collar bone. Doctors at Mackay Hospital estimated he may have two hours to live. His parents received a terse and no doubt horrifying telegram which read "Come immediately, condition very low." This led to Fred and Ivy Wriedt's first ever aeroplane trip as they rushed to Mackay to be by his bedside. After seven weeks in the hospital followed by another seven weeks in a Melbourne hospital, he somehow pulled through.

This accident did not diminish his love of the sea. He continued on merchant ships and competed in the sixth annual Sydney to Hobart yacht race in 1950.

The Merchant Navy went on to introduce him to two more loves: Tasmania and a young woman who lived there, Helga Burger. He fell in love with Tasmania the first time he sailed down the Derwent River and decided to move there in 1958.

Ken's mind was turning to settling down and he started to spend more time in Tasmania and less at sea. When ashore, he did various jobs, including working seasonally at a fruit company where Helga was one of the office employees. Helga was from Lower Saxony, her family migrating from Germany to Australia in 1951.

It was a rapid romance. They were married on Boxing Day 1959 in Hobart. Wriedt spent more time on land and less at sea after his marriage and the arrival of their daughters Sonya and Paula. He got a job in the Tasmanian Government Insurance Office (TGIO) and continued to work there until 1965 when he became Tasmanian state director of Community Aid Abroad, a job he held until he entered the Senate.

Into the Labor Party

As he settled into domestic life in Hobart, he finally joined the Labor Party in 1960. "I joined the Labor Party with no intention of running for Parliament, but it was put to me soon after joining that I should," he would later say.

This encouragement to run for parliament would have been partly as a result of his activism and organisational skills. He quickly became a branch secretary and then secretary of the Franklin Federal Electorate Division (now known as federal electoral councils).

He may not have had parliamentary ambitions when he joined the Labor Party in 1960, but the encouragement he received from members of the party didn't take long to lure him into putting his name forward. In 1961, he nominated for preselection for Franklin in the House of

Representatives. He lost the preselection and ran again in 1963, but again fell short. On neither occasion did the candidate successful in the preselection win the seat.

He then turned his attention to state politics. He won the right to contest the state seat of Franklin in 1964 as one of the eight Labor candidates for seven seats under the Hare–Clark proportional representation system but wasn't successful. He not unreasonably thought after this latest setback, "Maybe this is not my cup of tea."

A pivotal point in his career came in 1966.

Wriedt didn't seek preselection for the 1966 federal election, but instead became campaign manager for his friend Neil Batt's run for the seat of Denison. This was a difficult year for Labor. The Vietnam War was still popular with the Australian people and the new Prime Minister Harold Holt had reinvigorated the government, but Wriedt advised Batt to confront the Vietnam War head-on and explain to voters his reasoning for opposing it, rather than trying to minimise it as an issue. He also brought his considerable organisational skills to the campaign and developed a rudimentary – but for the time, cutting-edge – form of voter targeting. Door-knockers were despatched across the electorate. Their task was not to persuade voters, but to ask the person answering the door whether they always voted for the same party or considered themselves swinging voters. Residents who indicated they were "rusted on" to a particular party received no more attention from the campaign. Voters who indicated they were open to changing their vote received a personal visit from the candidate.

As a result, Denison was one of only two seats across Australia to record a swing to Labor. Whereas Labor's vote nationally fell by 4.5%, Batt increased the Labor vote in Denison by 6.2%, forcing the sitting Liberal MP to preferences.

A friendship with Batt was cemented. Their careers would intersect in ways that neither of them could have predicted in 1966, but their friendship would last for decades.

Wriedt's skills were also brought to the attention of senior party figures. While Wriedt had assumed his parliamentary career was over before it had started, the Tasmanian Labor Party's most senior federal representative, Lance Barnard, encouraged him to put his name forward for preselection for the ticket in the 1967 half-Senate election. Longstanding Senator Nick McKenna was retiring from politics, so there was a vacancy to be filled.

He followed Barnard's advice and put his name forward for preselection at the Tasmanian State Conference. In these days of less rigid factionalism, the result of the ballot was unpredictable. It resulted in success for Wriedt, winning second place on the party's Senate ticket, behind the sitting Senator Bob Poke. He forced fellow merchant-mariner Ray Sherry into the unlikely third spot on the ticket (Sherry would go on to win Franklin in 1969). Ironically, given that Lance Barnard was the one who had encouraged him to run, the other candidate he defeated in the preselection was Michael Barnard, nephew of the senior figure and member of a Tasmanian Labor dynasty. Michael would go on to enter the State Parliament and serve as deputy premier.

Half-Senate elections are no longer the norm in Australian politics, as governments avoid the challenge of a "national by-election", a chance for the people to send the government a message. Following the massive triumph of 1966, the 1967 Senate election was a setback for the Holt government, although Gough Whitlam's first electoral test as leader did not translate into an increase in Labor senators. Across the country, the Holt government lost two Senate seats to the

DLP. Tasmania was a status-quo result, with Labor and the Liberal Party retaining two seats each and the independent Senator Reginald "Spot" Turnbull being re-elected.

And so, after a comparatively short period of seven years of activism in the Labor Party, Ken Wriedt found himself elected to the Australian Senate.

Into the Senate

He took his place in the Senate on 1 July 1968. Between the election and the new senators taking their place, Harold Holt had gone missing, presumed drowned, and John Gorton had become prime minister. The scene was set for a titanic battle between Whitlam and the successors of Menzies.

Wriedt's maiden speech in the Senate was a blend of his domestic and international interests. He railed against the "shameful and futile war in Vietnam", condemned the Holt government's handling of the purchase of F-111 aircraft and strongly supported the two-airlines domestic air policy. Interestingly, he also called for the establishment of a national superannuation scheme, something which would have to wait for the advent of the Keating government.

Aviation policy dominated his early years in parliament. He spent many hours dealing with the JetAir scandal (an allegation that William McMahon as Foreign Minister had mishandled the purchase of aircraft for foreign aid to Cambodia and that a deal had been done for a good price for the government to purchase the aircraft in return for JetAir being allowed to compete with TAA and Ansett in Australia). He was also active in the parliamentary discussion of Sir Peter Abeles' attempt to take over Ansett between 1970 and 1972 (Abeles would eventually succeed in 1979).

His interests in foreign affairs and international relations continued. He became one of the key Tasmanian organisers of the anti-war moratorium movement.

His policy horizons were further expanded when Labor leader in the Senate, Lionel Murphy, asked him to serve on the Senate Select Committee on Security and Exchange. This committee, chaired by his Tasmanian Liberal Senate colleague Peter Rae, was established to examine whether insider trading should be specifically banned in corporations law. Remarkably, there was no explicit ban on company officers sharing confidential information with friends and family to make money in share trades. What restrictions did exist on corporate behaviour like insider trading were very limited in scope and difficult to enforce. In addition, most corporate regulation was governed by state laws (the various stock exchanges were still state-based) so regulation was fragmented. The stock market boom of the late 1960s meant attention was drawn to this hole in corporate law. The committee was established to determine whether the law should be tightened. Wriedt and his Labor colleagues on the committee needed little convincing. Senator Rae was equally determined to reform the law but received considerable pressure from his Liberal colleagues who, extraordinarily, saw no need for government intervention to stop insider trading. Rae was a courageous politician who withstood the pressure.

The committee recommended that "fundamental reform" was required, with insider trading specifically banned and that an Australian Securities Commission be established to enforce corporate law. The inquiry process was long and the committee did not issue its final report until 1974. The Whitlam government fell before the report's recommendations could be enacted. It would be a long and slow process over decades but the recommendations of the Rae

Committee would eventually form the basis for corporate law reform in Australia.

Minister for Primary Industry

Like every Labor member of parliament, Wriedt's life was changed irrevocably on 2 December 1972, as Whitlam finally led Labor to victory after 23 years in the wilderness.

There was no time to lose for the new government, with Whitlam and his deputy Lance Barnard forming the first (and so far only) duumvirate cabinet in history so that they could begin the process of reform after 23 long years. As an aside, Whitlam's decision to appoint himself and Barnard only is an interesting insight into his lack of regard for the Senate, which he considered a fundamentally undemocratic institution, to be treated with general disdain. He could easily have appointed a temporary "quad" cabinet by adding the Senate leaders Lionel Murphy and Don Willesee. This lack of regard for the Senate would, in due course, contribute to great tension between Whitlam and Wriedt.

Wriedt had been a diligent senator but was not necessarily an obvious candidate for the ministry. The only historical evidence of any discussion with his colleagues on being a possible minister in a Whitlam government is the record of a conversation between Wriedt and Member for Hindmarsh Clyde Cameron in 1970. He and Cameron recorded quite different versions of this conversation. Cameron's version is not flattering to Wriedt, but nor is it necessarily accurate.

Wriedt was a member of the party's National Executive from 1970 to 1980. Writing in his diary years later, in 1976, Cameron asserted that he lobbied Wriedt to vote in support of federal intervention in the Victorian branch of the party to remove the radical left-wing Secretary

Bill Hartley and impose a State Executive more interested in electoral victory than the ruling group. According to Cameron's version, he told Wriedt that he would be a minister in the Whitlam government, and so should vote for intervention to help bring that eventuality about. Cameron asserts that Wriedt was surprised and said, "Me! You must be joking." Cameron also claimed than when he told Whitlam he had held out the prospect of a ministerial birth to shore-up his support for intervention, Whitlam exploded in anger because Wriedt was not worthy of such support. Under Wriedt's version, recorded in oral history by the National Library many years later, Wriedt simply laughed when Cameron raised the prospect of promotion. Cameron's version suffers because Wriedt was not a natural supporter of Hartley and would have been strongly inclined to support intervention based on his actions before and after (in 1976 he would lead the calls for the expulsion of Hartley from the party over the Ba'ath Party loans scandal, which will be dealt with later in this chapter). Indeed, Wriedt seconded Cameron's motion for intervention – hardly the actions of a waverer.

In any event, when the Caucus came to vote on who would serve in the cabinet on a more permanent basis, Wriedt put his name forward in the first round of ballots. He claimed not to have campaigned among his colleagues for a vote. He was, however, on the influential "Whitlam–Barnard ticket" of preferred ministers. We can safely surmise that, just as Barnard had urged him to run for the Senate five years earlier, the deputy prime minister had been influential in urging Whitlam to include his fellow Tasmanian on the preferred list.

He only received 36 primary votes from his 97 Caucus colleagues. This placed him behind Senate colleagues John Wheeldon and Justin O'Byrne. When preferences were distributed he rocketed to 49 votes and was catapulted into the cabinet.

Then came the allocation of portfolios by Whitlam. Given his experience, Wriedt may well have hoped and expected Transport or Navy in the ministerial allocations (he also pined for Foreign Affairs, but this was optimistic for a first-time ministerial appointment). Jenny Hocking has described Wriedt's appointment as Minister for Agriculture as a "surprising move",[7] which is a fair summation. The accepted frontrunners for the role were Labor's rural members of the House of Representatives: Al Grassby (Riverina), Rex Patterson (Dawson) and Doug Everingham (Capricornia). Of the three, it was Patterson who was most interested in agricultural policy and wanted the job. But as historian and speech writer Graham Freudenberg explains, Whitlam "believed that a minister in the House of Representatives in a marginal seat would be too vulnerable to industry lobbying and parochial pressures".[8]

In 1972, agriculture represented 47% of Australian exports (compared to 11% today) and also represented a very substantial budget outlay because of the array of subsidies and bounties that had grown over 23 years of Liberal–Country Party rule. To be Minister for Agriculture in the Whitlam government was a substantial job, not only because of the importance of primary production to the economy, but also because there would be a significant and substantial reform agenda in the portfolio. Wriedt freely acknowledged that he knew nothing about agriculture as he set about the task. "I don't know the difference between a Corriedale and Merino," he quipped. His staff joked that they would have to walk behind him on farm visits and whisper "cows go moo, sheep go baa" so he wouldn't get his farm animals confused. Country Party leader Doug Anthony made the obligatory complaint that always comes from the party when Labor appoints an agriculture minister from the city. "It's an insult," he predictably opined.

Wriedt dealt with the cynicism and his lack of knowledge by throwing himself into the task, mastering his brief and making himself accessible to rural advocates. By the end of his time as minister, even ferocious opponents of the Whitlam government's agricultural policy would credit his work ethic and understanding of the issues.

His consultative and incremental style of reform was in contrast to Whitlam's more aggressive approach, and there would be tension between the two of them on matters of policy. They were, however, as one on the need for reform in agricultural policy.

The policy approach of the Whitlam government in agriculture could best be summarised as seeking to transform policy from being in the producers' interest to being in the national interest. This was hugely controversial, especially for producers!

Whitlam and Wriedt inherited a complex array of policy interventions designed to benefit agricultural producers (especially very large ones), which skewed production decisions very significantly. As future agriculture minister John Kerin described it: "Under the policies known as McEwenism, the Liberal Country Party coalition had indulged in nearly every form of agricultural protection, assistance and subsidisation known to mankind."[9]

As Whitlam himself put it:

> The very largest producers usually acted as the spokesmen for rural industry. Independent assessments by government departments or inquiries were rarely developed to scrutinise their demands. The large producers advocated policies which suited their financial interests but not necessarily those of small producers or country towns... it thus became the task of my Government to rationalise the uninformed, unrepresentative and inequitable nature of rural policy in Australia.[10]

In keeping with Whitlam's point that agricultural policy had built up in an ad hoc way with little regard to rationality or the national interest, the last agricultural white paper had been produced in 1952. And so in 1973 Wriedt commissioned the production of a review of agricultural policy led by the Deputy Secretary of the Department of Overseas Trade Stuart Harris, the eminent economist and bureaucrat Sir John Crawford and the economist Fred Gruen. Unsurprisingly for a process dominated by economists, the review emphasised the need for fewer subsidies and a more market-driven approach to agricultural policy.

Because this review was underway, the most controversial agricultural decisions came towards the end of 1974 and into 1975.

In the meantime, Wriedt set about reforming the various marketing and production boards that were strewn throughout the portfolio. Under the Country Party, these boards had consisted almost entirely of producer interests. Again in the words of Whitlam, "Ken Wriedt ended decades of large producer domination of the boards of wool, dairy, apple and pear marketing authorities by creating an increased number of positions for representatives of employees and the Australian Government and appointing members with special qualifications."[11]

During the course of 1973, the Whitlam government also set about the task of reforming the longstanding Tariff Board, transforming it into the Industries Assistance Commission (IAC). For the first time, agricultural subsidies and bounties were to be referred to the commission to assess whether they were in the national interest.

The two most controversial elements of agricultural policy, however, were not referred to the IAC, much to Wriedt's chagrin. Instead, the decisions to reduce the floor price for wool and to abolish the superphosphate bounty were taken by cabinet, against Wriedt's recommendation on both occasions. Eventually, he prevailed on the wool floor-price but he was defeated in the matter of the bounty. The decision to abolish the superphosphate bounty is remembered to this day as one of the Whitlam government's most "courageous" decisions. In the judgment of Wriedt, the fact that he was overruled on the bounty would alter Australian political history, as is discussed further below.

Since 1970, a ministerially prescribed floor price for wool had existed. This floor price, effectively subsidised by the government, was designed to smooth the rough edges of the volatile wool market and give producers a more stable income. This mechanism was possible because the Australian Wool Commission would buy wool when the market price was below the floor price and hold it to be sold when prices recovered.

In May 1974, as part of his effort to get the fiscal situation under control, Acting Treasurer Bill Hayden demanded the floor price be reduced from $2.50 a kilogram to $2. Wriedt resisted this in the cabinet, but Hayden carried the day.

The matter still had to go to Caucus for approval. The cabinet decision leaked before the Caucus discussion and there was very strong resistance from the wool industry. A protest was planned for Parliament House. In the Whitlam government, strict cabinet solidarity did not apply and ministers could seek to overturn cabinet decisions they disagreed with. There are varying versions of how the Caucus meeting played out. By Wriedt's recollection, he did not actively oppose the submission but answered "It should stay where it is" when Caucus members demanded to know "What does Ken think?" Other versions have Wriedt declaring he was in an invidious position because he disagreed with a position he was meant to recommend. In any event, a combination of Wriedt's opposition and Caucus concern for the political ramifications saw Caucus overturn the cabinet decision by a vote of 52 to 29. Author and journalist Paul Kelly would describe this as "the most decisive rebuff of the Cabinet in the three year history of the Whitlam Government".[12]

Wriedt was even more strongly opposed to the abolition of the superphosphate bounty in 1974 but did not prevail on this occasion. The bounty had been introduced in 1941. In the words of Whitlam, it was "a wartime measure designed to increase both farm productivity and farmer education on the need to overcome the serious phosphorous deficiency in Australian soils".[13] It was not paid to farmers directly, but was paid to fertiliser producers to reduce the price of the product. The Menzies government had abolished the bounty in 1950 due to the massively increased farm incomes as a result of the Korean War boom. It had been reintroduced in 1963 in the face of declining farm incomes. Now, the agricultural policy review led by Harris, Gruen and Crawford again recommended its abolition as part of their general support for less intervention and in the face of rising farm incomes.

Wriedt opposed the abolition in cabinet. He argued the government should use their newly installed powers to refer the bounty to the IAC so that the case for reform could be built over time. Again, Hayden as Acting Treasurer was desperate for budget savings and wanted the $56 million bounty cut without delay.

This time, there was no overturning the decision. Wriedt was not keen to announce a decision he profoundly disagreed with. The cabinet decision was made on 22 January 1974. The anger Whitlam felt with his relevant ministers was evident in his account written more than a decade later:

> When I returned to Australia on February 13, I found that the Cabinet decision had not been announced. My colleagues the Treasurer Frank Crean and Primary Industry Minister Wriedt had been haggling for three weeks over who should announce

the glad tidings. It did not occur to them they could make a joint announcement. I intervened to end the delay by announcing the decision on February 15. Due to the competitive courage of my colleagues, I became the subject of subsequent invective and a public campaign launched against the decision to abolish the bounty.[14]

Whitlam was disingenuous if he really believed the biggest problem with the decision to abolish the bounty was the (lack of) announcement strategy or that he would have avoided much of the opprobrium for the decision if he had not announced it personally.

A large campaign of anti-Whitlam-government rallies ensued around the country. Whitlam got a taste of the anger when he opened the Lardner Agricultural Show in the Gippsland region on 19 February, just four days after the announcement. A large group of protestors disrupted his speech. Whitlam, in his words, tried to "placate" the protestors by pointing out that "never has a government done so much to reduce costs. My government is the first in forty years to reduce tariffs for farming implements and equipment. Your incomes have trebled in three years. You've never had it so good."[15] Pointing out that costs were down was not likely to win over the protesting farmers but employing Harold Macmillan's phrase that they'd "never had it so good" was certainly not likely to "placate" the farmers. It had the opposite effect.

Whitlam was forced into calling an election for 18 May 1974 when the coalition blocked supply. If Whitlam had known he'd be facing the people so soon, he might not have been so insistent that the bounty decision be made so urgently and may have found Wriedt's suggestion of a reference to the IAC more appealing.

Wriedt certainly had the view that the anti-Whitlam campaign unleashed in rural Australia had very significant implications for the future of the Whitlam government. He argued that, without the bounty decision, Labor would have won the last Senate seats in New South Wales and Queensland. If he was right about that, Whitlam would have controlled the Senate and the 1975 Dismissal could not have occurred.

There is quite a lot of evidence to support Wriedt's contention. The Senate results in New South Wales and Queensland were very close. In a close election, the Whitlam government actually increased its vote in urban areas by 1% (to 52.6%). In contrast, Labor's rural vote fell by 0.2% (to 43.3%). The Liberal Party's urban vote lifted by 2.1% but its rural vote lifted by 4.4%.

In the words of Clem Lloyd and Gordon Reid:

> The Government was left tantalisingly short of control in the Senate. Its national result rose significantly on the previous Senate election in 1970, but was still 2.3% below the 1972 House of Representatives figure. In the weeks after the campaign the Labor government seemed about to pick up five seats in each of the six states and a sixth in New South Wales to give it the 31 it needed for control. As a second best alternative five seats in each state would have given it a blocking majority in its own right in the Senate. Ultimate distribution of preferences denied the Government a fifth seat in Queensland and sixth in NSW leaving it with 29 seats.[16]

In such a tight scenario, and with Labor's rural vote falling (which also led to the loss of the seats of Riverina, Hume and Wide Bay), we are entitled to conclude that Wriedt was almost certainly right about the impact of the superphosphate bounty decision. There were certainly other factors at play as well. For example, the Liberal Party embarked on a deliberate strategy of voter suppression by organising a very large number of Senate candidates (there were 73 candidates in New South Wales for example, by the far the greatest number since Federation). There was no such thing as above-the-line voting in 1974, and all squares had to be numbered in perfect sequence for the vote to count. Inflating the number of candidates was a tactic to increase the number of informal votes at Labor's expense. But even factoring in this and other issues, it is possible to surmise Labor could have won a Senate majority without the superphosphate decision. The events of 1975 would have played out very differently if Whitlam had commanded a Senate majority.

While the bounty and wool-price decisions were the most high-profile elements of agricultural policy, Wriedt's agenda was full. In fact, as he later pointed out, despite the unpopularity of the Whitlam government's agriculture policy, only one measure was reversed by the Fraser government: the superphosphate bounty.

The other things that he worked on survived as his legacy. He abolished the butter bounty to encourage dairy farmers to diversify into other products. He did so as part of a broader readjustment assistance package for dairy farmers. He worked with Minister for Overseas Trade Jim Cairns to expand access for Australian products in Asian markets (including China following diplomatic recognition) to offset the impact of Britain joining the European Community. Under Wriedt's stewardship, the government also increased the emphasis on research and development in agricultural policy. In this vein, he worked to establish the National Animal Health Laboratory in Geelong. This represented the largest investment in agricultural science in Australian history. The Laboratory wasn't complete when Labor left office and cuts and delays in the Fraser years meant it wasn't finally established until 1985. Although fairly low-profile, it has become a very important national institution and is internationally recognised as one of the world's foremost research laboratories in relation to infectious diseases. The Morrison government in 2019 expanded the Laboratory and rebadged it as the Australian Centre for Disease Preparedness.

1975

Wriedt started 1975 as a cabinet minister and ended it in Opposition. In the meantime, he had become leader of the government in the Senate. The year would also be one of great tension between Whitlam and Wriedt. Building on their disagreement over the superphosphate bounty, these two senior figures disagreed fundamentally about strategy and tactics in this most tense and tumultuous of years.

When the Caucus leadership positions were declared automatically vacant after the 1974 election, Wriedt challenged Lionel Murphy for the party's leadership in the Senate. He would later describe this move as "stupid" and reveal that he was urged to do so by Whitlam. This is an indication of how much Whitlam and Murphy's relationship had deteriorated. It is also a sign that Whitlam at that time had come to value Wriedt and saw him as the best alternative to Murphy. Murphy easily saw off the challenge from Wriedt and felt no ill will towards him.

If Whitlam's strategy was to set Wriedt up for the succession to the leadership should Murphy depart politics, it worked. When Whitlam appointed Murphy to the High Court in February 1975, Wriedt won the ballot against two of his closest friends in the Caucus: the Minister for Repatriation (now Veterans Affairs), the cerebral John Wheeldon, and the Minister for Media Doug McClelland. The friendship among the three was unaffected by the ballot.

To be elected leader of the Labor Party in the Senate in 1975 was to be thrown into the beginning of a constitutional maelstrom. The

Liberal and Country parties, under the leadership of Bill Snedden, had forced the 1974 election by blocking supply (now known as the appropriations), and thus starving the government of the funds necessary to operate. Whitlam had won the election but, as noted above, had fallen tantalisingly short of a majority in the Senate.

The tone for 1975 was set in February. Murphy's resignation from the Senate created a vacancy not only for the Senate leadership but also in the Senate itself. Casual vacancies in the Senate were and are filled by a joint sitting of the relevant State Parliament. This was usually a ceremonial affair, with the parliament simply endorsing the choice of the former senator's party. Not in 1975.

To replace Murphy, the Liberal Premier of New South Wales Tom Lewis defied convention and nominated the independent long-serving Mayor of Albury Cleaver Bunton instead of Labor's nominee Peter Westerway. The coalition had the numbers in a joint sitting of the New South Wales Parliament, and Bunton's appointment was rubber stamped.

Shortly after Wriedt's elevation to the leadership, Malcolm Fraser challenged Snedden for the leadership of the Liberal Party. The party was looking for a stronger leader, even more determined to oust Whitlam. They found one in Fraser.

Labor's numbers in the Senate suffered a further blow with the death of Queensland Senator Bert Milliner in June 1975. The precedent having been set a few months earlier, the Country Party Premier Joh Bjelke-Petersen needed no encouragement to strike a further blow to the Whitlam government. He nominated Albert Field. Field was a member of the ALP but was not Labor's nominee. In fact, he had written directly to Bjelke-Petersen making his services available to serve as a senator and vowed never to vote for Whitlam government legislation.

The Labor senators except for Wriedt boycotted Field's swearing-in as a senator. Wriedt swivelled his chair and turned his back on the ceremony, declining to shake Field's hand afterwards. This display of anger in the much more genteel of the two chambers underlined Labor's anger at the trashing of democratic norms and the seriousness of the looming situation. Field's appointment meant there were 31 non-government senators to 27 for the government.

The appointment of Field was all the more portentous given the timing. Field was appointed on 3 September. On August 27, the supply bill had passed the House of Representatives and was sent to the Senate.

On 15 October, Fraser announced that the Liberal and Country Party senators would not be voting for supply until an election was called, citing the Khemlani loans affair (the seeking of government finance from unconventional and disreputable sources for the government-funded expansion of minerals extraction) as the reason.

Whitlam and Wriedt differed on how to handle the crisis. Both had legitimate points to support their argument.

Whitlam's position was a principled one. He had called an early election in 1974 faced with the blocking of supply, and the people had spoken. How many times was he to accede to their tactics? If they could force an election at will by blocking supply, they would simply keep doing so until they prevailed. Government would be impossible in such circumstances. Whitlam's argument was strengthened by the undemocratic nature of the filling of the casual vacancies (Bunton would not vote to block supply but Field was not voting at all while his appointment was subject to High Court challenge under section 44 of the Constitution due to a possible office of profit under the Crown). Nevertheless, what claim the Senate had to be a democratically elected house had been traduced in 1975. Finally,

Whitlam was confident that he could wear down at least one or possibly more Liberal senators to cross the floor and grant supply if he could apply enough pressure. There is undisputed evidence to support this final point and strong grounds to believe that if Kerr had not dismissed the government on 11 November, supply would have been granted soon after.

Wriedt's view was that a general election was inevitable and time was not the friend of the Whitlam government. While he conceded that the government's defeat was likely in a general election, he contended that dragging the dispute out over a longer period would result in a deeper defeat and a longer consignment to Opposition. Also (although with hindsight), he felt that the stigma of the Dismissal was devastating for the government's electoral chances. His attitude would also have been impacted by his thorough disapproval of Rex Connor's and Jim Cairn's behaviour in the loans affair. He also supported Hayden in resisting attempts to find "innovative" ways of financing government activities to enable the government to carry on without a supply bill. As the minister representing the prime minister and treasurer in the Senate, he had answered more questions about the loans affair than any other member of the government. "It was galling for me to have to defend the indefensible," he would later concede.

Who was right? Despite the indefensible activities of Connor and Cairns, Whitlam certainly had principled reasons for resisting the blocking of supply by an undemocratic chamber resulting in a fresh election. In a counter-factual world, perhaps an election earlier in 1975 called by Whitlam would have led to a less heavy defeat and a return to government by, say, 1980. But we don't have the luxury of counter-factual history with any certainty.

In any event, Wriedt was in a small minority in both the cabinet and the Caucus. When he expressed his views at a Caucus meeting in 1975, the only person to agree with him was John Wheeldon.

Having decided to tough it out, Whitlam was dismissed by the governor-general at 1 p.m. on 11 November. Fraser was sworn-in as prime minister at 1.30 p.m. Blissfully unaware of these events, Wriedt took a walk around the parliamentary rose garden to clear his head before the resumption of the Senate at 2 p.m.

In this, the most controversial day in Australian political history, the events of the hours after the Dismissal are also controversial.

Having been dismissed by the governor-general at Yarralumla, Whitlam did not return to Parliament House. He could have convened an urgent cabinet or Caucus meeting. He could have walked into the House to move a motion of no confidence. He could have consulted a wide array of colleagues informally. He did none of these things.

Instead, Whitlam took the six-minute drive from Yarralumla to The Lodge and had lunch. He called a small number of colleagues to consult there after lunch, including the Deputy Prime Minister Frank Crean, the leader of the House Fred Daly and Whitlam's senior staffer John Mant. The Secretary of the Department of Prime Minister John Menadue was there briefly before being called away by the new prime minister.

No-one thought to invite the leader of the Labor Party in the Senate.

At The Lodge, the assembled group agreed to move a motion of no confidence in the new government on the floor of the House of Representatives. No thought was given to the Senate tactics.

When the Senate resumed at 2 p.m., Wriedt again moved the supply bills. Doug McClelland had been working with the Clerk of the Senate on a form of words for the motion to approve supply to maximise pressure on the Opposition, particularly the wavering senators.

Wriedt was shocked when the Liberals' Senate leader Reg Withers leant across the table and indicated the Liberals would be supporting supply. Wriedt briefly thought the battle had been won and the government had been saved. "I was quite confident that if anything of substance affecting [supply] had occurred I would have been advised, probably by a visit from the prime minister,"[17] he later wrote.

He started to work out what had happened as the supply bills moved quickly through the Senate with bipartisan support.

Senator John Button came into the Senate chamber and whispered to him: "The government has been sacked". "Rubbish," was Wriedt's reply. Button countered: "Well, they are packing up in Whitlam's office".

Supply had been passed before Wriedt could confirm what had transpired. Had he known that he was now the leader of the Opposition in the Senate, not government leader, he would have requested the President of the Senate, his Tasmanian colleague Justin O'Byrne, to adjourn the Senate while he consulted with Whitlam. It wasn't to be.

Students of the Dismissal differ about the implications of Whitlam's failure to inform Wriedt of the Dismissal. Paul Kelly and Troy Bramston argue the error was impactful: "The reality is that Kerr was dismissing Whitlam because he did not have supply. He could not therefore accept a Fraser government that did not have supply. The pivotal question on the afternoon of 11 November was supply. Fraser knew this. He needed to secure supply to advise Kerr to call a general election."[18]

Wriedt himself, while furious at the oversight and humiliated by it, did not regard the passage of supply as fundamental to events of the day. He argued that Fraser would have been able to quickly get Withers sworn-in as a minister and thus give him the right to move a "money bill", with the Liberals then using their numbers to ensure speedy passage of supply.

While Wriedt may have been correct, there is one element missing from his analysis: the role of the President of the Senate. If more thought had been given to Senate tactics, it is possible that Senator O'Byrne as President could have simply chosen not to take the Chair in the afternoon of 11 November, removing the ability of the Liberals to pass supply. Alternatively, he could have taken the Chair briefly and then exercised his prerogative to adjourn the chamber. The presiding officers of each chamber have great discretion in determining when their house will sit. At the very least, Labor's senators could have made the early days of the Fraser government very difficult. But they could only do this if they were informed.

Wriedt was angry about Whitlam's failure to involve him in the post-Dismissal conversations for the rest of his life. He had every right to be. We will never know what would have happened had Wriedt's strategy been adopted over the course of 1975. As it was, the Fraser government received the biggest majority in the history of federation at the election on 13 December. Safely ensconced in the Labor Party's number-one Senate-ticket position, Wriedt was returned to the Senate.

The Wilderness Years

The events of the Dismissal brought the Whitlam–Wriedt relationship to the breaking point. The years 1975–1977 would see the relationship rupture.

Things did not get off to a good start for the pair when they both supported challenges to the other for their respective leaderships.

In the automatic leadership ballot after the election defeat, Whitlam faced two challengers: Frank Crean with the support of left wingers, and Lionel Bowen with support from the right. Neither of the strongest challengers to Whitlam were available at this time. Hawke was not in parliament and Hayden was too traumatised by the hectic last days of the government and the near loss of his seat in the election to want to run. Wriedt's entry in the *Biographical Dictionary of the Australian Senate* contends he voted for Crean. It is unclear that this is true, given his views were much closer to Bowen's. What is certain is that he did not vote for Whitlam.

Regardless, Whitlam won comfortably enough, receiving 36 votes to Bowen's 14 and Crean's 13. Lionel Bowen is now primarily remembered as Bob Hawke's loyal deputy in government, but as the 1970s continued he became a credible candidate for the leadership. He and Wriedt became firm friends.

Whitlam encouraged and supported a challenge to Wriedt for the Senate leadership from Jim McClelland. Wriedt handily saw off the challenge 38 votes to 25. Incidentally, this was the same margin by which the deputy leader Jim Keefe (described by Susan Ryan as a "warm hearted fellow totally lacking in leadership skills"[19]) saw off a challenge from McClelland for deputy leader. Effectively, the Whitlam–Wriedt working relationship was over. Whitlam appointed him Shadow Minister for Education, a job he did not seek and did not want.

If there was any hope of rapprochement for the leaders in the House and the Senate, it was lost with revelation of the Iraqi loans affair. In the public consciousness, this affair tends to be conflated with the Cairns–Connor loans affair. In fact, it was quite separate although one consistent feature was Whitlam's readiness to engage in highly unorthodox financing methods.

In early 1976 it was revealed that Whitlam, ALP National Secretary David Coombe and former Victorian Secretary Bill Hartley had sought to raise $500,000 in loans from the Iraqi Ba'ath Party to help finance Labor's election campaign. Labor had not just been smashed in the election, but was very heavily in debt. The fact that the money had been promised but not delivered was hardly a defence against the storm of protest that ensued. The true horror of the Ba'ath regime was not yet known in 1975 (Saddam Hussein was effectively in control of Iraq by 1975 but had not formally taken power). But enough was known that sensible people should have known better than to have anything to do with them. Enough was known for there to be widespread anger and disbelief in the Labor Party. Whitlam's leadership was in danger, but he was inadvertently helped by Bob Hawke observing from outside parliament that Whitlam should be removed. This generated sympathy for Whitlam and sparked the always strong instinct of the parliamentary Labor Party that it should jealously guard its privileges against outside interference. No leadership challenge emerged at this time.

Despite the fact there was no challenge, Wriedt made his views very clear. At the stormy Caucus meeting that discussed the Iraqi debacle, he rose to his feet to move a motion. It was an extraordinary thing for a Senate leader to do. It is difficult to nominate any other public disagreement between a House and Senate leader as spectacular as this one in the history of the Labor Party. Wriedt's motion is worth reproducing:

> That the Leader be required to give an unqualified assurance that he will in future consult with the Parliamentary Executive and/or parliamentary leaders on any matter of substance which concerns the welfare of the Parliamentary Party and unless such an assurance be given, he be asked to resign.

If it is possible, his speech in support of his motion marked an even bigger breach with Whitlam. The Caucus was unaware of the Iraqi loan at the time of the last leadership ballot, Wriedt pointed out. If it had been aware, it is likely Whitlam would not have been elected.

Hence, it would be proper for Whitlam to resign as leader and allow the Caucus a fresh ballot. This was as far as Wriedt got. The Caucus Chair, left-wing senator and Whitlam supporter Bill Brown, declared the Senate leader's motion out of order and refused to allow him to speak. (Kim Beazley Senior resigned from the Shadow Cabinet in protest at the Iraqi loans affair.)

There is no record from either Whitlam or Wriedt as to whether they ever discussed the affair in private.

In the 1970s, long overseas trips by political leaders were more acceptable than today. Wriedt had a long period as acting leader of the Opposition in mid-1976 when both Whitlam and the new deputy leader Tom Uren were away overseas. This period coincided with the Fraser government's dismantling of Medibank. Wriedt made clear on behalf of the Parliamentary Labor Party that it, not Bob Hawke's ACTU, would decide Labor's position and the Caucus would not be bound by any agreement between the Fraser government and the ACTU. He also gave the televised address in reply to Fraser's address to the nation on the future of Medibank.

The question of the Labor Party leadership was not going to go away. Under new Caucus rules that had been adopted in the aftermath of the 1975 defeat, the leadership was automatically declared vacant halfway through the term, in May 1977. By now, Hayden had recovered his emotional balance and was available to challenge Whitlam. Hayden was urged by his colleagues to overcome his doubts about his own abilities and capacity to defeat Fraser. Hayden originally decided to challenge Tom Uren for the deputy leadership, but his colleagues (primarily Paul Keating) convinced him that the deputy leadership was a dead-end, and he must strike for the top job. He was the best alternative to Whitlam and, for those keen to block Hawke's ascension, it made sense to change leaders before Hawke made it to parliament. Bowen was originally determined to run (and would have challenged Whitlam if Hayden had not run) but he vacated the field to allow Hayden a clear run.

Wriedt had doubts about Hayden's capacity to overcome his shyness and still harboured some resentment at Hayden's role in insisting on the decision to abolish the superphosphate bounty. Nevertheless, he was strongly of the view that the Labor Party could not move on and put itself in a strong position to win an election while Whitlam remained leader and so gave Hayden his vote. It wasn't enough. Hayden had started the race as favourite, but Whitlam retained very considerable political skills. Enough Caucus members were convinced that it would be an unacceptably humiliating way to end the career of the man who led Labor to victory after 23 years to dump him as leader in a Caucus ballot. This, together with Whitlam's rusted-on support, was enough. He prevailed over Hayden by the narrowest of margins: 32 votes to 30.

A two vote margin was hardly enough to end leadership speculation (especially as Whitlam's margin consisted of himself and his son Anthony, who had entered parliament). Nor did Whitlam help calm matters when in September he made public comments supporting Indonesia's occupation of East Timor, along the way claiming that the East Timorese forces had killed more Timorese than the Indonesian Army. This was incendiary. Since losing office, both the ALP Federal Conference and the Caucus had carried resolutions opposed to the Indonesian occupation.

The Caucus was in revolt. Wheeldon moved a motion censuring Whitlam. Extraordinarily, the motion was carried by 31 votes to 17 (with five abstentions). It is unthinkable today that a modern Labor leader would survive a vote of censure from the Caucus. Even more extraordinarily, Wriedt voted with the majority. Again, by today's standards, any member of the Executive, let alone the Senate leader, would feel obliged to resign from the Executive if they felt they had to support a vote of censure in the leader. The relationship between the House and Senate leaders by now was completely unworkable.

Whitlam knew he did not have a realistic chance of winning the election in 1978. However, by now Fraser was extremely unpopular. Whitlam's hope was to win enough seats to make the party a viable force for the election after next and to retire with dignity after the election having done so.

It wasn't to be. Despite his unpopularity, Fraser knew he could beat Whitlam. In order to forestall any chance that the Labor Party might switch to a more viable leader (a move he would carry out again less successfully a little over five years later), Fraser called a snap poll for 10 December 1977. There was only a 1% swing back to Labor and a gain of two seats (mainly as a result of redistributions), meaning Fraser still had a commanding majority of 48 seats in the House of Representatives. Whitlam vacated the party leadership on election night.

The path was now clear for Hayden to take the leadership. But first Lionel Bowen tested the numbers. They were close. Hayden defeated Bowen by 36 votes to 28. In the words of Paul Kelly, the close vote "was testimony to the persistent doubts about Hayden in Caucus".[20] It is not clear who Wriedt voted for. He was personally closer to Bowen and had well-established doubts about Hayden. Clyde Cameron's diary records Bowen confiding in him that he thought he had probably lost Wriedt's vote to Hayden.

In any event, the Whitlam era, with all its glories, achievements, frustrations and contradictions, was over. Wriedt had wanted a more stable, consultative leader. Hayden certainly had those qualities. But it did not take long for the misgivings Wriedt had in Hayden to come to the fore. Wriedt suggested that the group of four leaders meet regularly and informally on Thursday nights in sitting weeks to compare notes on the week that had been and discuss the week ahead (Bowen was deputy leader having defeated Tom Uren, Wriedt had been re-elected unopposed as Senate leader and John Button had been elected Senate deputy leader). Hayden agreed at first but after a couple of weeks simply stopped turning up and the meetings petered out. Wriedt noted in his short book *Some Thoughts* published in his retirement that Hayden was a "natural loner" not suited to collegiate leadership.

Hayden appointed Wriedt to the portfolio he had always hankered for: Foreign Affairs. In this portfolio he had the opportunity to condemn Fraser's recognition of Indonesian jurisdiction over East Timor and called for greater aid for the Pacific. He also kept up his strong interest in Middle Eastern affairs, forged on his sea journeys through the region.

The efforts of the parliamentary party were now focused on securing a majority in the election due in 1980. Fraser remained unpopular and Hayden presented a fresh and less divisive face as Opposition leader. Nevertheless, the odds were long. Hayden had a huge deficit of seats to make up and five years wasn't a long time to allow the controversies of the Whitlam government to recede.

Wriedt's mind turned to what role he should play in bringing about the defeat of the Fraser government, which he reviled. This led to the biggest gamble of his political life.

As Senate leader, with a secure preselection, he was able to look forward to years of effectively guaranteed seniority in the Federal Parliamentary Labor Party. So why would he throw this away? Because he was concerned that only three years out of his long parliamentary career might be spent in government. If Labor was going to form a government, they needed to win seats in Tasmania. All Tasmanian seats had been lost in 1975 and none had been regained in 1977. His profile and popularity would make him a formidable candidate should he try for a lower house seat, so that's what he decided to do.

Hayden came to see him in his office in 1979 to encourage him to put his name forward for the seat of Denison. Presumably, Hayden had heard this was something he was contemplating doing. But even before Hayden's visit, Wriedt had decided to do it.

Wriedt's move took many by surprise. It was unusual to risk a safe Senate seat in order to snatch a seat of the Liberals. Some assumed he was angling for the leadership of the party. This is not correct. There is no reason to reject his assertion that he was simply seeking to give the Labor Party its best shot at winning government. He wrote later: "I did so knowing that I was putting all at risk and that, if unsuccessful, it would mean the end of my career in federal politics but I regarded the Fraser government as a disaster for Australia and the return of a Labor Government under Bill's leadership was more important than my own personal fortunes."[21]

Winning Denison was to be no easy task. It had been held by the Liberals between 1946 and 1972. A brief Labor interregnum had been ended by the election of Michael Hodgman in 1975. Hodgman had been in the State Parliament before running for Federal Parliament and was a member of Tasmanian political royalty, being a third-generation Liberal politician (his son Will would later form the fourth generation). He was loquacious and didn't mind controversy, which meant his profile was fairly high for a backbencher. His majority in Denison was not huge, having been re-elected in 1977 with 53.1% of the two-party preferred vote.

Wriedt said later he did not need to wait for election night to know his gamble had not paid off. Public polling showed him winning, but he was more pessimistic. Despite the national issues being dominated by tax and the economy, a strong "right to life" campaign was run in Denison with the high-profile anti-abortion campaigner Margaret Tighe making several trips to the seat. Wriedt had not been particularly active or radical on social issues like abortion. In fact, he had supported state aid to Catholic schools in internal party debates and had opposed the expulsion of socially conservative Brian Harradine from the party. However, Hodgman was a high-profile Catholic and vocal on such issues. An internal party poll shown to Wriedt during the campaign showed 80% of Catholic voters supported Hodgman. Wriedt knew many of these would be low-income voters who otherwise would have supported him. This theory was borne out on election night when swings to Wriedt came through in high-income areas of the electorate, but traditional Labor areas showed swings to Hodgman.

Another quirky local issue that impacted on Denison was a classic Cold War tactic. The Labor Premier Doug Lowe had negotiated with the Soviet government (during a trip to Moscow) to have a Russian floating dock brought to Hobart to enable more ship repairs and stimulate the economy. At first, the Department of Foreign Affairs approved the deal. But, urged on by Hodgman, Fraser vetoed it, and a "red scare" campaign was run by Hodgman against Wriedt and Labor.

Wriedt secured a 0.7% swing on a two-party preferred basis. The swing across the country was 4.23%. Any objective analysis would conclude that his candidacy underperformed. This is a view he concurred with. He was philosophical, saying later of his gamble: "If I had not done it, I would have condemned myself for not being game and for protecting my empire, my safe Senate seat and the leadership. I would never have forgiven myself for being gutless."

He declared his political career over and did not anticipate making a comeback at any level. He took nine months off, time spent with Helga and their daughters as well on their boat (*The Helga-Anne*).

After the break, Wriedt took a job as Tasmanian State Executive Director of the Bicentennial Authority, with the task of lifting the profile of the celebrations then eight years away.

But it wasn't too long before the entreaties began, asking him to run for State Parliament. At age 53, his friends and supporters felt he had more to give public life. It was again felt his public profile would assist the campaign. This was not about the party leadership. Despite the fact the Tasmanian Labor government was going through difficult times, it had been in office for all but three years since 1934. Tasmania was the most loyal of all Australian jurisdictions to the Labor Party. For many, it was unthinkable that they would lose. The plan was that Wriedt would join the cabinet on his election.

The urgings of his friends eventually worked, and he nominated and won preselection for the seat of Franklin (Tasmanian state electorates are the same as federal electorates, with members elected under the complicated Hare–Clark proportional system. In 1982 the five seats elected seven members each.)

He nominated for Franklin rather than Denison because there was a vacancy for preselection, and one created under dramatic circumstances. Doug Lowe was one of the Labor members for Franklin and became premier at the young age of 35 in 1977. He was a relatively successful and uncontroversial premier until the powerful Tasmanian Hydro-Electric Commission proposed building a dam on the Gordon River. This would flood the Franklin River Valley and was known as the Gordon-below-Franklin Dam.

This was proposed not only to produce electricity, but also to generate employment. The proposal was extraordinarily divisive both within the Labor Party and across the Tasmanian and wider national population. Environmentalists were pitted against advocates of economic development and job creation. While the majority of the Tasmanian population supported the proposal, the politics remained extremely difficult.

Eventually, Premier Lowe proposed a referendum which would decide between two dam options and the "no dams" alternative. But Lowe was overruled by the pro-dam Executive of the Labor Party which issued an instruction to the premier and Caucus that "no dams" was not to appear as an option on the referendum ballot paper. The Caucus went into meltdown, carrying a motion of no confidence in Lowe as leader. Lowe resigned not only as premier but also from the Labor Party, sitting in the parliament as an independent. He also contested Franklin as an independent.

Despite all this, the expectation was that Labor would hold on to office under the new Premier, Harry Holgate. It wasn't to be. A massive 17% swing against Labor saw the party reduced from 20 seats to 14. (A year later, Bob Hawke's federal Labor Party, which made a virtue of opposing the Franklin Dam, didn't win a seat in Tasmania, despite a landslide mainland win.)

Wriedt topped the poll in Franklin, outperforming all the sitting state MPs. The view that he would be an electoral asset at the state level was borne out. Yet his plan to become a minister in the Holgate government was rent asunder. Instead, he was soon prevailed on to become leader of the shell-shocked party. Only one colleague, Julian Amos, attempted to run against him, but withdrew due to lack of Caucus support. Wriedt, whose political career had been over two years earlier, was effectively the almost unanimous choice of the Caucus to take the leadership. He was elected unopposed.

Being the unopposed choice of his Labor colleagues hardly made the task of leadership easier. He inherited a dispirited and divided Caucus. He later complained that only half his Caucus was willing to do any work, the other half being too used to being in government and too dispirited by life in Opposition. Having served in the Federal Parliament for so long, he also found what he regarded as the amateurish procedures (and very rudimentary Parliamentary Library resources) of the Tasmanian Parliament extremely frustrating.

Most of all, the new Gray Liberal government was experiencing a considerable and prolonged honeymoon. The Liberal Party could be pro-dam without qualification whereas the Labor Party was split between protecting its environmental credentials and trying to promote its job-creation credibility. The pro-job position was the overwhelmingly popular one at the time. Gray made Prime Minister Hawke (and effectively the entire Labor Party) a bogeyman in Tasmania for using the Commonwealth's treaty-making power to ban the Franklin Dam proposal as being out of keeping with our international environmental obligations. Gray was also a master of the tactic of divide and conquer. He forged a relationship with Kelvin McCoy, the firebrand left-wing state secretary of the Federated Engine Drivers and Firemen's Association (FEDFA). Together these unlikely allies engineered the creation of the "Organisation for Tasmanian Development" which campaigned for the Franklin Dam and against the Labor Party.

Gray was an effective politician. But Wriedt, who had had effective and respectful relationships with political colleagues across the spectrum since he had entered politics, could not abide him. He was suspended from the House of Assembly for saying that Gray had been "raised in the gutter and is still in the gutter". There was no love lost. Wriedt, participating in the oral history project for the National Archives after he had finished his term as leader, said that Gray "would be the worst, lowest political animal that I have encountered in the political world. There would be no-one I would hold in greater contempt. He is a liar. He is devious. He is arrogant."

Wriedt tried valiantly to promote other issues which better suited Labor politically. Drawing on his federal experience he devoted his maiden speech as a member of the House of Assembly (and leader) to demolishing Fraser's proposed New Federalism policy which would have enabled state income taxes to better fund services. Unfortunately for Wriedt, Neville Wran, the most effective politician of his day and at the height of his powers as Premier of New South Wales, effectively scuttled New Federalism and that bogeyman was removed from Wriedt's armoury.

The Franklin Dam controversy was effectively the only game in town in Tasmanian politics. Gray played the issue shrewdly, even spectacularly but not realistically threatening to secede from the Commonwealth over the issue.

Such were the travails of Tasmanian Labor that the National Executive intervened into the Tasmanian branch, taking control of the administrative wing of the party. This was done against the wishes of Wriedt as state leader who saw no point in such an action and thought it undermined his message that Tasmanian Labor was a serious outfit ready for government. His federal colleagues were not particularly concerned to assist their state counterparts. Wriedt and Hawke had never had a warm relationship. He had resented Hawke's interventions in parliamentary matters and had said so. He would lament later that Hayden had called him on the night of his defeat in

Denison in 1980 and told him he would help him if the opportunity to do so ever presented itself. "Well, the opportunity came along in 1983 but I think Bill had forgotten about Ken Wriedt by then,"[22] he said.

Hence the 1986 state election was fought on issues that suited the incumbents, not Wriedt. The result was probably inevitable. While Labor and the Liberals emerged from the 1986 election with the same number of seats as they entered the campaign with, the Liberal vote actually increased by 5.7% and the Labor vote fell by a further 1.7% after the big swing in 1982 (independent former premier Doug Lowe retired at the election, meaning his vote was available for other parties and this election marked the decline of the Australian Democrats as a force in Tasmanian politics).

This result caused two records to be set: Robin Gray became the first Liberal premier to be re-elected since John McPhee in 1931. Less happily, Wriedt became the first Labor leader in Tasmanian history not to serve as premier.

It did not take him long to work out his future as Labor leader was limited. He had only entered state politics and become leader at the behest of friends. He did not resist the suggestion that his old friend Neil Batt should become leader. Batt had entered State Parliament in 1969 and been deputy premier. But he had left politics in 1980 to take up a humanitarian role in Bangladesh. His return to politics in the 1986 election made him available for the leadership.

Wriedt continued in the Tasmanian Parliament and supported Batt. But Tasmanian politics was about to take a dramatic turn. Batt became the second Labor leader not to serve as premier when he was replaced as leader in December 1988. Michael Field challenged Batt for the leadership, arguing that he presented a better chance for Labor at the election. Field defeated Batt by one vote, in an 8–7 result.

The 1989 election was a close one. While Labor's vote fell a further 0.4% from Wriedt's 1986 defeat, the Liberal vote fell 7.28%. There was a surge for the Greens, then led by Bob Brown. The loss of two Liberal seats meant Gray was one seat short of a majority. The ensuing events did not reflect well on Gray's Liberal Party and vindicated Wriedt's longstanding views of Gray's character. When Labor and the Greens signed a coalition agreement delivering a majority on the floor of the House, Gray did not resign. Instead, he advised the Governor Sir Phillip Bennett to dissolve the House for another election. Bennett took the rare step of declining to accept the advice of his premier. This was a proper exercise of the vice-regal prerogative, as Bennett knew that Field could successfully form an administration. Gray still declined to resign, as convention indicated he should. Instead he held on until the House sat. But not even he could hold on after his candidate for speaker was defeated on the floor of the House. It was then that he finally resigned the premiership and Field formed a government.

Gray's constitutional obstreperousness was not the biggest scandal of the post-election period. Not long after the election, it emerged that the chairman of the logging company Gunns (and owner of substantial Tasmanian media interests), Edmund Rouse, offered newly elected Labor MP Jim Cox a bribe of $110,000 to cross the floor and keep Gray in power. Cox (who had previously won a Logie as Tasmania's most popular TV personality) quite properly reported the attempted bribe to the police. Rouse was sentenced to three years in prison. A Royal Commission found no evidence that Gray had direct knowledge of the attempted bribe. However, it did find that he had acted "deceitfully and dishonestly" in keeping a $10,000 donation from Rouse at his home (in his freezer no less).

Rouse's ruse having failed, Michael Field was sworn in as Premier in June 1989. Wriedt was elected to cabinet (unlike former premier

Harry Holgate). Field allocated him the substantial portfolios of Police and Transport. He was back in power at last, but it wasn't to last long enough for him to make a substantial impact. His health was starting to fail him. In October 1990 he decided to retire both as a minister and from parliament.

Retirement

Wriedt's health was not good enough for him to continue as a minister, but he enjoyed his retirement. It gave him a chance to spend much more time on his real loves: his family, the sea, cricket and the AFL, poetry and classical music.

He boasted that following his retirement he didn't miss a single ball of first-class cricket bowled at Hobart's Bellerive Oval, watched the Derwent flow by their waterside house, and listened to an inordinate amount of classical music each day.

He wrote regular letters to the editor on a range of eclectic issues. In 1991, he published the short book *Some Thoughts*. While it contained some anecdotes from his life, it was not a memoir. As the title suggests, it was a potpourri of thoughts and ideas on politics, international affairs, religion, music and poetry.

He began a one-man campaign to have the Derwent River renamed Derwent Harbour because he argued the features of the waterway are more in keeping with that nomenclature. It is far beyond the nautical knowledge of this author to adjudicate on his claim.

His only return to more active political involvement came in 1995 when Paula surprised her parents by expressing a desire to follow her father into Tasmanian politics. She won preselection to contest Franklin on the Labor ticket for the 1996 election and Ken became her campaign manager. The campaign was enough to see her secure 5.6%

of the vote. This result surpassed the vote of a sitting Labor member and secured her election.

His family regarded 2007 as one of his happiest years, as it combined a rare double: the election of a federal Labor government and a Geelong AFL flag. But 2007 also saw his diagnosis with Parkinson's disease. This, combined with a prostate cancer diagnosis saw his health begin a fairly rapid decline.

He survived long enough to celebrate 50 years of marriage with Helga on Boxing Day 2009. Helga was his full-time carer as his health declined. She died suddenly in September 2010. After five decades together, she pre-deceased her husband by just a month. His death in October, at the age of 83, was more expected. He was accorded a state funeral in Hobart, with his daughters Sonja and Paula (who had left politics) providing eulogies, along with the then Premier David Bartlett and former federal colleague Barry Jones. Jones read a message from Whitlam that praised Wriedt's role in agricultural policy during their time in office and did not touch on their differences.

Conclusion

Ken Wriedt was not a lucky politician. Federal Labor politicians in the 1960s and 1970s knew life in Opposition was their most likely lot, but his timing was particularly bad. After three short, tumultuous and unsatisfying years in office, he risked everything to help the party, in a gamble that failed. He was then prevailed on to switch to state politics but did so at a time at which what had been effectively a permanent Labor government was drawing to an end. By the time the political cycle turned, and Labor was back in office, he was growing too ill to be an effective senior minister.

Every successful reforming government needs dreamers and senior members who are rooted in common sense to provide a balance. Whitlam, Connor and Cairns were dreamers. They thought big thoughts and pursued an expansive agenda. Wriedt was one of several who provided a pragmatic ballast to the Whitlam government. Perhaps if Wriedt, Hayden, Bowen and the other pragmatists had had more influence, that government would have been longer lived and its substantial achievements even greater.

His caution and common sense did not mean he was not a reformer. On the contrary, he crammed a lot of change into his term as Agriculture Minister. While controversial, his reforms were grounded in good sense and sensible policy. The reforms he implemented have stood the test of time.

Wriedt wasn't steeped in Labor history or a long-term activist before entering politics. He sometimes found the party and politics frustrating. He never let that frustration dull his commitment to the cause or his willingness to make great sacrifices for it.

The broad brushes of history won't reflect his decency and complexity. He'll always be primarily noted for the role he played (or didn't play) on the most dramatic day in Australian political history. Wriedt was philosophical about that, as he was about most things in life. He saw his political career as just part of his life, in which he was constantly in search of deeper meaning. "It's the search for the good things, the truthful things, the beautiful things that's important. That's what counts in the final analysis." He was in search of the good things, and he did good things in the cause of Labor. For this, his life deserves remembering and celebration.

NOTES

Introduction
1. The one exception is John Dedman, who had a fine biography written by Andrew Spaull. However, the book is not well known and is hard to get, so Dedman still needs more attention.

Chapter 1: Gregor McGregor
1. Norman Makin, personal letter to Scarfe, referred to in J Scarfe, "The Labour Wedge: The First Six Labor Members of the South Australian Legislative Council". Honours Thesis for the University of Adelaide School of History and Politics, 1968, p. 102.
2. *Morning Post*, "Opposition Tactics. Tariff Schedule Conflict. Ministerial Triumph". Reproduced in *From Our Special Correspondent: Alfred Deakin's Letters to the London Morning Post*, Volume One 1900–1901. Australian Parliamentary Library, Canberra, 2019, p. 248.
3. Gregor MacGregor was an outrageous international conman. See David Sinclair, *The Land That Never Was: Sir Gregor MacGregor and the Most Audacious Fraud in History*. Boston, Da Capo Press, 2004.
4. Scarfe, p. 106.
5. See https://adelaidecityexplorer.com.au/items/show/326?tour=28&index=5.
6. *The Biographical Dictionary of the Australian Senate*, "Gregor McGregor".
7. Ross McMullin, *So Monstrous a Travesty: Chris Watson and the World's First National Labour Government*. Scribe, 2004, p. 29.
8. John Faulkner and Stuart Macintyre (eds), *True Believers: The Story of the Federal Parliamentary Labor Party*. Allen & Unwin, Sydney, 2001, p. 28.
9. Ross McMullin, *Light on the Hill*, Oxford University Press, Oxford, 1991, p. 51.
10. G Sawer, *Australian Federal Politics and Law, 1901–1929*. Melbourne University Press, Melbourne, 1956, p. 110.

Chapter 2: Lilian Locke
1. Suffragettes are regarded as those in Britain who resorted to violence to bring about their aims. The term suffragist applies to campaigners for the female vote who used more traditional methods of campaigning.
2. Newspaper clipping of 22 January 1904 held in the State Library of New South Wales, Lilian Locke clipping collection. The title of the newspaper is not recorded.
3. Sharon Clarke, "Sumner Locke Elliott: Writing Life". Doctor of Philosophy Thesis, Department of English, University of Wollongong, 1995, p. 65.
4. Betty Searle, *Silk and Calico: Class, Gender and the Vote*. Hale & Ironmonger, 1988, p. 16.
5. Ibid., p. 34.
6. B Kingston, *The World Moves Slowly: A Documentary History of Australian Women*. Cassell, Sydney, 1977, p. 65.
7. J Bomford, *That Dangerous and Persuasive Woman: Vida Goldstein*. Melbourne University Press, 2016, p. 67.
8. N Dyrenfurth, *Heroes and Villains: The Rise and Fall of the Early Australian Labor Party*. Australian Scholarly Publishing, North Melbourne, 2011, p. 32.
9. L Locke, "Women's Organiser at Work". *The Tocsin*, 12 April 1905.

NOTES

10 *The Weekly Times*, 18 March 1905.
11 *Southern Mail*, 4 November 1904.
12 Untitled newspaper clipping for 22 January 1904 held in "Collection of newspaper cuttings, broadsides and other ephemera relating to the political and other activities of Lilian Locke Burns" held at the State Library of New South Wales.
13 Clarke, p. 70.
14 Searle, p. 40.
15 Clarke, p. 72.
16 Statement by Jessie Locke to the Supreme Court of New South Wales, 19 July 1927. Accessed by the author, with thanks to the Registrar of the Supreme Court.
17 Clarke, p. 136.
18 Ibid., p. 1.
19 Ibid., p. 4.
20 Ibid., p. 86.

Chapter 3: Frank Tudor

1 Norman Makin, *Federal Labour Leaders*. Union Printing, Sydney, 1961, p. 74.
2 The Mills building in Nicholson Street in Abbotsford still exists and is a site of heritage significance. Advertisements at the time indicated it was the largest hat factory in Australia. The factory was named after the Denton Hat Factory in the UK, Britain's most significant hat manufacturer. See Collingwood Historical Society (www.collingwoodhs.org.au).
3 Kim Beazley, "The Quiet Man. Leaders of Labor". *The Canberra Times*, 15 February 1966, p. 8.
4 Take the early subjects of this book, for example. McGregor and Dedman were both Presbyterians, Tudor a Congregationalist and Locke an adherent of Christian Science.
5 Janet McCalman, "Tudor, Francis Gwynne (Frank) (1866–1922)", *Australian Dictionary of Biography*. National Centre of Biography, Australian National University. http://adb.anu.edu.au/biography/tudor-francis-gwynne-frank-8874/text15583, published first in hardcopy 1990, accessed online 5 February 2020.
6 Beazley, p. 8.
7 Makin, p. 70.
8 Beazley, p. 8.
9 W Hughes, *Hansard*, 4106 P 24, April 1918.
10 F Tudor, *Hansard*, P2932, 11 January 1918.
11 Denis Murphy, *TJ Ryan: A Political Biography*. University of Queensland Press, Brisbane, 1990, p. 307.
12 *Rockhampton Morning Bulletin*, 20 September 1903.
13 McMullin, *Light on the Hill*, p. 113.
14 Murphy, p. 311.
15 Ibid., p. 315.
16 Ibid., p. 316.
17 Ibid., p. 328.
18 Ibid., p. 459.
19 Ibid., p. 447.
20 Ibid., p. 445.
21 Makin, p. 74.
22 *The Worker*, 25 September 1919.
23 *The Argus*, 23 September 1919.
24 *Official Report of the Federal Conference of the Australian Labor Party, 1919*, p. 106.

25 *The Argus*, 4 October 1919.
26 Murphy, p. 479.

Chapter 4: John Dedman

1 Stuart Macintyre, *Australia's Boldest Experiment: War and Reconstruction in the 1940s*. New South, Sydney, 2015.
2 Don Whitington, *The House will Divide*. Georgian House, Melbourne, 1954, p. 72.
3 Kim Beazley, *Father of the House: The Memoirs of KE Beazley*. Fremantle Press, Fremantle, 2009, p. 50.
4 Andrew Spaull, *John Dedman: A Most Unexpected Labor Man*. Hyland House, South Melbourne, 1988, p. 3.
5 LF Crisp, *Ben Chifley*. Longman Greens, Sydney, 1968, p. 197.
6 McMullin, *Light on the Hill*, p. 201.
7 John Curtin Prime Ministerial Library. Oral History interview with John Dedman. Conducted by Hazel de Berg, 6 October 1967.
8 Ibid.
9 Spaull, p. 7.
10 Ibid., p. 20.
11 Ibid., p. 27.
12 Arthur Calwell, *Be Just and Fear Not*. Lloyd O'Neil, 1972.
13 John Edwards, *John Curtin's War*. Penguin Books, 2017.
14 Jan Beaumont, *Australia's War, 1939–1945*. A&U Academic, 1996, p. 63.
15 Macintyre, p. 103.
16 McMullin, *Light on the Hill*, p. 221.
17 Diary of Gavin Long, 20 May 1943. Australian War Memorial.
18 Andrew Spaull, "John Johnstone Dedman: Australia's First Federal Minister for Education (1941–1949)", *History of Education Review*, 21, no. 1, 1992, p. 1.
19 Ibid.
20 Margaret Vaghese and Stephen Foster, *The Making of the Australian National University*. ANU Press, Canberra, 1996, p. 4.
21 CB Schedvin, *Shaping Science and Industry: A History of Australia's Council for Scientific and Industrial Research 1926–49*. CSIRO Publishing, Canberra, 1987, p. 62.
22 Frederick White, "CSIR to CSIRO: The Events of 1948–1949", *Public Administration*, vol. XXXIV, no. 4, December 1975, p. 52.
23 Ibid.
24 Schedvin, p. 62.
25 John Curtin Prime Ministerial Library.
26 Calwell, p. 57.
27 Crisp, p. 193.
28 Ibid., p. 194.
29 Spaull, *A Most Unexpected*, p. 169.
30 The seat of Ballarat was known as Ballaarat until 1977.
31 Spaull, *A Most Unexpected*, p. 2.
32 John Curtin Prime Ministerial Library.
33 Ibid.
34 McMullin, *Light on the Hill*, p. 340.

Chapter 5: Gertrude Melville

1 R Cavalier, *Power Crisis: The Self-destruction of a State Labor Party*. Cambridge University Press, Cambridge, p. 14.

NOTES

2   J Lang, *I Remember*. Invincible Press, Sydney, 1956, p. 196.
3   M Hogan, "The 1925 Election". In M Hogan and D Clune (eds), *The People's Choice: Electoral Politics in 20th Century New South Wales*. Sydney University and NSW Parliament, 2001, p. 314.
4   G Freudenberg, *Cause for Power: The Official History of the NSW Branch of the Australian Labor Party*. Pluto Press, Sydney, 1991, p. 139.
5   Ibid., p.182.
6   J Hagan and K Turner, *A History of the Labor Party in New South Wales 1891–1991*. Longman Cheshire, Melbourne, p. 152.
7   Ibid., p. 155.
8   D Clune, "1959", in D Clune and M Hogan (eds), *The People's Choice: Electoral Politics in 20th Century New South Wales*. The Parliament of New South Wales and University of Sydney, Sydney 2001, p. 355.
9   G Witherspoon, "Delaney, Colin John (1897–1969)". *Australian Dictionary of Biography*, National Centre of Biography, Australian National University. http://adb.anu.edu.au/biography/delaney-colin-john9945/text17617, accessed online 8 August 2020.
10   R Menzies, *The Measure of the Years*. Cassel, Sydney, 1970, p. 8.

Chapter 6: Ken Wriedt

1   Unless otherwise stated by footnote, all quotes from Ken Wriedt in this chapter are taken from the Ken Wriedt oral history interviews, National Archives.
2   J Hocking, *Gough Whitlam: His Time*. The Miegunyah Press, Melbourne, 2013, p. 107.
3   P Kelly, *The Unmaking of Gough*. Allen & Unwin, Sydney, 1976, p. 111.
4   A Reid, *The Whitlam Venture*. Hill of Content Publishing, Melbourne, 1976, p. 89.
5   S Ryan, *Catching the Waves*. Harper Collins, Sydney, 1999, p. 152.
6   K Wriedt, *Some Thoughts*. Keyline Press, Mornington, Tasmania, 1991.
7   Hocking, p. 31.
8   G Freudenberg, *A Certain Grandeur*. Sun Books, Melbourne, 1977, p. 256.
9   J Kerin, *The Way I Saw It; The Way It Was: The Making of National Agricultural and Natural Resource Management*. Policy Analysis and Policy Observatory, Melbourne, 2017, p. 240.
10   G Whitlam, *The Whitlam Government 1972–75*. Penguin, Sydney, 1985, p. 263.
11   Whitlam. p. 264.
12   Kelly, p. 111.
13   Whitlam, p. 270.
14   Ibid.
15   Ibid., p. 272.
16   C Lloyd and G Reid, *Out of the Wilderness: The Return of Labor*. Cassell, Melbourne, 1974, p. 414.
17   K Wriedt, "Meanwhile, Back in the Senate", in S Nolan, *The Dismissal: Where Were You on November 11, 1975?* Melbourne University Press, Melbourne, 2005. p. 36.
18   T Bramston and P Kelly, *The Dismissal: In the Queen's Name*. Penguin, Sydney, 2015. p. 233.
19   Ryan, p. 163.
20   P Kelly, *The Hawke Ascendancy*. Angus & Robertson, Sydney, 1984, p. 43.
21   Wriedt, *Some Thoughts*, p. 62.
22   Ibid., p. 63.

INDEX

Abeles, Peter, 196
Adams, Alderman, 156
Adelaide Critic, 36–7
Adelaide Herald, 36
The Age, 49, 59, 64, 82–3
Alldis, Septimus Denbigh, 146
Amos, Julian, 224
Ansett, 196
Anthony, Doug, 200
Anthony, Susan B., 24
Anti-Socialist Party,
  coalition with
  Protectionist Party, 19
The Argus, 60
Askin, Robin (Robert), 174, 176
The Austral, 53
Australasian, 59
Australian Consolidated
  Industries (ACI), 99
Australian Council of
  Churches, 136–7
Australian Council of Trade
  Union (ACTU), 217
Australian Country Party,
  74, 82, 83, 84
  coalition with Vic Labor
  Party, 94
  first Queensland seat, 86
Australian Democrats, 227
Australian Labor Party
  breakaway groups, 42, 52, 74, 141
  falling rural votes, 207
  Federal Executive, 130
  federal involvement in
  education, 90
  first federal deputy leader
  See McGregor, Gregor
  first female candidates, 41
  first female in
  organisational role, 24, 27–8

first majority
  government, 19–22, 40
impact of Hughes'
  conscription bill, 57–61
Melville's resignation
  from State Executive, 162
National Executive's
  intervention in
  Tasmania, 226
Protestant members, 53
relationship between
  House and Senate, 216–19
role in female suffrage, 24, 28
Tasmanian candidates, 37, 38
tradition of governing
  alone, 15
See also Federal
  Labor; Lang Labor
  government (NSW)
Australian Labor Party
Caucus
  conscription plebiscite, 40, 57–8
  first federal, 10–12
  Tudor's roles in, 55, 59–61, 84–7
Australian Labor Party
conferences
  federal/national, 36, 55, 57, 75, 77–80, 130, 152, 218
  interstate, 36
  NSW, 74, 75, 77–80, 144–6, 157–8, 162–3
  TAS, 189, 195
Australian National
University (ANU), 90, 118–21, 137
Australian Securities
Commission, 197

Australian Wool
  Commission, 203
Australian Workers Union
  (AWU), 74, 144, 146, 158
Aylmer, Gerald, 4
Bailey, Jack, 144
Bailey, John, 78
Baker, Frank, 116
Baker, Richard, 4, 9, 10
bank nationalisation, 132–3
Barclay, Aggie, 43
Barnard, Lance, 185, 195, 198
Barnard, Michael, 195
Barnes, John, 79
Bartlett, David, 230
Barton, Edmund, 13
Batt, Neil, 194, 195, 227
Beasley, Jack, 89, 105, 153
Beaumont, Jan, 106
Beazley, Kim Senior, 55, 81, 87, 90, 185, 217
Begg, Colin, 179
Benalla Standard, 64
The Bendigo Independent, 63
Bennett, Phillip, 228
Bent, Thomas, 13
Bicentennial Authority, 193
*Biographical Dictionary of the
  Australian Senate*, 215
The Biz, 155
Bjelke-Petersen, Joh, 209
Blakely, Arthur, 84
Bomford, Janette, 32
Bowen, Lionel, 214, 215, 218, 219
Bramston, Troy, 213
Bridges, Arthur, 180
The Brisbane Worker, 33–4
British Liberal Party, 91
Brock (McGregor), Charles, 5, 23
Brock, Fred, 5
Brock, Sarah *See* McGregor,
  Sarah (nee Brock)

INDEX

Broken Hill Trades Hall, 35–6
Broken Hill Women's Branch, 166, 168
Brown, Bill, 217
Brown, Bob, 228
Brownbill, Bill, 98
Brownbill, Fanny, 98
Bruce coalition government, 121
The Bulletin, 23, 188–9
Bunton, Cleaver, 209, 210
Burger, Helga, 193
Burns, George Mason, 36–43, 46–7, 49
Burt, Ellen, 52 *See also* Tudor, Ellen (nee Burt)
Bury, Les, 138–9
Butler, Walter, 153, 154
butter bounty, 207
Butterfield, Tom, 79
Button, John, 213, 220
Cabramatta–Canley Vale Council, 142, 155
Cahill, Joseph, 43, 69, 160, 161, 166, 170, 183
Cahill Labor government, 170–1, 174, 176–7, 182
Cain, John (Senior), 95
Cairns, Jim, 185, 187, 207, 211, 215, 231
Calwell, Arthur, 88, 102–3, 110, 120, 124, 130, 137
Cameron, Clyde, 198–9, 219
Canberra College, 118
Careful, He Might Hear You (Elliott), 25, 45–7
Carmody, Leo, 98
Carr, Bob, 182
'The Case against Bretton Woods Financial Agreement' (Ward), 130
'The Case for Bretton Woods' (Dedman), 130
Casey, Richard, 197, 34
The Catholic Press, 59–60
Catholic Social Studies Movement (the Movement), 163–4
Catts, James, 58, 75, 77, 78, 84

Cavalier, Rodney, 144
The Century, 110
Chambers, Cyril, 138
Charleston, David, 10
Charlton, Matthew, 85–6, 87, 145
Chifley, Ben, 105, 136, 149, 154
  appreciation for Dedman, 89, 105, 136
  as Minister for Post-War Reconstruction, 113–14
Chifley Labor government, 123–4, 135, 141
  bank nationalisation, 132–3
  campaign to join IMF and ITO, 129–31
  postwar rebuilding priorities, 125–36
  Snowy Mountains Scheme, 127–8
child endowment, 143, 146–7
Christian Science, 30
Church of Christ (Scientist), 30
Church of England, 25, 30
Clarke, Sharon, 42, 48–9
Clayton, HJR, 180
Clune, David, 170
Cohen, Lewis, 7
Coles, Arthur, 100, 103–4
Commonwealth Bank, 21, 55
Commonwealth Electoral Act, 10
Commonwealth Employment Service (CES), 125
Commonwealth Liberal Party, 22, 61–2, 206–7, 209
Commonwealth Reconstruction Training Scheme (CRTS), 127
Commonwealth Royal Commissions Act, 16
Commonwealth Scientific and Industrial Research Organisation (CSIRO), 90, 123

Community Aid Abroad, 193
conferences *See* Australian Labor Party conferences
Congregational Church, 53, 54–5
Conlon, Alf, 112, 118
Connor, Rex, 185, 211, 215, 231
conscription plebiscites, 51–2, 56–9, 65–72
Constitutional Convention 1897, 29
Cook, Joseph, 22, 61–2
Coombe, David, 215
Coombs, Herbert Cole 'Nugget', 89, 118, 119, 122, 123, 126
corporate law reforms, 197–8
Council for Scientific and Industrial Research (CSIR), 121–3 *See also* Commonwealth Scientific and Industrial Research Organisation (CSIRO)
Country Women's Association, 142
Cox, Jim, 228
Crawford, Annette Bear, 30
Crawford, John, 202, 204
Crean, Frank, 185, 204, 212, 214, 215
Crisp, Fin, 11, 90, 126–7
Curnow, Rupert, 113
Curtin, John, 98–9, 109, 152
  appreciation for Dedman, 101–3, 104–5, 113
Curtin Labor government, 104–21, 128
  austerity restrictions, 108–11
  Department of Post-War Reconstruction, 113–14, 119
  interventionist policies during WWII, 106–11
  Manpower Directorate, 106–7
  Production Executive, 104–7

237

Daily Telegraph, 165
Dairy Producers Association of Victoria, 94
Daly, Fred, 212
Darling, JR, 116
Dawson, Andrew, 10, 17
Day, Gertrude Mary *See* Melville, Gertrude
Day, Joseph, 142
Day, Mary Ann (nee Dunbar), 142
Deakin, Alfred, 2–3, 13–14, 15, 18
Dedman, James, 91
Dedman, Jessie (nee McEwen), 93, 137
Dedman, John Johnstone, 88–139
   Address in Reply, 100–1
   appointment as Director of Refugee Resettlement, 136–7
   appointment to War Cabinet, 105
   arrival in Australia, 93
   austerity restrictions and interventionist policies, 106–11
   campaign to join IMF and ITO, 129–32
   Curtin government ministry portfolios, 104
   dairy farming business, 93–4
   death, 138
   Department of Post-War Reconstruction ministry, 113, 114
   early life, academic achievement and WWI enlistment, 91–4
   elevation to Production Executive, 104–7, 116
   inaugural speech, 100–1
   involvement in local government, 95, 96–7
   involvement with Country Party, 90, 94–5
   joins Labor Party, 96
   key roles in Curtin and Chifley cabinets, 88–9
   as Minister for Defence, 128
   as Minister for Organisation of Industry, 107
   as Minister for Post-War Reconstruction, 115, 117–18, 128, 129
   as Minister for War Organisation of Industry, 115–16, 119–20
   postwar legacy, 90, 114–23
   preselection for Corio by-election, 98–9
   projects post-Chifley ministry, 136–8
   public duel with Ward over joining IMF, 130
   responsibilities for legislation 1946–1949, 133–5
   role in university education policy during WWII, 115–17
   state elections, 94–9, 112–13, 135
   tilt for deputy role in Chifley government, 123–4
   trenchant critics of, 110, 111
   war with media over austerity measures, 108, 110
   See also Australian National University (ANU); Commonwealth Scientific and Industrial Research Organisation (CSIRO)
Dedman, Mary (nee Johnstone), 91
Delaney, Colin, 171
Democratic Labor Party, 141, 170
Denton Hat Mills, 52
Department of Education, 114
Dooley, James, 145, 149
Dougherty, Tom, 158
Downer, John, 10
Downing, Reg, 160, 173, 177
Drakeford, Arthur, 105, 124, 130
Drayton Grange Commission 1902, 16
Drummond, John, 117
Dunbar, Mary Ann, 142
Dunk, William, 123
Dwyer, Kate, 142, 146, 147
Eddy, Mary Baker, 30
education, federal Labor involvement in, 90, 114–21
Edwards, John, 105
electoral systems
   first-past-the-post, 54
   Hare–Clark proportional representation, 194, 223
   manipulation, 65–6
   multi-member district, 43
   1901 elections, 9–10
   preferential voting, 84, 149
Elliott, Henry Logan, 41, 44
Elliott, Sumner Locke, 25, 41–5
   Locke as inspiration for literary works, 25, 45–7, 50
Evatt, HV, 88, 99–100, 102, 120, 124, 183
   denouncement of the Movement, 164
   groups loyal to, 164, 166, 181
   opposition to Dedman, 111
   opposition to Production Executive, 105
   sides with media over austerity measures, 108
Everingham, Doug, 200
Ewart, Ernest, 44
Ewers, Florence, 146
Factory Act, 35

INDEX

Fadden, Arthur, 102, 104, 105, 121, 137
Fairfield Council, 157
Fairfield Hospital, 155, 161
Farmers Association, 82
farmers' party *See* Australian Country Party
Farrar, Ernest, 158–9, 160
Farrar, Laurence, 160
Federal Conciliation and Arbitration Bill, 13–14, 16
federal elections
 half-Senate, 195–6
 1900s, 9–10, 12–13, 17–19, 54, 68
 1910s, 23, 40–1, 62–5, 73–84
 1920s, 145, 149
 1930s, 97–9, 149, 152–3
 1940s, 91, 123–4, 133–5
 1970s, 206–7, 210, 219
Federal Labor, 141, 149, 152, 153–4 *See also* Chifley Labor government
Federated Engine Drivers and Firemen's Association (FEDFA), 225
Federated Laundry Employees of Australia (SA), 36
Federation, keen proponents, 4
Federation Convention 1896 (SA), 9
Felt Hatters Union (UK), 53
Ferguson, Carlyle, 110
Field, Albert, 209–10
Field, Michael, 227, 228–9
Finlayson, William, 58, 59
Fisher, Andrew, 10, 11, 23, 74, 76
 McGregor's loyalty to, 2, 18
 prime ministership, 18, 19, 22, 40
Fisher Labor government, 19–22, 55–6
Florey, Howard, 120
Forde, Frank, 105, 123, 137, 138
Forgan-Smith, William, 83

Fowler, James, 17
Fowler, Lilian, 155
Franklin Dam, 223–4, 225, 226
Franklin Federal Electorate Division, 193
Fraser, Malcolm, 209, 212, 213
Fraser Liberal government, 207, 214, 217, 219
Free Trade Party, 11, 13, 16, 17 *See also* Anti-Socialist Party
Freeman, Josie, 168
Freeman, Neil, 113
Freudenberg, Graham, ix, 150, 154, 158, 189, 200
Full Employment White Paper, 126
Fuller, George, 40, 43
Fysh, Philip, 38
Game, Philip, 153
Gardiner, Albert, 58, 85
Garran, Robert, 118
Geelong Football Club, 189
Geelong Wool Mills rally, 35
Gibson, Ivo, 134–5
Glanville, Edith, 142
Glynn, Stephen, 118
Golding, Annie, 142
Golding sisters, 24
Goldstein, Isabella, 32
Goldstein, Vida, 24, 30–2, 37, 39
Good Neighbour Council, 142
Gorton, John, 196
Gosford Times and Wyong District Advocate, 40–1
Government Printing Office, 40, 71, 72
Grassby, Al, 200
Gray, Robin, 227, 228
Gray Liberal government (Tas), 225, 226, 228
Green, Catherine, 160
The Greens, 228
Greville, Henrietta, 41
Gruen, Fred, 202, 204
Guardian, 110, 192

Gunns, 228
Hagan, Jim, 164
Hall, David, 71–2
Hampson, Alfred, 63
Hansard documents, 71, 173, 180, 181
Hardie, Keir, 91
Hare–Clark proportional representation system, 194, 223
Harradine, Brian, 187, 189, 222
Harris, Stuart, 202, 204
Harrison, Eric, 121
Hartley, Bill, 199, 215
Hasluck, Paul, 188
Hawke, Bob, 214–15, 216, 218, 224, 225, 226
Hawke Labor government, 125
Hayden, Bill, 185, 215
 as Acting Treasurer, 203, 204, 211
 as Labor Party leader, 219–21, 226–7
 Whitlam leadership challenge, 217–19
Heffron, Bob, 162
Herald, 34, 98, 99
Higgins, Henry Bourne, 16
Higgs, William, 17, 57, 58, 59, 76
High Court, 132
Hills, Pat, 163
Hoban, Mrs S, 166, 168
Hocking, Jenny, 200
Hodgman, Michael, 221, 222
Hodgman, Will, 221
Hogan Labor government (Vic), 95
Holder, Frederick, 29–30
Holgate, Harry, 224, 229
Holloway, EJ (Jack), 75–6, 81, 130
Holman, William, 143, 159
Holman Labor government, 143
Holt, Harold, 101, 194
Holt Liberal government, 195–6

239

Houlihan, Tom, 94, 95
House of Representatives
   Dedman's inaugural speech, 100–1
   deputy leader role, 18
   first Speaker of, 29–30
   Labor Party representation, 12–13
Howard Liberal–National government, 125
Hughes, Billy, 18, 21, 23, 40, 51, 64, 159
   formation of National Labor Party, 40, 61
   on Tudor's integrity, 60–1, 87
   walks out of Labor Party, 52, 58–9
   See also National Labor Party
Hughes Labor government conscription plebiscite, 51, 52, 56–9, 143–4
Hughes Nationalist Party government, 83–4
   second conscription plebiscite, 65–9
   strategies to censor No campaign, 70–2
Hussein, Saddam, 216
Independent Socialist Labor Party, 42
Industrial Groups, 141, 158, 163, 183
   groups loyal to, 164, 166
Industrial Workers of the World, 42
Industries Assistance Commission (IAC), 202, 204
International Monetary Fund (IMF), 129–31
International Trade Organization (ITO), 129, 131–2
International Union of Workers, 62, 74
Iraq Ba'ath Party, 187, 199, 215–16
Irvine, William, 33

Jackson, Rose, 163
JetAir scandal, 196
John, Mrs S, 166, 167, 168
Johnstone, Mary, 91
Jones, Barry, 230
Jubilee Conference (1954), 162–3
Keating, Paul, 217
Keefe, Jim, 215
Kelly, Gus, 155–6
Kelly, Paul, 188, 203–4, 213, 219
Kerin, John, 189, 201
Kerr, John, 186, 211, 212
Khemlani loans scandal, 185, 210
Knox, James, 95
Krichauff, Friedrich, 7
Labor Call, 96
Lambert, William, 78
Lamond, Hector, 40
land taxation (federal), 20–1
Lang, Jack, 43, 110, 111, 141, 144, 159
Lang Labor government (NSW) 141, 143, 146–7, 153
   split between federal and Lang Labor, 149–54
Lardner Agricultural Show, 205
Lawson, Henry, 41
Lawson, John, 99
Lee, Mary, 24
Legislative Assembly for the Nationalists, 43
Legislative Council of New South Wales, 157–62
Legislative Council of South Australia, 4, 6
Lemmon, Nelson, 128
Lewis, Tom, 209
Ley, Thomas, 43
Liberal Country Party, 201, 202, 205, 209
Liberal Party *See* Commonwealth Liberal Party
Light, RA, 156
Liverpool Hospital, 155
Lloyd, Clem, 206

Locke, Agnes, 30, 48, 49
Locke, Blanche, 48–9
Locke, Helena Sumner, 41–2, 44, 45
Locke, Jessie, 43–5
Locke, Lilian, 24–50
   Christian Science principles, 48–9
   crisis of confidence in Labor, 38–9
   custody battle for Sumner, 43–5
   death, 49
   early life and activism, 25–8
   extent of loyalty to Labor, 31
   female equal pay argument, 34–5
   as inspiration in Elliott's literary works, 25, 45–7
   legacy, 50
   marriage to George Burns, 36–7
   move to New South Wales, 39–43
   North Queensland Women's Organising Committee, 38
   organisation of Tasmanian state elections, 34
   organisational and advocacy roles, 24, 27–8
   as paid organiser for Victorian Labor Party, 32–3
   as platform speaker at elections, 33–5
   pioneering role in Labor, 25
   relationship with Blanche, 48–9
   relationship with Goldstein, 30–2
   'Solitary' grief poem, 47–8
   suffrage and reform activities, 28–43
   trade union rallies, 35–6

INDEX

United Council for Women's Suffrage, 28, 30, 31, 32
  work in Women's Committee, 32–3
Locke, William, 26, 36, 43
Locke, William Senior, 26
Lowe, Doug, 222, 223, 224, 227
MacGregor, Gregor, 4
Macintyre, Stuart, 88, 110
Makin, Norman, 2, 51, 56, 77, 89, 104, 105
Maloney, Parker, 64
Manifold, Chester, 56
Mann, Tom, 32
Mannix, Jack, 157, 174, 179
Manpower Commission, 107–8
Mant, John, 212
The Martyrdom (Reade), 192
Maternity Allowance Act, 21
McAuliffe, Ron, 189
McCalman, Janet, 54–5
McCarney, Mrs, 167, 169
McClelland, Doug, 189, 191, 208, 212
McClelland, Jim, 215
McCoy, Kevin, 225
McDonald, Charles, 59–60
McEwen, Jessie, 93
McEwen, Walter, 93
McGirr, Greg, 145
McGirr, Jim, 128
McGirr Labor government, 155–6, 157
McGregor, Gregor, 1–23, 55
  candidate for 1896 Federation Convention, 9
  cause of blindness, 1–2, 4–5
  Deakin's assessment of, 2–3
  death and colleagues' tributes and honour, 23
  early life, 4–5
  election as Senate party spokesperson, 10
  enters political arena, 6–16
  as first federal deputy leader, 1, 11
  inaugural speech in Parliament, 12
  as leader of the Opposition in Senate, 22
  loyalty to Watson and Fisher, 2, 14–15, 18
  marriages, 5
  role in election speech campaigns, 19–20
  senate election performance, 12–13, 18
  South Australian Senate elections, 9–10
  speech-giving prowess, 1, 2, 8, 19–20
  as Vice-President of Executive Council, 14–15, 19–20
  work in Royal Commissions, 16–17
McGregor, Jane, 4
McGregor, Malcolm, 4
McGregor, Sarah (nee Brock), 5, 23
McKell, William, 138, 177
McKenna, Nick, 195
McLean, Allan, 16
McMahon, William, 196
McMullin, Ross, 14, 90, 111–12, 138
McPhee, John, 227
media/newspapers
  austerity restrictions, 108
  bias against Labor, 98, 99
  coverage of election of permanent leader of Opposition, 59–60
  coverage of Tudor's interstate campaigns, 63–4
  portrayal of women in local government, 155
  support for Hughes' re-election, 62, 63
  war between Dedman over austerity measures, 108, 110
  See also Sydney Morning Herald
Medibank, 217
Melville, Arthur, 142–3, 157, 183
Melville, Arthur Junior, 149
Melville, Brian, 175
Melville, Gertrude, 140–84
  birth of sons, 149
  calls for inquiry into police brutality and corruption, 170–82
  commissioned portrait of, 163, 184
  contest for Hurstville, 153–4
  death, 182, 183
  Downing's response to police brutality claims, 178–9
  election to Cabramatta-Canley Vale Council, 142, 154–7
  election to NSW Legislative Council, 157–62
  groups supporting motion for inquiry, 181–2
  inaugural speech in Parliament, 161–2
  involvement in WCOC, 163–4, 69
  legacy of, 183–4
  lobbying for widows' pension, 146–7
  marriage to Arthur Melville, 141, 142–3
  as member of State Executive, 141, 144–6
  opposition to Industrial Groups, 183
  preselection to NSW Parliament, 140, 142, 146
  report on overseas trip, 169
  response to Sheahan, 179

241

Sheahan's response to police brutality claims, 177–8
son as victim of police brutality, 175–6
support for Federal Labor, 141, 149, 152
Melville, Leonard, 149
Melville, Leslie, 129
Menadue, John, 212
Menzies, Robert, 113, 120–1, 128–9, 177
Menzies Liberal government, 97, 98, 105–6
  abolition of land tax, 21
  abolition of superphosphate bounty, 204
  coalition with Country Party, 99
  corruption scandal, 99
  double dissolution election, 138
  vetoes Dedman's appointment to UNICEF, 135
The Messenger, 96
Military Service Referendum Bill 1916, 58
Milliner, Bert, 209
Mills, RC, 119
Miners Association, 38
Morning Post, 2
Morosi, Juni, 185
Morrison government, 208
Munroe-Ferguson, Ronald, 72
Murphy, Denis, 67, 70, 71, 76, 84
Murphy, Lionel, 197, 198, 208, 209
National Animal Health Laboratory, 207–8 *See also* Australian Centre for Disease Preparedness
National Association of University Students, 117
National Labor Party, 40, 61, 62 *See also* Nationalist Party

National Library oral history project, 137, 199, 226
Nationalist Party, 40, 65–9, 70–2
New Settlers League, 142
New South Wales
  by-elections, 150–2
  electoral system, 43
  method of appointing magistrates, 172
  state elections, 43, 145, 146, 149–54
New South Wales Association of Women Workers, 40
New South Wales Labor Party, 141, 154
  advocacy for women and children's welfare, 147–8
  allegations of corruption against Executive, 145–6
  annual conferences, 74, 75, 77–80, 144–6, 157–8, 162–3
  battles for dominance, 143–6, 149–54
  child endowment legislation, 143
  first female candidates, 41
  formation of new majority group, 145–6
  Paddington branch, 143
  support for Ryan to move to federal platform, 77, 78
  See also Lang Labor government (NSW)
New South Wales Legislative Assembly, 146
New South Wales Legislative Council, 157–62, 170–3
New South Wales Police Force, 171
New South Wales State Conference, 74
New Statesman, 96, 192
New York Times, 192
Niemeyer, Otto, 151

North Queensland Women's Organising Committee, 38
Nyham, Miss, 167–8
obituaries, Locke, 49
O'Byrne, Justin, 199, 213, 214
O'Malley, King, 37, 55, 75, 83
One Big Union movement, 42, 74
Opperman, Hubert, 134, 135, 136
Organisation for Tasmanian Development, 225
Page, Jim, 86
Pankhurst, Emmeline, 24
Patterson, Rex, 200
Pearce, George, 10, 23, 56, 57
Playford, Thomas, 10
Poke, Bob, 195
political campaign, forms of, 2
Political Labour Council of Victoria, 28
Pollard, Reg, 95, 96, 134, 138
Portland Guardian, 32
Premier's Plan 1931, 127, 151
Press, Anne, 183
Preston-Stanley, Millicent, 43, 142, 146
property qualification franchise, 6
Protectionist Party, 11, 13, 16, 17, 19, 37–8
Public Service Act, 122
Publications Bill 1955, 162
Queen Elizabeth II, 161
Queensland
  first Labor majority government, 69–72
  Labor and Deakinite Liberals coalition, 69
  state elections, 68–9
Queensland Labor Party, 75
Queensland Worker, 36
Rae, Peter, 197
'ragged school' movement, 26
Re-Establishment and Employment Bill, 125

242

INDEX

Reid, Alan, 188
Reid, George, 13, 16, 19
Reid, Gordon, 206
Renfrey, Ivy, 190
Rivett, David, 119, 122
Rockhampton Political Association, 68
Roper, Edna, 164–5, 170–3, 179, 181–2
Ross, Lloyd, 116
Rouse, Edmund, 228
Royal Australian Navy, 21
Royal Commissions, 16–17, 85, 228
Russell, Edward, 58
Ryan, Susan, 188, 215
Ryan, Thomas (TJ)
  co-leadership with Tudor, 81–4
  election to Caucus Executive, 84–5
  No campaign to conscription, 69–72
  Royal Commissions, 85
  transfer to federal parliament, 75–84
Sawer, G, 22
Scarfe, J, 7
Schedvin, CB, 121–2
Scullin, James, 97, 150–3
Searle, Betty, 31, 42
Seddon, Anne, 26
Seery, Eva, 41
Senate elections *See* federal elections
Sheahan, Billy, 177–8, 181–2
Shedden, Frederick, 105
Sherry, Ray, 195
Smale, Alice, 53, 54
Smith, Edwin, 6–7
Snedden, Bill, 209
Snowy Mountains Hydro-Electric Commission, 128
Snowy Mountains Scheme, 127–8
Some Thoughts (Wriedt), 220, 229
South Australia
  Federation Convention (1896), 9
  federation referenda, 9

'Hundred of McGregor' honour, 23
Kingston Liberal government, 7–8
legislation to provide women with vote, 1, 7–8, 28, 29
Locke's trade union rallies, 36
Senate elections, 9–10, 12–13, 23
state elections, 6
South Australian Labor Party, 6, 7, 28
Spaull, Andrew, 90, 99, 115, 133
Spence, Catherine, 24
Spence, William, 19
SS *Drayton Grange*, 16
state elections *See under individual states*
State Library of New South Wales, 27, 166
Stegall, Julia Jane, 5
Stevens, Bertram, 153, 159
Storemen's Union, 40
Storey, John, 143
stump speeches, 2, 63
Sunday Sun, 109
superphosphate bounty, 202, 203, 204, 206–7
Suttor, JB, 145
Sydney Morning Herald, 59, 108, 110, 183
  coverage of Melville's call for inquiry into police brutality, 173, 174, 175, 176, 181
Symon, Josiah, 9, 10
TAA, 196
Tariff Board, 202 *See also* Industries Assistance Commission (IAC)
Tasmania
  Denison seat, 37, 38, 194–5, 221–2
  Franklin Dam controversy, 223–4, 225, 226
  Locke's organisational campaigns, 34

state elections, 34, 194–5, 224–5, 227, 228–9
Tasmanian Government Insurance Officer (TGIO), 193
Tasmanian House of Assembly, 188
Tasmanian Hydro-Electric Commission, 223
Tasmanian Labor Party, 28, 220
  Locke as delegate to Interstate Conference, 36
  Nationalist Executive's intervention in, 226
  state conferences, 189, 195
  support for Ryan to move to federal platform, 75, 78
  voter-targeting campaign, 194–5
  Wriedt as leader, 225, 226
Theodore, Ted, 71, 151
Tighe, Margaret, 222
The Tocsin, 28, 33, 38
Tomlinson, Samuel, 7
Toowoomba Chronicle, 63
Tudor, Alfred Gwynne, 53, 54
Tudor, Francis Gwynne (Frank), early life, 52–4
Tudor, Frank, 51–87
  Armistice speech, 73
  co-leadership with Ryan, 81–4
  commitment to Congregational Church, 53, 54
  death and state funeral, 87
  election campaigns, 54, 62–5, 73–84
  ill health, 82–3, 85
  initiation of establishment of Commonwealth Bank, 55

interest in trade unionism
and community
activities, 53
as leader of the
Opposition in Senate, 56
leadership in adverse
conditions, 51–2, 65,
87
marriage to Alice Smale,
53–4
as Minister for Trade
and Customs, 55–6
opposition to
conscription policy,
51–2, 56–7, 66
as permanent leader of
the Opposition, 60–1
political moderatism,
54–5
remarriage to Fannie
Mead, 54
roles in Labor Caucus,
55
Victorian Trades Hall
Council, 53
work experience in UK
and US, 52–3
Tudor, John Llewellyn, 52
Turnbull, Reginald 'Spot',
196
Turner, Jim, 164
Turner, Ken, 158
United Australia Party, 98
United Builders Labourers
Society, 5
United Council for
Women's Suffrage, 28, 30,
31, 32
United Kingdom
Felt Hatters Union, 53
'ragged school'
movement, 26
suffragettes and women's
right to vote, 24, 28
United Labor Party of
South Australia, 6 *See also*
South Australian Labor
Party
United Nations Children's
Emergency Fund
(UNICEF), 135

United States
One Big Union
movement, 74
suffragettes and women's
right to vote, 24, 8
United Trades and Labor
Council of South
Australia, 6
Universities Commission,
116
University of Edinburgh,
92, 116
University of Melbourne,
118 *See also* Canberra
College
University of Sydney, 120
Uren, Tom, 217, 220
Varghese, Margaret, 118
Victoria
by-elections, 97–9
first-past-the-post
electoral system, 54
milk boards, 94, 95
state elections, 94–5, 97,
112–13, 135
Victorian Farmers' Union,
94 *See also* Australian
Country Party
Victorian Labor Party
coalition with Country
Party, 94
conferences, 33
Locke as paid organiser,
32–3
opposition to Ryan's
transfer to federal
parliament, 75–6, 79,
80
See also Women's
Committee
Victorian Legislative
Assembly, 98
Victorian Life Saving
Society, 53
Victorian Parliament
House, 10
Victorian Trades Hall
Council, 28, 30, 32, 53
Vietnam War, 137, 194,
197
Vigilance Society, 30

Waiting for Childhood
(Elliott), 46
Walker, Ronald, 119
Wallace, Con, 81
War Precautions Act, 70
Ward, Eddie, 89, 91, 105,
124, 125, 129
preselection for
by-election, 151, 152
public duel with Dedman
over IMF, 130–1
Warton, Leo, 134
Watson, John Christian
(Chris), 10, 11, 13, 18,
55, 57
McGregor's loyalty to,
2, 14–15
prime ministership,
14–16
Watt, William, 73
Webb, James, 153, 154
Webster, Ellen, 160
Webster, William, 57
The Week, 63
West, John, 150, 151
Western Australia, women's
right to vote, 29
Westerway, Peter, 209
Wheeldon, John, 199, 208,
212, 218
White, Frederick, 122
White, Patrick, 45
Whitington, Don, 90
Whitlam, Anthony, 218
Whitlam, Gough, 137–8,
231
failure to inform Wriedt
of dismissal, 212–14
lack of regard for senate
and senators, 186, 198,
208, 212
relationship with
Wriedt, 214–17
Whitlam government, 185,
198–208, 210
agricultural reforms and
reviews, 185–6, 200–7
anti-Whitlam campaigns
in rural areas, 205–6
corporate law reforms,
197–8

244

INDEX

dismissal of, 186, 212
federal involvement in education, 118
loans scandal, 199, 210, 215–17
resistance to blocking of supply, 210–11
Whitlam in Opposition, 215–19
widows' pension, 146–7
Willesee, Don, 198
Wilson, Alex, 100
Withers, Reg, 186, 213
Witherspoon, Garry, 171
Woman's Christian Temperance Union, 30
women
  advocacy for equal pay, 34–5, 161–2
  first female elected to local government, 142
  first Labor member of Victorian Legislative Assembly, 98
  first Labor Party elected member to NSW Parliament, 140
  first Labor Party preselected member to NSW Parliament, 142, 146
  first NSW Labor candidates, 41
  right to vote, 1, 7–8, 13, 28, 29
  suffrage activism and reforms, 24, 28–39
  See also United Council for Women's Suffrage
Women's Central Organising Committee, 147, 162–3, 183
  commissioning of Melville's portrait, 163, 184
  divisions in, 163, 164, 166–9
  Melville's resignation from Presidency, 164–5
  support for Melville's motion for inquiry, 181

Women's Committee, 32–3
Women's Political Association, 31, 49
Wood Royal Commission (1995), 182
wool floor-price, 202–3
World Bank, 129
World Trade Organization, 131
Wran, Neville, 77, 226
Wriedt, Frederick, 190, 192
Wriedt, Helga (nee Burger), 193, 223, 230
Wriedt, Ivy (nee Renfrey), 190, 192
Wriedt, Kenneth Shaw, 185–231
  affinity with Buddhism, 191–2
  as Agriculture Minister, 185, 188–9, 231
  attempt to transfer to House of Representatives, 188
  birth of daughters, 193
  as campaign manager for Batt's Denison seat, 194–5
  as campaign manager for Paula Wriedt, 229–30
  commission of review of agricultural policy, 202
  death, 230
  early Senate years, 196–8
  education and naval career, 190–3
  inaugural speech in Tasmanian Parliament, 226
  lasting reform legacies, 231
  legacy as Agriculture Minister, 207–8
  marriage to Helga Burger, 193
  as Minister for Primary Industry, 198–208
  as National Executive, 198
  opinion on Gray, 225–6

  opposition to abolition of superphosphate bounty, 202, 204
  opposition to wool floor-price, 202–3
  as Police and Transport Minister (Tas), 228–9
  preselection for 1967 half-Senate election, 195–6
  preselection for Franklin (House of Representatives), 193–4, 223
  relationship with Hawke, 226–7
  relationship with Hayden, 219–21
  relationship with Whitlam, 186–7, 208, 214–17
  retirement, 229–30
  risks Senate seat for Denison, 221–2
  Senate Select Committee on Security and Exchange, 197–8
  as Shadow Foreign Affairs Minister, 220
  as Shadow Minister for Education, 215
  time as leader of the Senate, 208–14
  transition from federal to state politics, 188
  Whitlam's failure to inform of dismissal, 186, 212–14
Wriedt, Paula, 193, 229–30
Wriedt, Sonja, 193, 230
Zeehan and Dundas Herald, 34

ABOUT THE AUTHOR

Chris Bowen is one of Labor's most experienced parliamentarians. He entered Parliament in 2004 and has held a wide range of portfolios, including being Treasurer, Shadow Treasurer, Minister for Immigration and Minister for Tertiary Education.

He served as Interim Leader of the Labor Party in 2013, and is currently Shadow Minister for Climate Change and Energy.

He has degrees in economics, international relations and the Indonesian language. He is the author of three previous books: *Hearts & Minds* (2013), *The Money Men* (2015) and *On Charlatans* (2021).

He lives in Smithfield in Western Sydney with his wife Rebecca, their children Grace and Max, and two very cheeky Labradors, Ollie and Toby.

Ingram Content Group UK Ltd.
Milton Keynes UK
UKHW040653090723
424784UK00004B/90